Windows Performance Analysis Field Guide

Windows Performance Analysis Field Guide

Clint Huffman

ELSEVIER

AMSTERDAM • BOSTON • HEIDELBERG • LONDON
NEW YORK • OXFORD • PARIS • SAN DIEGO
SAN FRANCISCO • SINGAPORE • SYDNEY • TOKYO

Syngress is an imprint of Elsevier

Acquiring Editor: Chris Katsaropoulos
Editorial Project Manager: Benjamin Rearick
Project Manager: Priya Kumaraguruparan
Designer: Matthew Limbert

Syngress is an imprint of Elsevier
225 Wyman Street, Waltham, MA 02451, USA

Library of Congress Cataloging-in-Publication Data
Huffman, Clint, author.
  Windows performance analysis field guide / Clint Huffman.
    pages cm
  Includes index.
  1. Windows (Computer programs) 2. Debugging in computer science. 3. Client/server
computing–Equipment and supplies. I. Title.
  QA76.76.W56H84 2014
  004'.36–dc23

2014017844

British Library Cataloguing-in-Publication Data
A catalogue record for this book is available from the British Library

ISBN: 978-0-12-416701-8

For information on all Syngress publications,
visit our website at http://store.elsevier.com/syngress

This book has been manufactured using Print On Demand technology. Each copy is produced
to order and is limited to black ink. The online version of this book will show color figures
where appropriate.

Dedication

This book is dedicated to all of the Microsoft support professionals and the Microsoft Premier Field Engineering (PFE) organization. None of us will ever know everything, but together, we can solve anything. This book is a reflection of everything I have learned and will still learn from all of you. Microsoft and my manager, Mikel Hancock, have given me the opportunities that I always dreamed of and have genuinely cared about my family and I. Thank you!

Acknowledgments

Thank you to Mark Russinovich and David Solomon for the incredible training on Windows Internals and for writing the Windows Internals book series where much of this knowledge is put to use in the field.

Thank you to Mark Minasi for his PC Upgrade and Maintenance (big blue book) that got me started on computer systems.

Thank you to Yuri Diogenes, Mario Hewardt, Mark Russinovich, Aaron Margosis, and Ed Wilson for their experiences and insight into writing books. They helped inspire this one.

Thank you to Yong Rhee, Jeff Stokes, and Carl Luberti for the technical accuracy of the Performance Monitor chapter and the boot performance chapter and for helping me with many ETL tracing questions. You guys are the best in the industry at ETL trace analysis!

Thank you to Bruce Worthington, Qi Zhang, and Emily Langworthy for the very detailed feedback and technical accuracy of the disk performance chapter.

Thank you to Holger Hatzfeld for the technical accuracy and feedback on the Performance Monitor chapter.

Thank you to Ed "The Scripting Guy" Wilson for providing Powershell examples throughout this book.

Thank you to Daniel Pearson for the technical accuracy of the Performance Monitor chapter and for all of the high-quality feedback.

Thank you to Matthew Reynolds for the technical accuracy of the boot performance chapter and all of the great boot performance traces. You are the best boot performance analysis guy out there!

I would like to thank the following people for always being very helpful and patient with all of my technical questions over the years:

Mark Russinovich, Aaron Margosis, Andrew Richards, Landy Wang, Pavel Lebedynskiy, Bruce Worthington, Qi Zhang, Joe Laughlin, Shane Creamer, Antonio Neves, Stephen Cole, Ben Christenbury, Ken Brumfield, Benny Lakunishok, Bhumit Shah, Bruce Adamczak, Ewan MacKellar, Chris Davis, Brian Wilhite, Leonardo Fagundes, Mark Fugatt, Daniel Pearson, and Kevin Anderson.

Thank you to Joseph Joe Holly for being a great friend all of these years and providing valuable feedback on this book.

Thank you to my parents, Malcolm and Sheila Farrant and David and Rebecca Huffman, for always being up for a beer, conversation, support, love, and plenty of computer problems for me to solve. Hi mom! I wrote my first book!

Thank you to Don Smith, Kevin Anderson, Robert Hensing, and Mike Leuzinger for being great friends and for getting me serious about Microsoft technologies.

Thank you to my cousin, James "Jimmy" Streck, who has always shared my excitement and passion for computers and video games over the years. Thanks for all of the fun! "They say it can destroy the universe... or worse!" – MST3000

And finally, the biggest "thank you" to my wife, Maggie, and my daughter, Paige, for supporting me and loving me unconditionally. I love you both!

Biography

No one knows everything, but together we can solve anything.

 Originally from Dayton, OH, Clint Huffman joined Microsoft in 1999 supporting Web technologies and Microsoft load testing tools and later worked as a testing consultant helping people with load testing at the Microsoft Services Labs. There, he found a passion for solving Windows performance issues. In 2006, he joined Microsoft Premier Field Engineering (PFE) to take on Microsoft BizTalk Server performance issues only to find that most issues could be diagnosed by analyzing operating system resources. Some may say that performance analysis of Windows is more of an art than a science. Well, Clint strives to make it as much of a science as possible and to bring it to the masses. Clint is probably best known for the Performance Analysis of Logs (PAL) tool, which simplifies the analysis of performance monitor logs.

Vital Signs Workshop: Clint teaches the Vital Signs workshop (originally created by Shane Creamer), which is a 3-day workshop that covers Windows architecture and how to identify performance bottlenecks.

Products: Clint primarily supports Microsoft Windows Server, Microsoft BizTalk Server, Microsoft Internet Information Services (IIS), and scripting (VBScript or Powershell) technologies at Microsoft Corporation for Microsoft PFE.

PAL Tool: Clint wrote the free and open-source PAL tool, which saves you time by analyzing performance counter logs. You can check out the tool at http://pal. codeplex.com.

Clint's Windows Performance Analysis in the Field Blog: Clint blogs about the Windows performance issues he encounters in the field at http://blogs.technet.com/clinth.

Facebook http://www.facebook.com/clint.huffman
Twitter http://twitter.com/clinth
E-mail clinth@microsoft.com
Resume http://bit.ly/ClintHResume

Contents

Foreword

I have had the privilege to know and to work with Clint Huffman for more than a decade at Microsoft. He is the consummate professional and is genuinely empathetic when it comes to working with customers. He is also a great teacher, as I found out when I was doing a Train the Trainer for a VBScript class I wrote a long time ago.

Since then, I had the opportunity to observe him at conferences, such as TechEd, where I could hear the questions that customers asked and how he responded to them. He is in a word great.

So what does this have to do with *Windows Performance Analysis Field Guide*? Well, in my experience, a person who is a great teacher, and is excellent at working with customers, is better able to get the point across in book fashion. Clint does this in the extreme.

It is well known that Windows, especially on a server, can benefit from some performance tuning. Why? Well, consider the millions of different ways that a server can be deployed. Consider the thousands of different processes those servers are expected to serve. Think about the literally infinite number of combinations of processes, services, applications, and network infrastructure that can impact performance of your Windows servers.

If all you have is a single Windows server, doing file sharing, and maybe authentication for a small number of Windows clients, then this book is not for you. But if you work with dozens, hundreds, or even thousands of servers, all of which are running different combinations of processes, services, etc., then this book is an absolute must.

When I first met Clint, he was working in the Microsoft Premier labs, doing performance analysis for large customized applications and some really wild network configurations. He has since moved to be a Premier Field Engineer (PFE). For those of you who have not heard about PFE, they are the best of the best of the best! When Clint says this is a field guide, he is not being metaphorical—he is being literal, this book was written in the field, and his target audience is in the field.

Therefore, what you have is the book on performance analysis by the guy who has pioneered many of the techniques he mentions in the book. In fact, it is a perfect combination. As Renault said in *Casablanca*, "this is the beginning of a beautiful friendship." Get the book; you can thank me the next time you see me.

Ed Wilson, MCSE, MCSD, MCDBA
Microsoft Scripting Guy
Author of *Windows PowerShell Best Practices*

Introduction

Like any good medical technician might say, if you are in an emergency situation with your Windows or Windows Server computer, then consider opening an urgent case with Microsoft Support. With that said, go to the Start Here chapter of this book to begin troubleshooting the issue.

Why is my computer slow? That is the fundamental question and purpose of this book. Before I joined Microsoft, I assumed that there was a person buried deep who knows everything. Years after I joined Microsoft, I realized that no one knows everything, but together, we can solve anything. I took it as my life's goal to accumulate the necessary knowledge to troubleshoot performance problems and consolidate it. Ultimately, I strive to make performance analysis easy enough for my parents—very nontechnical—to solve on their own, but the reality is that even the most experienced support professionals struggle with these problems. I hope you find this book helpful in your own "adventures."

WHO SHOULD READ THIS BOOK?

The "Windows Performance Analysis Field Guide" book is intended for experienced IT professionals and developers who want to know how to identify and troubleshoot common performance problems in Microsoft Windows and Windows Server.

Start here

1

INTRODUCTION

This book is intended to be a guide through the self-help process of troubleshooting performance issues with Microsoft Windows and Windows Server. As always, if you are in an emergency situation with your computer system, then immediately call Microsoft Support. Otherwise, start at this point in the book for guidance on where to start. The rest of this book covers more detailed concepts and procedures.

IS IT A PROBLEM WITH BOOT OR SHUTDOWN PERFORMANCE?

A healthy computer running Microsoft Windows 7 or later should be usable after powering it on in about 60 seconds—this includes the time after logging (postboot). A healthy Windows Server computer might take a bit longer due to specialized hardware. If your system is taking longer than the expected amount of time to be usable, then it is worthy of more investigation. Go to Chapter 11 "Boot Performance" to learn more about how to troubleshoot boot and shutdown performance.

IS IT A HARDWARE OR SOFTWARE SYSTEM HANG?

A "complete hang" by this definition is where the system does not respond to any input from the keyboard or mouse for more than 1 minute after the system has already booted. If the system responses every few seconds, then it is not a complete hang. If the system is slow during boot, then go to Chapter 11 "Boot Performance" to learn how to do a boot trace and other tips and tricks for improving boot performance. Otherwise, continue reading. Troubleshooting boot failures is not covered by this book.

There can be many causes of a complete hang and an important troubleshooting step is to determine if it is a hardware or software hang. A trick that Kevin Anderson showed me was to simply press the Num Lock key or the Caps Lock key on the keyboard. If the respective lights on the keyboard do not toggle on and off when the key is pressed, then it is likely a hardware hang. Go to section "Common environmental and hardware-induced performance problems" later in this chapter. Otherwise, it is more likely a software-related hang. Go to section "General slow system performance" later in this chapter.

TROUBLESHOOTING HARDWARE SYSTEM HANGS

As mentioned earlier, it is beyond the scope of this book to troubleshoot hardware conditions, but I'll focus on some common conditions.

Review the System Event Logs

Whether it is a hardware or software system hang condition, if the system is ever in at a point where you can get to the Windows desktop, then try to go to the system event logs and search for possible hardware failure messages.

TIP

The system event logs can provide vital clues to system hangs and delays.

Potential cause: Busy or malfunctioning hardware

Malfunctioning hardware such as physical memory modules, hard drives, optical drives, and USB devices can cause the system to hang and/or respond slowly. Hardware devices that have been dropped, broken, misrepaired, or simply had coffee spilt into them are obvious (a friend of mine's wife had this happen several times by accident), so I'll focus on the not so obvious hardware problems. By the way, if a system or device ever does get water in it, then DO NOT POWER IT ON! Take the battery out and place the device or components into a bag of rice and let it sit in there until completely dry, which might take several days.

TIP

If a computer or device gets wet, DO NOT POWER IT ON. Remove the battery and place everything in a bag of rice for a few days to allow it to dry out.

My friend, Don, once had a system that hung for 3 seconds every 30 seconds. We had a difficult time figuring out why the system was hanging like that. Once we started removing USB devices, it became clear that it was a malfunctioning sound device for recording live music. This is one of the many reasons to consider Microsoft logo'd devices when possible since they are less likely to cause problems.

Hardware Diagnostics

Hardware manufacturers typically provide diagnostic tools in the BIOS or downloadable tools from their Web site to help find problems with their respective hardware. Consider running these tools if you suspect a hardware problem.

Potential cause: Virtual machine host

If the system is a virtual machine (a computer running on top of another computer) and hangs, then the host system might have exhausted its resources or throttled the virtual machine's resource usage. Go to section "Virtual machine considerations" in Chapter 10 "Processor".

Potential cause: Power and/or excessive temperatures

Excessive heating and cooling can cause device to perform poorly or malfunction.

Go to section "Common environmental and hardware-induced performance problems" later in this chapter for troubleshooting power and heat problems.

COMPLETE OR PARTIAL SYSTEM HANGS

This section assumes the system eventually hangs after the system boots up normally. If the system hangs during boot, go to Chapter 11 "Boot Performance"; otherwise, continue.

During a complete system hang after the system has been running for a while, if the keyboard lights are working fine, then it is likely a software condition causing the system to hang or to appear to hang. Very busy or poorly written drivers are the common causes of this condition.

Potential Cause: High Processor or Disk Usage

If the system is responsive every few seconds, then that is more likely a high resource usage condition such as processor or disk.

Go to Chapter 10 "Processor" for processor monitoring and troubleshooting.

Go to Chapter 3 "Storage" for disk monitoring and troubleshooting.

Potential Cause: Lack of Kernel Pool Memory

If there is no evidence of high processor or disk usage (detailed in Chapters 3 and 10) during the system hang, then the system might be out of memory in one or more various ways. A complete system hang that lasts indefinitely—meaning no update to the user interface in several minutes—might indicate a lack of kernel nonpaged pool memory.

Go to Chapter 5 "Kernel Memory" for kernel pool memory monitoring and troubleshooting.

Potential Cause: High Processor Interrupts or DPCs

This symptom is commonly associated with either high kernel-mode processor usage or frequent processor interrupts.

I was playing a PC game once and it played fine for many hours until the game and the system suddenly began to stutter and pause frequently. This had happened a few times already and this time I was prepared with a Windows Performance Recorder (WPR) trace in the background. Microsoft Support assisted me with the analysis of the ETL trace and discovered that the device driver for my USB head-phones was issuing a high number of deferred procedure calls (DPCs). Once I updated the USB driver on my Windows 7 laptop, the problem never occurred again.

Go to Chapter 10 "Processor" for both user-mode and kernel-mode processor monitoring and troubleshooting.

PROCESS TERMINATED UNEXPECTEDLY

If a process/application is crashing regularly, then it is often due to poorly written code or unexpected environmental conditions. A process crash dump can be captured that can provide evidence of what led to the crash by using debugging tools such as ADPlus.exe (part of the Debugging Tools for Windows) or ProcDump.exe (part of Windows Sysinternals). Collecting a process crash dump is discussed in Appendix B Collecting Process Memory Dumps.

If the process is crashing due to an out of memory condition such as a System. OutOfMemoryException, then it is most likely running out of its private, virtual address space. Go to Chapter 4 "Process Memory" for monitoring and troubleshooting process virtual address space conditions.

When a process/application is running slow (not crashing the application), then it could be due to a lack of one or more system resources. Continue reading for more information about monitoring and troubleshooting system resources.

GENERAL SLOW SYSTEM PERFORMANCE

If you have ruled out hardware problems and if the system becomes slow after usage, then there could be many reasons for it being slow. This book cannot address all performance problems, but the primary purpose of this book is to help identify and troubleshoot common conditions.

If you are in a hurry and need to quickly identify a system performance problem, then this section of the book will guide you. This book covers commonly used troubleshooting tools used by Microsoft. See Appendix A Tools for more information on the various tools discussed in this book.

IF ON THE CONSOLE/DESKTOP OF A SINGLE SYSTEM

If you are logged in with administrator rights (required for nearly every troubleshooting step in this book), then Task Manager and Resource Monitor are great tools to start with simply because they are built into the operating system.

Task Manager can be brought up quickly by pressing Ctrl+Shift+Esc at the same time. Go to the Performance tab and determine which resource is overwhelmed. Resource Monitor can be started by clicking the Resource Monitor link on the Performance tab of Task Manager.

If CPU is busy then go to section "Identifying high processor usage using Task Manager" in Chapter 10 "Processor". CPU usage (synonymous with "processor" in the context of this book) is considered busy when it sustains a value at or near 100%.

If available physical memory (RAM) is low, then go to section "Identifying a low available physical memory condition using Task Manager" in Chapter 8 "Physical Memory". Memory usage refers to the percentage of physical memory (RAM) that is in use. A sustained value of over 75% (25% available) is considered high.

Be aware that physical memory is just one of the several memory-related resources that the system can run out of:

- Go to section "Identifying application virtual address space problems using Performance Monitor and the application event log" in Chapter 4 "Process Memory" to learn more about process virtual address space.
- Go to section "Monitoring system-committed memory with Task Manager" in Chapter 6 "System Committed Memory" to learn more about system-committed memory.
- Go to section "Initial indicators of Pool Paged and Pool Nonpaged kernel memory" in Chapter 5 "Kernel Memory" to learn more about free system page table entries (PTEs), pool paged kernel memory, and pool nonpaged kernel memory.

If Disk is busy, then go to section "Disk analysis using Task Manager and Resource Monitor" in Chapter 3 "Storage". Disk is available on Windows 8 and 8.1 by default for each fixed disk drive. Use "diskperf –y" at an administrator command prompt to have Disk show up in Task Manager on Windows Server 2012 and Windows Server 2012 R2, but be aware that the disk performance data in Task Manager can be resource-intensive. A busy disk is one that is at or near 100% **active time** with a relatively high **average response time**. Be aware that the **average response time** field in Task Manager is generally much higher than the actual average response time of the disk. The performance counter **\LogicalDisk(*)\Avg. Disk sec/Transfer** is more reliable.

If Ethernet (network) is busy, then go to section "Monitoring network utilization using Task Manager" in Chapter 9 "Network". Each wired and wireless network interface should show in Task Manager. Task Manager only shows the overall data throughput of each network interface and it does not show network delays. Network delays often cause applications or services to delay by waiting on network resources. TCP/IP connection delays (Latency (ms)) can be seen in Microsoft Resource Monitor on the TCP Connections pane on the Network tab.

NOTE

The Windows Sysinternals tools (http://www.sysinternals.com) deserve an honorable mention here because they can run on nearly any version of Windows or Windows Server without installation. Just download and run. These tools are covered throughout this book as relevant.

IF MONITORING ONE OR MORE SYSTEMS

When the need arises where you need to monitor more than a few systems, it becomes impractical to monitor the systems using console/desktop tools. Performance counters are arguably the most practical way of gathering performance information from remote systems; therefore, performance counters are discussed throughout this book. Monitoring and collecting performance counter data is discussed in detail in Chapter 2 "Performance Monitor."

To get started, I recommend going to section "Using the PAL tool to create a data collector template" in Chapter 2 "Performance Monitor". It walks through using the PAL tool (a tool I created in collaboration with the open-source community) to create a Performance Monitor data collector template that can be used to gather the appropriate performance counters for the operating system and specific server products. Once the performance counter data collector has created a counter log, the counter log can be analyzed using the PAL tool on a non-production system such as a workstation. Think of the PAL tool as an easy button for this book where all of the performance counter thresholds mentioned in this book are already preprogrammed into the tool. The result is an HTML report of red, green, and yellow alerts. For more information about the PAL tool, go to Chapter 12 "Performance Analysis of Logs (PAL) Tool."

NOTE

Microsoft Windows Management Instrumentation (WMI) classes are another method of gathering performance data remotely from other systems, but WMI data is generally more resource-intensive than performance counters. WMI classes are discussed throughout the book as they become relevant.

If any of the processor instances of **\Processor Information(*)\% Processor Time** have a sustained value of greater than 75, then go to section "Identifying high processor usage using Performance Monitor" in Chapter 10 "Processor".

If **\Memory\Available MBytes** is less than 10% of the installed/usable physical memory, then go to section "Identifying a low available physical memory condition using Performance Monitor" in Chapter 8 "Physical Memory". This counter measures the amount of physical memory that can be reused without incurring a disk IO. The less available memory, the more likely there will be increased disk IO, which can cause system-wide delays if the disk becomes overwhelmed. Disk overwhelmed criteria is covered in Chapter 3 "Storage."

The following Powershell command can be used to identify the amount of usable physical memory of a given system:

```
gwmi  Win32_ComputerSystem  -ComputerName  localhost  |  SELECT
TotalPhysicalMemory
```

Replace localhost with a remote computer system name, IP address, or DNS name. Administrator rights and DCOM connectivity are required to the target system. Keep in mind that the result of the Powershell command is in bytes and the performance counter is in megabytes.

Be aware that physical memory is just one of the several memory-related resources that the system can run out of:

- Go to section "Identifying application virtual address space problems using Performance Monitor and the application event log" in Chapter 4 "Process Memory" to learn more about process virtual address space and the **\Process(*)\Virtual Bytes** performance counter. Note: Task Manager and Resource Monitor do not provide a field equivalent of process virtual bytes, which is the amount of in-use (non-free) virtual address space within a process.
- Go to section "Monitoring system-committed memory with Performance Monitor" in Chapter 6 "System Committed Memory" to learn more about system-committed memory.
- Go to section "Initial indicators of Pool Paged and Pool Nonpaged kernel memory" in Chapter 5 "Kernel Memory" to learn more about free system PTEs, pool paged kernel memory, and pool nonpaged kernel memory.

If any of the instances of **\LogicalDisk(*)\Avg. Disk sec/Transfer** has a sustained value greater than 0.025 (25 ms), then go to section "Disk analysis using Performance Monitor" in Chapter 3 "Storage". This counter measures the average response time of every I/O request related to the specified logical disk. This threshold is not an indicator of a problem, but it just indicates that more investigation is needed.

If any of the instances of **\Network Interface(*)\Bytes Total/sec** is greater than 30% of the network adapter's connection speed (**\Network Interface(*)\Connection Bandwidth**), then go to section "Monitoring network utilization using Performance Monitor" in Chapter 9 "Network". Keep in mind that this counter only shows the over-all data throughput of each network interface and it does not show network delays. Network delays often cause applications or services to delay by waiting on network resources. TCP/IP connection delays (Latency (ms)) can be seen in Microsoft Resource Monitor on the TCP Connections pane on the Network tab.

COMMON ENVIRONMENTAL AND HARDWARE-INDUCED PERFORMANCE PROBLEMS

It is beyond the scope of this book to cover hardware performance in any great detail, so I'll cover the most common conditions.

POWER USAGE ANALYSIS

Does your laptop have poor battery life? To help identify unnecessary power usage, which is commonly associated with poor performance, at an administrator command prompt, run the command:

Powercfg /energy

This command will monitor the system for 1 minute and produce an HTML report of power usage.

If the PowerCfg report doesn't help, then continue reading for tips on avoiding performance problems due to hardware.

ENSURE THE COMPUTER IS PLUGGED IN WITH THE PROPER POWER ADAPTER

If the computer system cannot draw enough power, then the hardware may malfunction or operate at lower-power levels, which typically results in slower performance.

I have heard of a case where a lower wattage power supply was attached to a laptop that needed more. The laptop performed poorly even when the original equipment manufacturer's (OEM) power supply was later attached to it. In this case, the BIOS had to be updated to reset the hardware back to normal operation.

ENSURE THE HARD DRIVES AND OPTICAL DRIVES ARE RUNNING AT FULL PERFORMANCE

Some computers support the option to run the hard drives and optical drives (CD/DVD) in an "acoustics," "quiet," or "low-power" mode to reduce the sound and/or power consumption of the device. This is certainly a valid concern but can lead to poor boot performance and general slow performance when using these devices. This setting is typically in the BIOS or with vendor-specific software.

REVIEW THE SYSTEM'S POWER PLANS

Power reduction is an important consideration when running on battery or even running hundreds of servers in a server room. The default power plan of Windows and Windows Server is to reduce the processor's power usage by lowering its clock speed or putting the processors in a "parked" mode when not needed. When the processors are needed, the system automatically unparks the processors from a low-power state to a full-power state.

There are many other options in the power plans and they are worth reviewing to customize your experience.

IS THE SYSTEM OVERHEATED?

Hardware generally has safety mechanisms to save itself from permanent damage due to overheating by increasing fan speeds, forcing the device into a lower-power state, or various other ways. Lower-power usage generally results in lower heat generation.

As mentioned earlier, make sure that the proper power supply is attached. A power supply that has too much output might result in over whelming the hardware or lead to increased heat.

Ensure the fans are operating normally as well. Dust, dirt, cigarette smoke, and other things that might find its way into the computer can jam or significantly degrade the fan's performance. Be sure to regularly blow dust and other foreign objects out of the system. As Mark Minasi always says, "Dust is a fantastic insulator of heat."

CONCLUSION

This chapter serves as a starting point for most readers to "jump" into the problem and work toward a solution. This book is designed to cover common performance problems of Windows or Windows Server that are not directly hardware-related.

Want to learn more with a live instructor? Microsoft Premier Field Engineering (PFE) (my team) offers the Vital Signs and Vital Signs Advanced workshops that take students through a myth-dispelling Windows architecture and performance monitoring experience, going from simple counter thresholds to advanced debugging visualizations—much of which is covered in this book. The workshop is available to Microsoft Premier customers. To learn more about getting a Microsoft Premier Support contract go to http://www.microsoft.com/en-us/microsoftservices/support.aspx.

I certainly don't know everything, so if there is something that this book has not covered, then tap into my network of friends—the real source of knowledge—using their contact information later in the text.

Windows Performance Analysis Industry Experts and Their Contact Information

We keep a current list of Twitter handles of industry experts on Microsoft technologies at http://social.technet.microsoft.com/wiki/contents/articles/15539. twitter-handles-of-industry-experts-on-microsoft-technologies.aspx.

Bruce Adamczak

Twitter @BruceAdamczak (https://twitter.com/BruceAdamczak)

Bhumit Shah

Twitter @bhumitps (https://twitter.com/bhumitps)
E-mail: bhumits@live.com

Chris Davis

Twitter @ChrisDavis9z (https://twitter.com/ChrisDavis9z)

Clint Huffman

Twitter @ClintH (https://twitter.com/ClintH)

Ewan MacKellar

Twitter @ewanmackellar (https://twitter.com/ewanmackellar)

Jeff Stokes

Twitter @WindowsPerf (http://twitter.com/WindowsPerf)

Mark Fugatt

    Twitter @mfugatt (https://twitter.com/mfugatt)
    Blog: http://blogs.technet.com/mfugatt

Matthew Reynolds

    Twitter @MatthewMWR (https://twitter.com/MatthewMWR)

Moti Bani

    E-mail: moti.ba@Hotmail.com

Robert Smith

    E-mail: sandude@outlook.com

Yong Rhee

    Twitter @YongRheeMSFT (https://twitter.com/YongRheeMSFT)

Performance monitor

You know PerfMon, it's like your own little internet inside your computer, in the sense that everything you need to know is in there, you just can't find it.

Richard Campbell (host of the RunAs Radio podcast)

INTRODUCTION

This chapter provides practical facts and common usage of Windows Performance Monitor and other tools related to collecting and managing performance counter logs.

INTRODUCTION TO PERFORMANCE MONITOR

Windows Performance Monitor ("Perfmon" for short) applies to many aspects of collecting performance data in Windows and Windows Servers such as live monitoring, data collection, and data management and reporting of performance counter data, event tracing for Windows (ETW) data, and system information data.

In Microsoft Support, we regularly use Perfmon for gathering performance counter data from customer systems to help identify problems. The impact of gathering the data is almost always trivial, yet it provides a wealth of information. With that said, gathering unnecessary data over a long period of time can be overwhelming without proper planning.

The point of this chapter is to provide practical facts and common usage of Performance Monitor and related tools. The help documentation of Performance Monitor is available in the article "Overview of Windows Performance Monitor" at http://technet.microsoft.com/library/cc749154.aspx.

WHY DO YOU NEED TO KNOW PERFORMANCE MONITOR?

Actually, you don't really need to know Performance Monitor—it is simply a means to an end, the "end" being the ability to effectively measure system and application performance. Tools will come and go, but knowledge of the internals of the Windows and Windows Server operating systems will ultimately allow you to find the right tools. Performance Monitor is already part of the operating system (no need to download it or install it), can reliably collect performance data, and has enough data to get an idea of the conditions. These factors alone make it a standard tool for any software professional.

Windows Performance Analysis Field Guide. http://dx.doi.org/10.1016/B978-0-12-416701-8.00002-8

With that said, Performance Monitor is not always the best tool for every performance problem. Throughout this book, I will cover various tools that provide varying levels of detail toward resolution.

WHAT ARE PERFORMANCE COUNTERS AND CAN WE TRUST THEM?

Performance counters are bits of code that monitor, count, or measure events in software, which allow us to see patterns from a high-level view. They are registered with the operating system during installation of the software, allowing anyone with the proper permissions to view them.

This concept isn't much different from managing a restaurant. You can certainly try to be at the restaurant 24/7, but that is impractical and even impossible to know everything that is going on. By placing monitors at key parts of the restaurant such as the number of guests per hour, the number of orders queued, the amount of food supplies, and so on, the manager can take a step back and can identify problems, see patterns emerge, and predict future trends.

When a developer writes software, it can be difficult to measure the performance of the software when it's being written and when it is limited to a developer's workstation. The developer can certainly step through the code with a debugger, but this induces frequent pauses that are not part of the normal flow of execution. Furthermore, once the software is in production, the developer has very few ways of monitoring the code paths taken by the software. Therefore, performance counters can help measure key parts of the software.

Like all software, the reliability depends on the quality of code and environmental factors. In most cases, performance counters are highly reliable once you understand what and how they are measuring. With that said, even the best written performance counters can become ridiculously inaccurate by something as simple as a clock problem with the processor—a problem we dealt with in 2008 (http://support.microsoft.com/kb/938448/en-us). In addition, virtualization of computers can skew the measurements of processor related counters not because of bad code, but due to how threads are scheduled between the virtual computer, the hypervisor, and the hardware.

In summary, once you understand how the counter is collected, you can better judge its reliability.

BASIC USAGE

This part of the book covers the basic usage and commonly used features of Performance Monitor.

STARTING PERFORMANCE MONITOR

Performance Monitor can be started in many ways. The easiest way is to press the Windows key, type "perfmon," and then click Performance Monitor. The executable for it is located under the Windows directory at %windir%\system32\perfmon.exe where %windir% is the environment variable indicating where the operating system is installed. This means that Perfmon can be started from any command prompt or address bar by simply typing in "Perfmon" and pressing Enter. Next, it can also be started by opening a binary counter log file (*.blg), but this method is discouraged since it immediately adds all of the performance counters to the chart, which can be difficult to work with. Finally, the Perfmon snap-in can be added to a Microsoft Management Console (MMC), which can be a convenient way of administrating applications and services.

If Perfmon fails to start or if access is denied, then log in with a user account that is a member of the local Administrators security group.

NOTE

User accounts that have membership in the Performance Monitor Users or Performance Log Users security groups can view live Performance Monitor counters and Data Collector Sets, but cannot make changes to Data Collector Sets. Only user accounts with administrator rights can make changes to the features of Performance Monitor.

For more information on the security group membership needed to use specific features of Performance Monitor, go to the "Overview of Windows Performance Monitor" article at http://technet.microsoft.com/en-us/library/cc749154.aspx.

After starting Perfmon, ensure that the Performance Monitor node is selected in the tree view control on the left. If you don't see it, then try expanding Monitoring Tools. Once Performance Monitor is selected, it will show the counter instance **\Processor Information(_Total)\% Processor Time** by default (Figure 2.1).

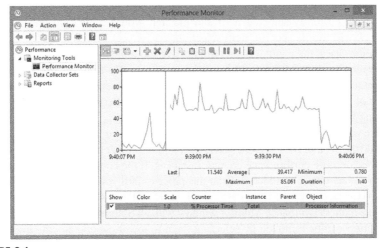

FIGURE 2.1

Initial view of Performance Monitor.

If you've worked with Windows and Windows Server for a long time, you might be wondering why the Processor Information object is loaded by default instead of the Processor object. The Processor Information object supersedes the Processor object due to the need to expose all of the possible logical processors supported by Windows and Windows Servers. With that said, the Processor object can still be used on 32-bit computers with 32 or less logical processors or on 64-bit computers with 64 or less logical processors.

ADDING AND REMOVING COUNTERS

Performance counters can be added to Performance Monitor by clicking on the green cross [+] button or by right-clicking anywhere within the chart area and then clicking Add Counters. Either action will show the Add Counters window allowing you to browse the counters available on the local computer. If you don't see names like Processor or Processor Information or if you see odd numeric names, then there might be corruption in the counters. If corruption is suspected, then go to the "Detecting and repairing corrupted performance counters" section later in this chapter to learn more about the condition and how to resolve it.

The initial view shows the counter objects (explained in more detail later in this chapter), which are logical groupings of counters. I like to refer to them as categories. Each counter object can be expanded to show all of the counters within it. Selecting a counter will reveal the instances of the counter object in the pane below it called **Instances of selected object**. Sometimes, the instances of a counter don't show up right away, so you might have to select another counter under the same counter object for the instances to show (Figure 2.2).

The counters and instances can be selected in a similar fashion as file lists in Windows Explorer. Keyboard combinations such as Shift-Click will select all items between the currently selected item and the item you are clicking on. Likewise, Ctrl-Click will toggle specific item selection.

In some cases, the counter object might have too many instances to show. When this happens, use the Search field just below the instances field to search for a specific instance. This commonly happens to the Process object when there are a large number of processes running. Figure 2.3 is an image of Performance Monitor while searching for counter instances.

Once you have selected the counters and instances that you want, click the Add button to add the counter path(s) to the pane on the right. Counter paths are expressions that define one or more performance counter instances. If the counter paths are not on the right, then they won't be added. Repeat this process until you have all of the counters that you want added to the right. Once finished, click the OK button. This will return you to the main Performance Monitor window with all of the selected counters loaded.

Counters can be removed by selecting them in lower pane, then clicking the red "X" button at the top. Alternatively, all counters can be removed by right-clicking the counter list and selecting Remove All Counters or by selecting all of the counters in the counters list (Ctrl-A) and pressing the delete key.

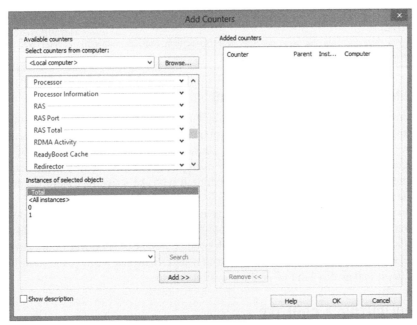

FIGURE 2.2

Initial view of the Add Counters window.

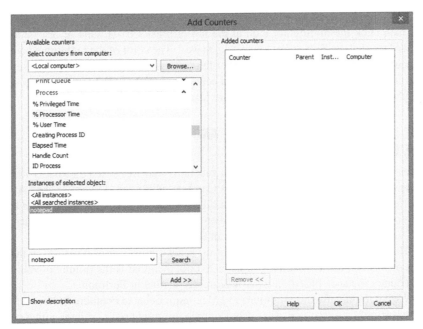

FIGURE 2.3

Searching for counter instances.

NOTE

If you plan on using the same counters again soon, then consider hiding the counters versus removing them.

HIDING AND SHOWING COUNTERS

A counter can be hidden from the chart by unchecking the Show checkbox, but the advantage is that it doesn't remove the counter from the list making it convenient to show again later. For added convenience, the space bar can be used to toggle the last selected counter to show or hide it. For example, when looking at process-related counters, I can quickly select a counter, hide it with the space bar, and then down arrow to the next one.

In the Windows XP days, we didn't have this feature and we had to use the delete button to remove unwanted counters from the list. Unfortunately, when we did this too fast, we ended up not knowing which counter we just deleted and would have to re-add all of the counter instances again and restart. Now that we have the show/hide feature, it makes this kind of analysis easier.

HIGHLIGHTING A COUNTER

There is nothing like having a lighthouse in a storm. When you have a lot of counter instances on the line chart, it can be difficult to distinguish which one you are looking at. This is when the counter highlighting feature is very helpful.

To highlight counters in the chart, select the counters that you are interested in and then click the highlighter icon at the top or press Ctrl-H. One of my students showed me that the Backspace key works as well. The color of the highlighted counters contrasts with the background color of the chart making it stand out. If the chart background is dark, then the highlighted counters are white. If the chart background is light, then the highlighted counters are black.

THE LAST, MINIMUM, AVERAGE, AND MAXIMUM FIELDS IN THE GRAPH

When counter data is collected, Perfmon generates statistics based on what is visible in the chart. The Last (also referred to as Current), Minimum, Maximum, and Average fields show the respective values for the selected counter instance. If more than one counter instance is selected, then the fields will show nine dashes (————————) indicating no data can be shown.

The best part about these fields is that the scale multiplier has no effect on them. This means that if the minimum value is 20,000, then that is the minimum value of the counter instance based on what is currently visible in Perfmon.

We commonly use the Minimum and Maximum fields of counters to determine if there is significant resource usage. For example, we might see a counter with a steep trend, but if the difference between Minimum and Maximum is only 10 MB, then it isn't significant enough to be of concern. There again, if the minimum value is 104,857,600 (100 MB) and the maximum value is 1,073,741,824 (1 GB), then we know that the process consumed 900 MB, which is significant.

Another helpful feature introduced by Windows Vista and Windows Server 2008 is the addition of digit groupings in the fields. Digit grouping is synonymous with the thousands separator—meaning that the value of 100000000 is displayed as 100,000,000 on systems with an English (US) locale making it easier to recognize large numbers. The symbol used to separate each thousands group is based on the locale of the currently logged on user.

If a number in a field is too large to display, then scientific notation is used to represent the number (Figure 2.4). A value such as 37,580,963,840 (35 GB) is too large for a field to display, so it is represented as $3.7580e+010$. This is not an error—it is scientific notation. It indicates that the decimal point must be moved to the right the number of times indicated after the plus (+) symbol. There are nine digits behind a gigabyte, so the number $3.7580e+010$ appears as roughly 37 GB, but after dividing each thousands group by 1024, the true answer is 35 GB.

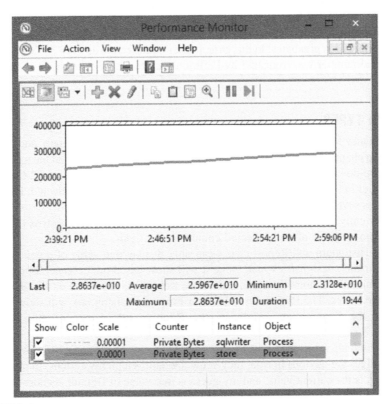

FIGURE 2.4

Performance Monitor showing scientific notation.

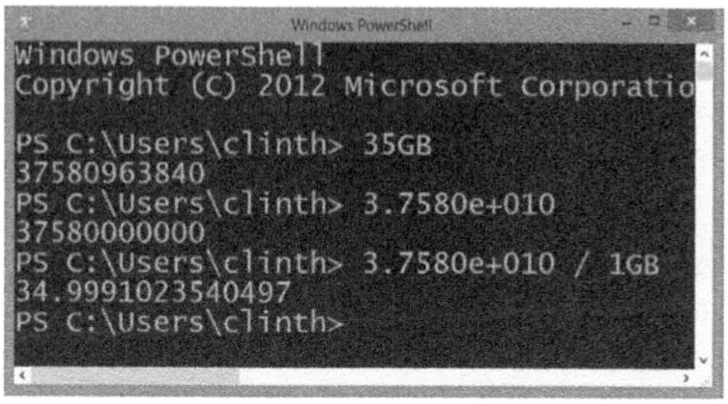

FIGURE 2.5

Numeric calculations using Powershell.

Powershell can be used to assist with interpreting large numbers. Powershell can convert values in gigabytes and return the number in bytes. For example, Powershell can convert the value 35 GB into the full numeric value 37,580,963,840 and, next, can convert scientific notation into a full numeric value. In Figure 2.5, I copied the value 3.7580e +010 from Perfmon into Powershell and it returned 37,580,000,000. Knowing what this value is in gigabytes would be nice, so I divided it by 1 GB to give me the number in gigabytes. In this case, it didn't quite return an even 35 GB because the actual number was truncated by Perfmon, but it is close enough.

GRAPH TYPES

Performance Monitor has three views of counter data: Line, Histogram, and Report view. To change the graph type, click on the third icon from the left on the top menu. The drop-down list will show Line, Histogram bar, and Report (Figure 2.6). The drop-down list will show Line, Histogram bar, and Report (Figure 2.6).

Earlier in this chapter, I mentioned that when counter data is collected, Perfmon generates several statistics (Minimum, Average, Maximum, and Last) based on the data currently being displayed. A line chart shows the data points across time and shows the statistics of each selected counter in the fields.

The Histogram and Report charts can only display one value of a counter at a time. Perfmon designates which value it will show based on the general properties of Perfmon. To change the statistical value, right-click anywhere on the chart and click Properties. The Performance Monitor Properties dialog box will show. Navigate to the General tab and locate the **Report and histogram data** section (Figure 2.7).

The default value shown in Report and Histogram charts is Default. While the other values are obvious in what they show, Default is a bit mysterious. In my experience, it is the current value and my guess is that value of Default is chosen by the creator of the counter object. In any case, when I use Histogram or Report charts, I commonly change this setting from Default to the statistical value I'm looking for just to be sure.

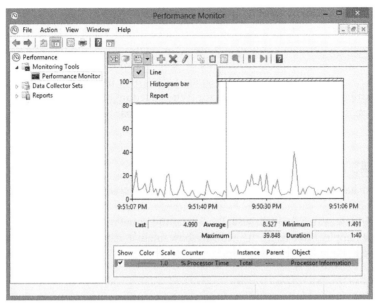

FIGURE 2.6

Changing chart types.

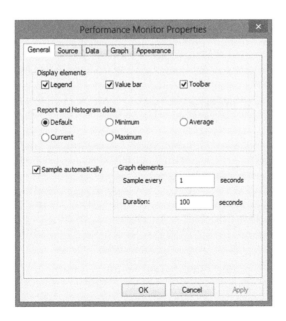

FIGURE 2.7

The general tab of Performance Monitor properties.

VIEW AS A LINE CHART

The line chart is the default view in Performance Monitor and is the most common way to view performance counters. It uses time on the x-axis and numeric values on the y-axis. Figure 2.8 shows the line chart of the Memory object counters.

This view is best for displaying counter values over time and for showing all of the statistics of a single counter instance. When needing to see numeric values from many counters at the same time, use the Histogram bar or Report views.

VIEW AS A HISTOGRAM (BAR CHART)

Perfmon has a histogram view, which presents the counter values in a bar chart (Figure 2.9).

This view is helpful with visually comparing counter values.

For example, I like using this view to show the live instances of **Processor(*)\% Processor Time** to a live audience.

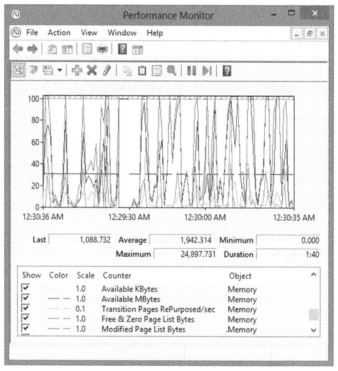

FIGURE 2.8

The Line chart view of Performance Monitor.

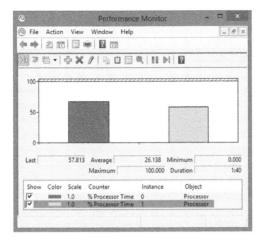

FIGURE 2.9

The Histogram view of Performance Monitor.

VIEW AS A REPORT

The Report view of Perfmon shows counter values in columns and rows similar to a spreadsheet. Each row represents one or more instances of a counter. This view is best for displaying the values of many counter instances at the same time. In Figure 2.10, I am using this view to compare the counter instances of C: and D: drives.

THE OVERHEAD OF VIEWING LIVE PERFORMANCE COUNTERS

A common question that I get from my customers and students is, "How much overhead (resource usage) will my computer take on when monitoring performance counters?" This question is important because systems under load typically have little room for additional load and we certainly don't want to make the condition worse. The answer to this question is "It depends."

First, it depends on if the counters are being monitored live or being logged by a data collector. When monitoring live, counters must be calculated—meaning a formula is applied to it—then displayed in the screen. If enough counters are added in this way, then it can have a slight impact on system resources. Second, when counters are logged by a data collector, the file format of the data collector determines if the counters are written in a "raw" or "calculated" format. Binary logs write in the "raw," while comma-separated value (CSV), tab-separated value (TSV), and SQL Server table logging require the counters to be calculated. As expected, calculated counter logging requires slightly more processor usage than raw counters. In any case, the overhead is trivial (less than 1% CPU) on modern systems. See the "Log format" section later in this chapter for more information on data collector log formats. Finally, it depends on the amount of free disk space.

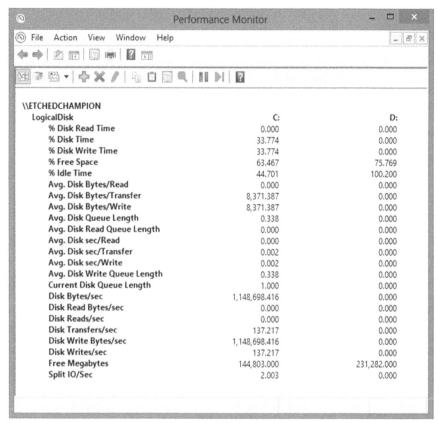

FIGURE 2.10

Report view of Performance Monitor.

Counter logs have been known to grow to several gigabytes if not managed properly. We don't want to run the system out of disk space and make problems worse. Ensure that the system has enough free disk space to handle your counter logging requirements.

VIEWING REMOTE PERFORMANCE COUNTERS

Counters available on remote computers (any computer that you are attempting to connect to other than the one you are interactively logged on to) can be viewed in Performance Monitor by providing the name of the computer in the **Select counters from computer** field in the **Add Counters** window. I commonly use this feature when engaged in a performance lab where all of the computers involved are on a local area network.

There are many conditions required to access remote performance counters. The following are common connection failures:

- *Wrong operating system or kernel version*: Microsoft Windows and Windows Server are "paired" with the same kernel version such as Windows 8 and Windows Server 2012. This means that they have been well tested together. Therefore, as a best practice, use the same versions of the Windows or Windows Server.
- *Network connectivity*: Ensure that the computer name is resolving to the correct IP address and MAC address on the target computer. Next, ensure that Distributed Component Object Model (DCOM) connectivity is not blocked by firewalls or other devices on the network. DCOM is a protocol that enables software components in Windows and Windows Server to communicate directly over a network. Performance Monitor uses DCOM to access performance counters on another computer. For more information on DCOM troubleshooting, see "Troubleshooting DCOM" at http://technet.microsoft.com/library/cc751272.aspx.
- *Appropriate rights*: Administrator rights are technically not required, but in many cases, it's just easier to use an account that has administrator rights on the target computer. See "Overview of Windows Performance Monitor" at http://technet.microsoft.com/en-us/library/cc749154.aspx for details on the security requirements of Performance Monitor features.
- *Remote Registry service*: This service must be running on the target computer to gain access to the performance counters. This is because your account needs access to the Perflib registry key at **HKLM\Software\Microsoft\Windows NT\CurrentVersion\Perflib** on the target computer. If you've ruled out all of the other common causes and solutions in this list and suspect access to this registry key might be a problem, then consider using Process Monitor (a Windows Sysinternals tool) on the target computer and then reviewing the trace to troubleshoot access to the registry.

Regarding the overhead of monitoring performance counters over the network, it will greatly depend on the number of counter instances being collected and the quality of the network connection. For example, I once monitored 30 critical performance counters from 10 servers at the same time. This caused the 100 Mb network adapter on the computer to become overwhelmed just from the monitoring.

SHOWING AND HIDING THE CONSOLE TREE

If you need additional screen space, then consider using the Show/Hide Control Tree control to show or hide the console tree on the left side of Performance Monitor (Figure 2.11).

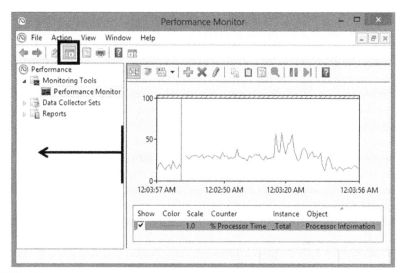

FIGURE 2.11

A screenshot showing the use of the Show/Hide Console Tree control.

COUNTER INSTANCES ARE NOT AUTOMATICALLY ADDED OR REMOVED

Perfmon does not automatically add or remove counter instances to the chart. Let's say we are looking at all of the instances of **\Process(*)\% Processor Time** and a new process starts to consume a large amount of processor usage. Even though we are looking at all of the instances of the counter, Perfmon will not automatically add or remove process instances as they come and go—we have to re-add the counters to the chart to see the new instances. This is why tools like Task Manager, Resource Monitor, or Process Explorer are better when actively monitoring processes.

GAPS IN PERFORMANCE MONITOR DATA

On occasion, Perfmon may have gaps (no data points) in the counter data. The cause of the gaps is most often attributed to a lack of resources at the time of the collection. Perfmon collects counter data at a Normal priority level, and when the system is low on resources, then the data collection is ignored and tried again at the next interval (Figure 2.12).

I was able to replicate this effect by using a CPU stress tool to consume 100% of the processors on my computer while monitoring several performance counters. At first, it had no effect on Perfmon. Then, I increased the priority level of the CPU stress threads to Above Normal and the gaps appeared. I doubt that this reproduction is the only cause of the gaps, but it does show that the explanation is plausible.

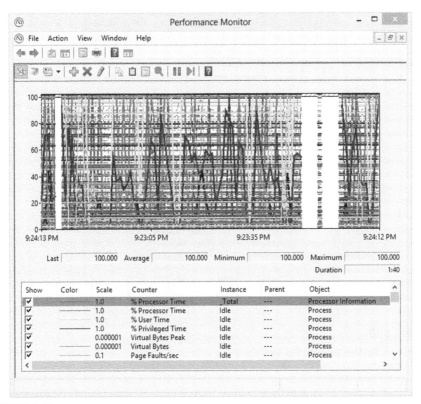

FIGURE 2.12

Performance Monitor showing gaps in the counter data collection.

The article "Overview of Performance Monitoring" at http://technet.microsoft.com/en-us/library/cc958257.aspx is old but explains how the gaps might occur. It talks about "System Monitor," which is an old reference to the chart control of Performance Monitor.

OPENING A COUNTER LOG

Counter logs are files that contain counter data and created from performance counter data collectors. Performance Monitor can open counter logs in binary (*.blg) format, comma separated value (*.csv) format, tab separated value (*.tsv) format, or from a database table through a data source name (DSN).

To open a counter log, press Ctrl+L or click the cube icon at the top of Performance Monitor. The Performance Monitor Properties dialog box will show with the Source tab selected. Click the Log files radio button, and then click Add. Select a counter log (*.blg, *.csv, or *.tsv) from the file system, click Open, and then OK.

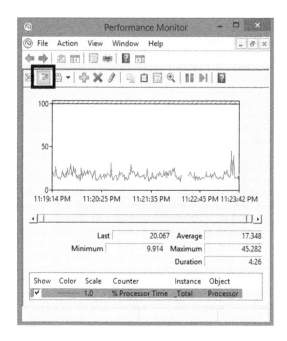

FIGURE 2.13

Performance Monitor with the View Data Log icon highlighted.

Note: when the log is loaded, the counter list is automatically cleared. This is normal behavior. Click the green plus button to add counters from the log into Performance Monitor (Figure 2.13).

Avoid double-clicking a counter log from Windows Explorer. This results in all of the counter instances automatically added to Performance Monitor, which can be resource-intensive and a bit disorienting. As a best practice, open counter logs from within Performance Monitor.

WARNING

Windows and Windows Server older than Windows Vista cannot open binary counter logs from newer operating systems.

The binary log format (*.blg) changed between Windows XP/Server 2003 and Windows Vista/Server 2008. This means that Windows XP and Windows Server 2003 and earlier operating systems cannot open binary counter logs recorded on Windows Vista, Windows Server 2008, or later operating systems. As a best practice, use a version of Windows or Windows Server that is Windows Vista or newer when viewing performance counter logs.

USING THE TIME RANGE CONTROL

Once a counter log is loaded in Performance Monitor, the time range control can be used to select a time range within the log and "zoom to" it. Performance Monitor displays up to 1000 data points in the line chart at a time, so it is sometimes necessary to use this technique to see more detail (Figure 2.14).

To see more details of a time range within a counter log, click and drag across a portion of the counter log and then either click the magnifying glass icon at the top or right-click and select **Zoom To**. The line chart will update to show more details of the counter log within the selected range (Figure 2.15).

You can go deeper and deeper into a time range so long as there is enough data. Keep in mind that the numeric fields under the chart update to reflect the statistics of the currently selected view. For example, the average value is the average of all of the data points in the current view—not the entire log.

To zoom out, double-click the time range control bar and either click the magnifying glass icon or right-click and select **Zoom To**. This will return you to the initial view of the counter log.

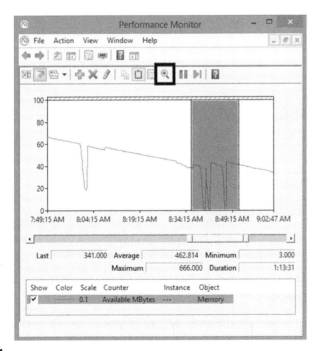

FIGURE 2.14

Selecting a time range within a counter log.

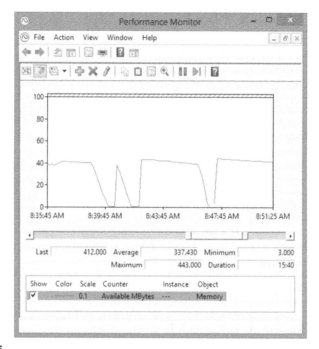

FIGURE 2.15

Zoomed into a portion of a counter log.

PERFORMANCE COUNTERS

This part of the book covers the syntax, usage, and quirks of performance counters.

COUNTER DESCRIPTIONS

Counter descriptions are a quick, "in-tool" reference about the counter you have selected. It can be viewed by checking the **Show description** checkbox but are only available when browsing local counters. Searching http://msdn.microsoft.com or http://technet.microsoft.com is always encouraged to learn more.

COUNTER PATHS

A counter path is a line of text that defines one or more counter instances. It is similar to a UNC path (\\server\share) but has a slightly different syntax. The path can include a computer name as the source for the counter data. If the computer portion of the path is omitted such as **\Processor(_Total)\% Processor Time**, then the local computer is assumed. An asterisk (*) is used as a wild card for counter instances (example: **\Processor(*)\% Processor Time**), for counter names (example: **\Processor(_Total)***), or both (example: **\Processor(*)***).

The syntax of a counter path is

\\Computer\Object(Instance)\Counter

Example:

\\Web01\Processor(0)\% Processor Time

Computer: The computer where the counter exists. If no computer is specified, the local computer is assumed.

Object: A logical grouping of counters such as Processor or Memory.

Counter: The name of the counter such as % Processor Time. An asterisk (*) indicates all counters.

Instance: A specific instance of a counter on the computer such as _Total or 0. An asterisk (*) indicates all instances.

COUNTERS ARE ALWAYS POSITIVE

Performance counter values are of type unsigned double, which is a decimal value that cannot contain a negative number.

UNIQUE INSTANCE NAMES

Every instance of a counter must have a unique name. Perfmon deals with this by adding a suffix of #x to each counter instance of the same name, where x is the lowest number available starting with 1. The Process object often has multiple instances with the same name and commonly uses this naming convention.

If there are three instances of svchost.exe, then Perfmon will have instances svchost, svchost#1, and svchost#2. If the process assigned to the instance of svchost#1 ends and a new svchost.exe begins, then Perfmon will assign it to svchost#1 even when svchost#2 is still active. This technique might seem strange, but it minimizes the number of counter instances.

The suffix has nothing to do with the PID (process identifier), but it serves Perfmon in a similar way by making them unique. The value of the counter **\Process(*)\ID Process** provides the PID of the process.

SPECIAL COUNTER INSTANCES

Some counter instances have a special purpose. The following special counter instances are commonly found in Windows and Windows Server:

- **<All instances>:** This is a user interface mechanism representing all of the instances of the currently selected counter object in the **Add Counters** dialog box.
- **_Total:** This instance is found on most of the core operating system counter objects. Despite the name, the value it represents differs between each counter object. For example, it represents the total of all of the instances of the

LogicalDisk Transfers/sec counter, but it represents an average of all of the instances of the Processor % Processor Time counter. The counter documentation might reference the value of _Total. If not, try adding all of the counter instances and determine what it represents.

- **_Global_:** This instance is commonly found in .NET-related counter objects and represents the sum of all of the counter instances of the respective counter.
- **PID in Process:** Windows XP, Windows Server 2003, and later support the ProcessNameFormat registry key, which changes the behavior of Perfmon to display the Process object instances with the name of the process and its process ID (PID) displayed as < ProcessName>_<ProcessID>.

WARNING

The ProcessNameFormat feature can significantly increase the number of counter instances in a counter log.

If too many counter instances are logged to counter logs due to the Process NameFormat feature, then consider disabling the ProcessNameFormat feature and using the "ID Process" counter under the Process object (**Process(*)\\ID Process**) to identify the PID of a process. This can help products such as Microsoft System Center Operations Manager (SCOM) management packs operate more efficiently.

SCALING COUNTERS

The values of performance counters don't always fit within the range of the line chart. When this happens, Perfmon plots the values at the top of the chart to indicate that the data points are off of the chart. I am often amused when a character in a movie refers to something being "off the charts." Why not increase the chart? In Perfmon, increase the chart range in the Graph tab of Performance Monitor Properties or change the scale multiplier of the counter to fit within the existing range.

Proper adjustment of a counter's scale will make it easier to see patterns. The scale of a counter is the multiplier used to plot the values on the chart. If the scale is 10, the counter values are multiplied by 10 and plotted on the chart as such. In Figure 2.16, most of the values of the Available MBytes counter are too high to plot on the chart and it prevents us from seeing the pattern of counter values.

The scale of a counter can be changed in the properties of the counter (Figure 2.17), which can be accessed by right-clicking anywhere in the chart and selecting Properties. Various features of the selected counter can be modified here such as color, width, and style. Unfortunately, only one counter can be selected for modification at a time, making it difficult to adjust a large number of counters. I changed the scale of the counter to 0.1 and then clicked OK resulting in a much better view of the counter shown in Figure 2.18.

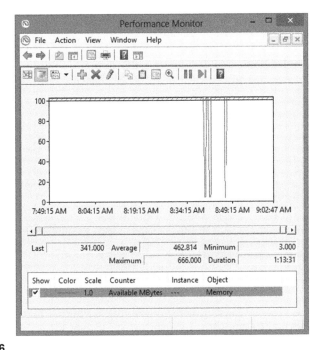

FIGURE 2.16

Counter data that is too high to plot in the chart.

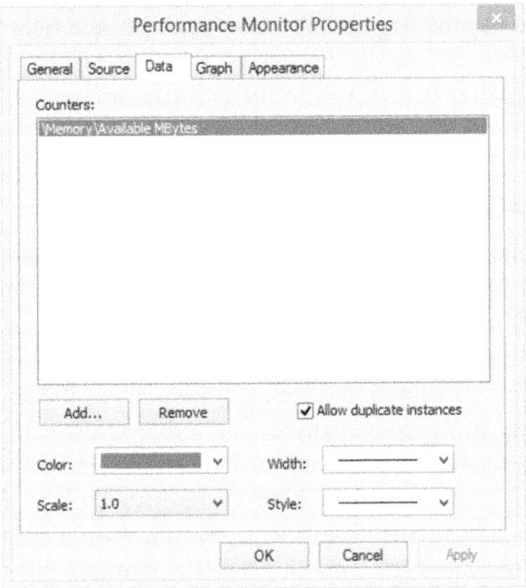

FIGURE 2.17

Counter properties.

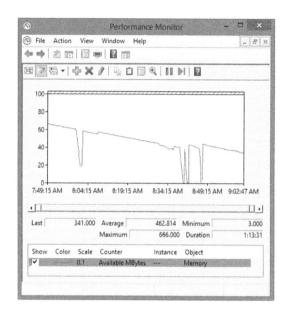

FIGURE 2.18

Counter data at an appropriate scale.

The values in the number fields (Minimum, Average, Maximum, and Last) are not multiplied by the scale, so looking at the fields is a reliable way to determine if a counter has actually exceeded a threshold or not. Use the values in the number fields first, and then use the line chart to show relative data over time. For example, an increasing trend might initially appear as a memory leak, until you look at the number fields and realize that it was an insignificant amount.

AUTOMATIC SCALING

One of my favorite features of Performance Monitor is the **Scale Selected Counters** feature, which was first introduced in Windows Vista and Windows Server 2008. This feature automatically changes the scale of the selected counters to a multiplier that fits within the current range of the line chart. This feature is very helpful when working with counters measured in different units such as the counters of the Memory object, which are in bytes, megabytes, and other units.

I discourage using this feature when there is a need to visually see which instances are the highest. If I am looking at the instances of **\Process(*)\Private Bytes** and automatically scaled all of them, then counters that are ten times larger than the others will be scaled down making it difficult to visually see which processes are consuming the most memory. When all of the counters are of the same type and unit, then consider simply increasing the maximum chart size until all of the counters fit.

CHANGING THE SCALE OF THE CHART

It is common for counters such as **\Process(*)\Virtual Bytes** to exceed the maximum size of the chart. When these are the only counters loaded in Perfmon, the easiest way to see which counters visually have the highest values is to increase the maximum size of the chart. This can be done by right-clicking anywhere on the chart, selecting Properties, and then navigating to the Maximum field on the Graph tab. A common practice that I use is to append a zero to the existing maximum value, click Apply, and repeat until all of the counters fit.

The Minimum size of the chart can certainly be changed, but I rarely need to change it.

DEFAULT SCALING IN LOG FILES

When viewing counters in a binary counter log (*.blg), each counter has a default scale multiplier appropriate to the counter so that they will comfortably fit between 0 and 100. For example, the **\LogicalDisk(*)\Avg. Disk sec/Read** counter has a default multiplier of 1000, so that a value of 0.020 is plotted in the chart with a value of 20 to represent 20 ms.

CSV and TSV counter logs default to a 1.0 scale, making counters such as **\Process(*)\Virtual Bytes** difficult to work with. This is because most processes consume more than 104,857,600 bytes (100 MB) and these numbers are immediately off the scale. The counter properties dialog box only allows one counter to be selected for modification at a time, so this means that modifying counters in mass to a specific scale is not possible. Since the counters are all of the same type and unit, it makes sense to just increase the maximum range of the chart until all of the counters fit. Unfortunately, the maximum size that the chart can go up to is 999,999,999, which is not large enough to display values roughly over 1 GB. And since processes often use more than 1 GB of virtual address space, this poses a problem.

An alternative is to select all of the counters and use the **Scale Selected Counters** feature to automatically change the scale of each counter to fit within the current range of the chart. Unfortunately, this makes visually seeing the largest counters difficult. Finally, the only other alternative is to just look at the numbers in the fields to see which is the largest or by using the report view of Perfmon. My advice is to simply do all of your counter logging in binary (*.blg) format, so that you get the benefits of the default scaling.

NOTE

Relog.exe is a command-line tool that can be used to convert CSV logs to binary (*.blg) logs, but logs converted in this way do not get the default scaling benefit with counter logs originally recorded in binary.

COUNTER CORRELATION

Look for correlations. A correlation is a statistical relationship between two or more sets of data. We commonly find correlations between resources such as disk queues and latency, working sets and available memory, and processors and power. Once you understand how Windows architecture works, the relationships between the resources make more sense and easier to identify. In Figure 2.19, the operating system's available memory inversely correlates to the working set of a Microsoft Biz-Talk Server process (BTSNTSvc.exe).

Finally, when tried and true analysis fails, it is sometimes necessary to explore related counters in an effort to identify undiscovered correlations or patterns. This is how we find new ways to troubleshoot problems and is an important step toward evolving beyond the basics.

DATA COLLECTORS

Data collectors are needed to record performance counter data into a log file. This part of the book covers how to create and manage data collector sets and data collectors.

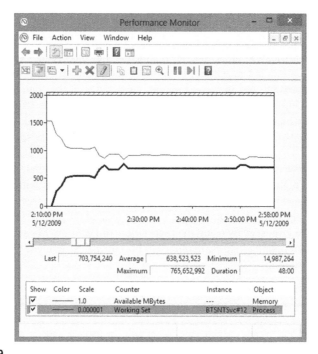

FIGURE 2.19

Performance Monitor displaying a correlation between two counters.

INTRODUCTION TO DATA COLLECTORS

Performance Monitor has data collectors that can collect performance counters event trace data, or system configuration information. It uses predefined or user-defined data collector sets to combine multiple data collectors into a single container for ease of administration.

Throughout this book, I often refer to a "counter log," which is file or Microsoft SQL Server table produced from a performance counter data collector. Creation and management of counter logs is covered later in this chapter.

Event trace data is more commonly known as ETW tracing and collect into an event tracing log (*.etl) file. These files typically contain high levels of detail on Windows performance and various other events depending on the providers collected. A basic analysis of this data is covered throughout this book. Performance Monitor is able to collect ETW data, but most ETW-related tools implement their own data collection, so the need to collect ETW data using Perfmon is rare.

System configuration information is limited to collecting registry key values which may be helpful with determining appropriate thresholds for counters.

In addition to collecting data, data collector sets can contain performance counter alerts. Each alert collects counter data from one or more specific counter instances—meaning it cannot dynamically collect data on transient counter instances that come and go—and then compares the counter values to a simple threshold of above or below a specific number.

Counter alerts are helpful when needing to take an automated action when a counter exceeds a threshold. I have used this feature to automatically create a hang dump of IIS worker processes when the ASP.NET execution times exceed 10 s. With that said, the simplicity of counter alert thresholds commonly results in the actions being repeated more often than expected, so consider adding logic into the script actions to prevent unnecessary duplication. For more information on creating data collector sets, see "Creating Data Collector Sets" at http://technet.microsoft.com/en-us/library/cc749337.aspx.

CREATING AND STARTING A PERFORMANCE COUNTER DATA COLLECTOR USING THE WIZARD

Data collectors are used to record performance counter data into a log file. This section walks you through how to create a performance counter data collector using the Performance Monitor user interface. When creating a data collector set, please consider the topics in the "Best practices for managing performance counter data collectors" section later in this chapter.

NOTE

This operation requires you to be logged in with an account that is a member of the Administrators security group.

---

1. *Start the wizard*: To start the wizard, open Performance Monitor, right-click on User Defined, select New, and then select Data Collector Set.
2. *Name the data collector set*: Give the data collector set a unique name that is descriptive of its purpose.
3. *Choose a data collector*: Select **Create manually**, and then click Next. I will discuss creating a performance counter data collector from a template later in this chapter. Next, select **Performance Counter**, and then click Next.
4. *Adding counters and adjusting the sample interval*: At the "Which performance counters would you like to log?" portion of the wizard choose a sample interval appropriate to the purpose of the counter log based on the "Selecting a sample interval" section discussed later in this chapter. Click Add to select the counter paths you wish to collect. See the "Selecting counter paths for a performance counter data collector" for more information on which counters to select. Once finished, click Next.
5. *Choose a file system location*: Performance Monitor defaults to the "% systemdrive%\PerfLogs\Admin\<Your data collector set name>" directory. I recommend choosing a healthy, non-critical non-overwhelmed logical disk to put the counter log on instead of the system drive. The system drive is critical to the operating system, and if it runs out of disk space, then it may lead to system-wide delays or other problems. Verify that the logical disk chosen to host the counter log file has enough free disk space to handle the intended counter log. For example, a 24 h counter log with a large number of counters will typically use about 300-500 MB of disk usage.
6. *Run with appropriate rights*: Administrator rights is not required to view performance counters and to start the data collector set creation wizard, but it is required to create and run data collector sets. If you are not logged in with a user account that has administrator rights, then provide the credentials of one that does. For details on the minimum security group memberships needed to use features of Performance Monitor, go to the "Overview of Windows Performance Monitor" article at http://technet.microsoft.com/en-us/library/cc749154.aspx. Click Finish to finish the wizard.
7. *Start the data collector set*: After considering the suggestions in the section "Best practices for managing performance counter data collectors" covered later in this chapter, select your newly created data collector set, right-click it, and then select Start. The data collector will begin writing to a counter log. If not, an error message might pop up with a reason and an event may be written to the system event log with more information about the start failure.

DELETING A DATA COLLECTOR SET

When a data collector set is deleted, the files associated with it will not be deleted. Therefore, if you intend to delete all of the files, then make sure that you know the output directory of where the files exist before deleting it.

To delete a data collector set, select it under the User Defined node and press the Delete key or right-click on it and click Delete.

STARTING AND STOPPING PERFORMANCE COUNTER DATA COLLECTORS

Data collector sets have a serial number that increments each time it is started. The serial number is used to create a unique output file, so that the existing file(s) is not overwritten. This means that under normal conditions, you can stop and then immediately start a data collector set without fear of it deleting or overwriting data. With that said, a data collector can be set up to overwrite the same file.

A performance counter data collector has a **File name format** field that is used to determine how the serial number of the data collector set will be used in the output. If the data collector set was created in the Performance Monitor user interface, then the **File name format** field is omitted and a new file system folder is created with computer name, date-time, and serial number in the pattern of Computername_yyyyMMdd-SerialNumber when the data collector set is started. As a best practice for managing counter logs, consider enabling the checkbox **Prefix file with computer name**, which will automatically put the local computer name into the output file.

If the data collector set was created using Logman (discussed later in this chapter), then the **File name format** field has the value of NNNNNN, which is a zero-filled value of the serial number such as 000001 for the initial name. Instead of creating a separate folder each time the data collector set is started, a new file is created with the serial number making it unique. For example, if SystemOverview is the value of the **Log file name** and if the serial number is 5, then the next file name will be SystemOverview_000005.blg.

CREATING A PERFORMANCE COUNTER DATA COLLECTOR TEMPLATE

Creating a data collector set is relatively easy, but can be time-consuming to create one on ten or more computers. A data collector set can be saved to a template file, which can make the creation of data collection sets easier by starting off with pre-defined settings.

Once you have a data collector set that has all of the counters and settings that you prefer, you can save it to a template file.

As a reminder, if a counter path in a data collector has a computer name in the path, then it will always try to collect the respective counter data from that computer. If the counter path does not have a computer name in the path, then it will assume the local computer.

A counter path that has a computer name specified: \\webserver01\Processor(*)*

A counter path that assumes the local computer:

\Processor(*)*

Before creating a template, look through the list of counter paths in the data collector and verify that the counter paths represent the data you wish to collect.

Finally, to save a template file, right-click on a data collector set and select "Save Template" as an XML file.

USING THE PAL TOOL TO CREATE A DATA COLLECTOR TEMPLATE

The Performance Analysis of Logs (PAL) tool is an open-source project that I started in 2007 to help me analyze performance counter logs. It is free for download at http://pal.codeplex.com. The PAL tool is covered in detail in Chapter 9, but I want to take this opportunity to let you know that it can be used to create counter log templates for most of the major Microsoft products and some third-party products.

Once the PAL tool is installed, open the PAL Wizard and navigate to the Threshold File tab. Select a threshold file that best matches the product or products that are installed. Keep in mind that you can always combine threshold files by using the Add button. Otherwise, use the System Overview threshold file, which is a detailed analysis of the Windows and Windows Server operating systems. Once you have a threshold file selected, click the Export to Perfmon template file button and choose a file format. HTM files are for Windows XP and Windows Server 2003 and earlier operating systems. XML files are for Windows Vista and Windows Server 2008 and later operating systems. TXT files are for input into the Logman command-line tool. All of these formats are intended to make it easy to create a performance counter data collector set that has all of the counters that the PAL tool analyzes (Figure 2.20).

CREATING AND STARTING A DATA COLLECTOR SET USING A TEMPLATE

Data collectors are needed to record performance counter data of a computer into a log file. This section walks you through how to create a performance counter log using a data collector set template.

NOTE

This operation requires you to be logged in with an account that is a member of the local Administrators group.

---

1. *Start the wizard*: To start the wizard, open Performance Monitor, right-click on User Defined, select New, and then select Data Collector Set.
2. *Name the data collector set*: Give the data collector set a unique name. The name will be used as part of the file name given to the counter log, so I recommend using a description of the kind of data you are collecting and the name of the computer or computers that the data collector is collecting data from such as "IIS_Web01." Having the name of the computer or computers in the name of the counter log make it easier to identify it.
3. *Choose a template*: Select **Create from a template**, and then click Next. The operating system might offer some templates that help with system diagnostics. Select one of the templates offered, or use a template file using the Browse button. Click Next.

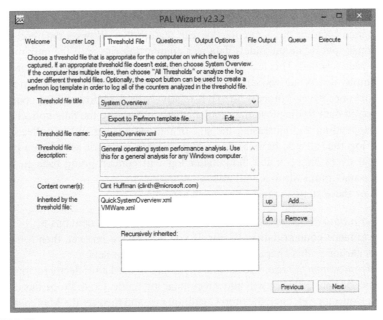

FIGURE 2.20

The Threshold File tab of the PAL Wizard.

4. *Choose a file system location*: Performance Monitor defaults to the "% systemdrive%\PerfLogs\Admin\<Your data collector set name>" directory. I recommend choosing a healthy, non-critical non-overwhelmed logical disk to put the counter log on instead of the system drive. The system drive is critical to the operating system, and if it runs out of disk space, then it may lead to system-wide delays or other problems. Verify that the logical disk chosen to host the counter log file has enough free disk space to handle the intended counter log. For example, a 24 h counter log with a large number of counters will typically use about 300-500 MB of disk usage.

5. *Run with appropriate rights*: Administrator rights are required to create and run a data collector set. If you are not logged in with an account that has administrator rights, then specify the credentials of a user account that does. For details on the minimum security group memberships needed to use features of Performance Monitor, go to the Overview of Windows Performance Monitor article at http://technet.microsoft.com/en-us/library/cc749154.aspx. Click Finish to finish the wizard.

6. *Start the data collector set*: Consider the suggestions in the section "Best practices for managing performance counter data collectors" covered later in this chapter, select your newly created data collector set, right-click it, and then select Start. It will begin writing to a counter log.

CREATING A CIRCULAR DATA COLLECTOR

Performance Monitor has a circular log file feature that allows a data collector to continuously overwrite the oldest data in a counter log file once the maximum file size has been reached. This feature is helpful when details are needed of a rare event. For example, if a Windows Server has a critical performance problem at a random time about once every 3 months, then it is relatively difficult to acquire a counter log with enough data to diagnose the problem. This is because the data collector is by default appending and increasing the size of the counter log. When collecting in a circular log file, all you have to do is stop the data collector set when a problem or critical event happens and the counter log will contain going back in time as far as the maximum file size will allow.

Follow these steps to create a circular log file:

1. *Select a data collector set*: Find a data collector set that contains a performance counter data collector. If you don't have one yet, then follow the steps earlier in this chapter on creating data collector sets.
2. *Set the maximum file size*: The maximum file size of the data collector set must be set before the data collector will allow a circular log mode. Go to Properties of a Data Collector Set, click the Stop Condition tab, and then set the Maximum Size. Choose a maximum file size that is large enough to contain enough data for the amount of time you wish to analyze in the log. A 300 MB maximum file size can generally handle up to 24 h of heavy counter data collected at a 1 min sample interval.
3. *Enable Overwrite and Circular*: Go to the Properties of the Data Collector and navigate to the File tab. Enable the checkboxes Overwrite and Circular. Click OK and start or restart the data collector set for these settings to take effect.

SELECTING A SAMPLE INTERVAL

Consider the purpose of the performance counter data collector when choosing a sample interval. If you are doing 20 min load test runs of an application, then a 15 s sample interval is a good starting point. If you are troubleshooting a memory leak that requires a few weeks of monitoring, then a 5 or 10 min sample interval is more appropriate. Also, consider the how the counter objects collect their data. Counters like **\LogicalDisk(*)\Avg. Disk sec/Read** provide an average value of read latency for all of the IOs that occurred since the last time the counter was collected. But counters like **\System\Processor Queue Length** are point-in-time counters where the value is what it is at the time it is collected. When high accuracy is needed, then sample often, but not so much as to overwhelm the counter log.

If you are still not sure of what sample interval to use, then start with an interval that will collect about 1000 samples though the duration of the data collection. The reasoning for this is Perfmon's line chart can only display up to 1000 data points at a time and the extra samples are hidden in an equal distribution. Limiting the counter log to 1000 or less samples prevents Perfmon from needing to hide some of the data.

SELECTING COUNTER PATHS FOR A PERFORMANCE COUNTER DATA COLLECTOR

Similar to selecting a sample interval, consider the purpose of the performance counter data collector when specifying the counters to collect. If you are troubleshooting an unknown problem, then adding all counters and instances of several counter objects may be appropriate, but at a cost of a large log size. If the purpose of the data collector is to do general monitoring of a server, then specifying the exact counters and all instances of those counters is appropriate. Finally, if you know exactly which counter instances you want to monitor and have a good understanding of data collectors, then specifying the exact instances of counters is appropriate. Choose counter paths that provide enough detail to cover the purpose of the data collector, but not enough to overwhelm it.

Considerations when selecting counters and instances:

- *All counters and all instances of a counter object* (**example: \Processor(*)***): Collection of all of the counters and instances of a counter object will collect the most data possible of the object. This is best for discovery and troubleshooting problems but has the most impact on log size and disk usage.

    Avoid using this option with counter objects that have a very high number of counters and instances such as the Thread object.
- *All instances of a counter* (**example: \Processor(*)\% Processor Time**): Specifying all instances of counters is a good balance between troubleshooting and log size.
- *Specific instances* (**example: \Processor(_Total)\% Processor Time**): Use caution when collecting specific instances of counters. This option will not collect transient instances of a counter such as processes that come and go but it is the least impactful when it comes to log size.

IMPACT OF COLLECTING COUNTER DATA

The impact of collecting performance counter data had a lot more overhead back in the Windows NT 4.0 days, but on modern computer systems, the overhead is relatively trivial. First of all, the actual impact depends on the number of counter instances being collected and the frequency of the sample interval. Next, consider the impact it will have on the network when collecting counters from remote computers. See the "Viewing remote performance counters" section earlier in this chapter for more details. Finally, consider the size of the counter log.

Avoid collecting counters with a large number of instances such as the Thread object unless specifically needed. The Thread object creates a series of counters for each thread on the system. Modern systems can handle millions of threads, so when you multiply this by the number of counters in the Thread object, you can get a lot of counters being logged.

Technically speaking, when Performance Monitor collects counter data, it collects all counters and instances of a counter object and then filters it to the specified counters and instances if needed. This means that it requires less processor overhead to collect all counters and instances of a counter object, but again, it can have a significant impact on the counter log size.

MANAGING THE SIZE OF COUNTER LOGS

The counter log sizes can vary greatly based on the number of counter instances, the frequency of sampling, the log file format, the duration of the log, and if it is in a circular format. In my experience, collecting a 24 h log at 1 min sample intervals with about 20 of the most common counter objects (all counters and instances of the objects) typically results in a 200-400 MB log file.

The text-based counter log formats CSV and TSV are significantly smaller than the binary (*.blg) format. This is because CSV and TSV collect the data as "cooked" or "formula applied," while binary collects the data as "raw." Initially this sounds like text-based counter logs are the better, but unfortunately, text-based counter logs do not collect transient counter instances that come and go after the data collector has started. This means that if you start a performance counter data collector in CSV format capturing all instances of the Process object and restart the worker processes of IIS, then the counter log will be missing the data of the new IIS worker processes. This is because the text-based data collectors are unable to make schema changes to the log file. To prevent missing counter instance data, I highly recommend to always, always, always collect in binary (*.blg) log file format. If you require the data in a parse-able, text-based format, then consider using the Relog.exe command-line tool (discussed later in this chapter) to convert the log from binary to text.

Log files can become very large especially if the data collector was only intended to run for a few days. This is one of the reasons why I recommend setting a stop condition on the data collector set. If you intend to collect data for 24 h, then specify an overall duration of 24 h. The point here is to avoid conditions that could lead to a counter log unintentionally running a system out of disk space (Figure 2.21).

If you end up with an extremely large counter log, then consider using the Relog. exe command-line tool (discussed later in this chapter) to create smaller, more manageable counter logs from the existing counter log.

NOTE

Relog is a command-line tool that can create smaller, more manageable counter logs from extremely large counter logs. For more information, see the Relog-related sections later in this chapter.

CREATING A "BLACK BOX" DATA COLLECTOR

We generally recommend that each Windows or Windows Server computer in your environment should have a "black box" data collector. The term "black box" refers to the data recorder of an aircraft used to record detailed data about the aircraft with the purpose of analyzing it after a crash. In this case, a "black box" data collector refers to a data collector that will record details about computer system until there is a problem with it.

Follow these steps to create a "black box" data collector:

1. *Create a circular log file*: Follow the steps in the "Creating a circular data collector" section earlier in this chapter to create a circular data collector. Use a maximum file size that is large enough to accommodate the intended window of time.

FIGURE 2.21

The default stop conditions of a data collector set.

2. *Set to binary log file format*: Unlike the text-based log file formats, binary is able to record transient counter instances that come and go. This is important when using a data collector that will be running for a long time.
3. *Consider the following list of counter paths in the performance counter data collector*:

   \Cache\Dirty Pages
   \Cache\Lazy Write Flushes/sec
   \LogicalDisk(*)\% Free Space
   \LogicalDisk(*)\% Idle Time
   \LogicalDisk(*)\Avg. Disk Bytes/Read
   \LogicalDisk(*)\Avg. Disk Bytes/Write
   \LogicalDisk(*)\Avg. Disk Queue Length
   \LogicalDisk(*)\Avg. Disk sec/Read
   \LogicalDisk(*)\Avg. Disk sec/Write
   \LogicalDisk(*)\Current Disk Queue Length
   \LogicalDisk(*)\Disk Bytes/sec
   \LogicalDisk(*)\Disk Reads/sec
   \LogicalDisk(*)\Disk Transfers/sec
   \LogicalDisk(*)\Disk Writes/sec
   \LogicalDisk(*)\Free Megabytes
   \Memory\% Committed Bytes In Use
   \Memory\Available MBytes
   \Memory\Cache Bytes
   \Memory\Commit Limit

\Memory\Committed Bytes
\Memory\Free & Zero Page List Bytes
\Memory\Free System Page Table Entries
\Memory\Long-Term Average Standby Cache Lifetime (s)
\Memory\Pages Input/sec
\Memory\Pages Output/sec
\Memory\Pages/sec
\Memory\Pool Nonpaged Bytes
\Memory\Pool Paged Bytes
\Memory\System Cache Resident Bytes
\Network Inspection System\Average inspection latency (sec/bytes)
\Network Interface(*)\Bytes Received/sec
\Network Interface(*)\Bytes Sent/sec
\Network Interface(*)\Bytes Total/sec
\Network Interface(*)\Current Bandwidth
\Network Interface(*)\Output Queue Length
\Network Interface(*)\Packets Outbound Errors
\Network Interface(*)\Packets Received/sec
\Network Interface(*)\Packets Sent/sec
\Network Interface(*)\Packets/sec
\Paging File(*)\% Usage
\PhysicalDisk(*)\Avg. Disk Queue Length
\PhysicalDisk(*)\Avg. Disk sec/Read
\PhysicalDisk(*)\Avg. Disk sec/Write
\PhysicalDisk(*)\Current Disk Queue Length
\PhysicalDisk(*)\Disk Bytes/sec
\PhysicalDisk(*)\Disk Reads/sec
\PhysicalDisk(*)\Disk Writes/sec
\Process(*)\% Privileged Time
\Process(*)\% Processor Time
\Process(*)\Handle Count
\Process(*)\ID Process
\Process(*)\IO Data Operations/sec
\Process(*)\IO Other Operations/sec
\Process(*)\IO Read Operations/sec
\Process(*)\IO Write Operations/sec
\Process(*)\Private Bytes
\Process(*)\Thread Count
\Process(*)\Virtual Bytes
\Process(*)\Working Set
\Processor Information(*)\% DPC Time
\Processor Information(*)\% Interrupt Time
\Processor Information(*)\% of Maximum Frequency
\Processor Information(*)\% Privileged Time

\Processor Information(*)\% Processor Time
\Processor Information(*)\% User Time
\Processor Information(*)\DPC Rate
\Processor Information(*)\Parking Status
\System\Context Switches/sec
\System\Processor Queue Length

The justification of each of these counter paths is discussed throughout this book.

4. *Start the data collector set*: Once the modifications are set, start or restart the data collector set.

TIP

You can save the list of counter paths in an ANSI or Unicode text file and use it as input into the command-line tool Logman for easy creation. See details of using Logman later in this chapter.

TIP

After you create a "black box" data collector, consider saving it and reusing it as a template on other computers.

AUTOMATICALLY STARTING A DATA COLLECTOR SET AFTER A REBOOT

Data collector sets do not automatically start again after a reboot and there are no settings within it to configure this behavior. This can make it difficult to keep a data collector running all the time.

A relatively easy way to solve this problem is to create a scheduled task to start the data collector set every time the system starts. The command below uses the command-line tool, Schtasks, which is part of the Windows and Windows Server operating systems. It will create a scheduled task that will start the data collector set named "SystemOverview" when the system starts. It uses the command-line tool Logman (discussed later in this chapter) as its action.

```
schtasks /create /tn \Microsoft\Windows\PLA\SystemOverviewOnStart /sc
onstart /tr "Logman start SystemOverview" /ru system
```

In this case, I am creating the scheduled task in the Performance Logs and Alerts (PLA) location of Task Scheduler and naming it SystemOverviewOnStart. The reason I am using a name that is different than the data collector set is because when the SystemOverview data collector set was created, a scheduled task with the same name was automatically created and associated with the data collector set (Figure 2.22).

Now that the scheduled task is created, the data collector set should be running after a reboot. Keep in mind that the serial number will increment each time it is started. If you wish to merge the counter logs created from several restarts of the data collector

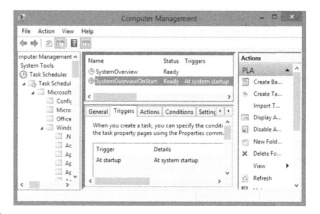

FIGURE 2.22

Task Scheduler showing a user-defined task.

set, then consider using the Relog command-line tool discussed later in this chapter to merge the logs into a single log. For more information on the Schtasks command-line tool, go to "Schtasks" at http://technet.microsoft.com/library/cc725744.

If you prefer Powershell, then the Set-ScheduledTask cmdlet can be used instead of the Schtasks command-line tool. This cmdlet was first introduced in Windows 8 and Windows Server 2012. For more information, see the article "Set-ScheduledTask" at http://technet.microsoft.com/library/jj649814.aspx.

I have a blog entry on this subject called "How to create a "black box" performance counter data collector" at http://blogs.technet.com/b/clinth/archive/2014/05/23/how-to-create-a-blackbox-performance-counter-data-collector.aspx.

BEST PRACTICES FOR MANAGING PERFORMANCE COUNTER DATA COLLECTORS

Performance counter data collectors are relatively easy to create, but there are many aspects to consider that can lead to undesirable results. The following is a list of best practices to consider when managing performance counter data collectors:

1. *Output to a noncritical disk*: If possible, set the output counter log file to a logical disk that is not critical if it runs out of disk space such as avoiding the system drive. It is certainly not good to run any logical disk out of space, but if the system disk is out of space, then the system could become unstable.
2. *Add the computer name to the output file*: Once you have a large number of counter logs, it might be difficult to determine where the logs came from. Try to include the computer name of the computer the log was capturing in the name of the log file. If you are collecting counter data from multiple computers into the same counter log, then consider a name that best describes the contents.

3. *Set a stop condition*: Set the data collector set to the intended size, time, or duration. This can prevent unintended disk space usage.

4. 1000 *samples*: Performance Monitor can display up to 1000 samples, so try to keep the sample count in the log to around 1000. See the section "Selecting a sample interval" discussed earlier in this chapter for more information about setting an appropriate sample interval.

5. *Use the binary log format*: Text-based counter logs are significantly smaller than binary but can miss transient counter instances; therefore, it is safer to log in binary (*.blg) format, which happens to be the default. If you need the counter logs in text file format, then consider logging in binary first and then converting them to CSV or TSV using Relog.exe. Keep in mind that analysis of text-based counter logs in Performance Monitor has some disadvantages. See section "Default scaling in log files" earlier in this chapter for information.

6. *Use local counters*: When possible, gather counters local to the computer. First, when gathering remote counters from a computer in another time zone, Performance Monitor uses the date-time stamp of the computer doing the data collection. The need to constantly adjust for the time zone difference can make it difficult to work with the counter log. Next, gathering local counters significantly reduces the chance of gaps in the counter data. Finally, there is no network overhead when gathering local counters.

7. *Use data collector templates from the PAL tool*: The PAL tool is specifically designed to analyze counter logs using the thresholds discussed throughout this book. Use the tool to export a data collector template with the counters it analyzes, and then use the template to create a performance counter data collector. This will produce a counter log that has all of the counters that the PAL tool will analyze.

8. *Restart after a reboot*: If you need the data collector set to start again after a reboot, and then consider using Task Scheduler. For more information, see the section "Automatically starting a data collector set after a reboot" discussed earlier in this chapter.

9. *Create Data Manager rules*: Data collector sets have Data Manager features that allow you to set the maximum free disk space size and many other options as criteria to remove unnecessary counter logs. Set rules that are appropriate for your needs. For more information on Data Manager, see "Manage Data in Windows Performance Monitor" at http://technet.microsoft.com/en-us/library/cc765998.aspx.

10. *Consider a circular log*: Binary circular log files will overwrite the oldest data in the file when the maximum size of the log is reached. Therefore, it can run infinitely and never consume more space than what is specified as its maximum.

11. *Establish a counter log management solution*: Once you have a few hundred counter logs to manage, it may be necessary to establish a counter log solution that can "roll up" and aggregate the data into larger views such as

a 6-month or 1-year view of several computers and/or logical groups of computers. You can certainly build your own solution using products like Microsoft SQL Server, but keep in mind that Microsoft System Center Operations Manager is designed to manage counter data in an enterprise environment. Also, I recently came across a product called SysTrack (http://www.lakesidesoftware.com/end_user_experience.aspx) that is designed to do enterprise data collection and performance analysis.

TOOLS

Windows and Windows Server have several tools related to Performance Monitor built into the operating system. This part of the book covers the common usage of the command line tools Logman, Lodctr, and Relog.

LOGMAN

Logman.exe is a command-line tool that manages data collector sets either locally or remotely. It is a part of the OS, and it was first introduced in Windows XP and Windows Server 2003. This tool is a great way to automate the creation of counter logs on many computers from a single workstation.

Older operating systems such as Windows XP or Windows Server 2003 will not be able to manage newer versions of Windows using Logman. As a best practice, use the same version of Windows or Windows Server when managing remote computers.

REMINDER
Administration of data collectors requires a user account that is a member of the Administrators group of the target computer(s).

CREATING AND MANAGING A PERFORMANCE COUNTER DATA COLLECTOR USING LOGMAN

The syntax below shows how to create a data collector set where <Name> is the name of the data collector and <CounterPath> is a counter path describing the counter instances separated by a space. Any number of counter paths can be added in this way. Some counter paths such as Network Interface have a space in the name that requires the path to be enclosed within double quotes. Technically, this command creates a data collector set with a performance counter data collector as the only data collector:

```
Logman create counter <Name> -c <CounterPath> <CounterPath>
```

The data collector does not start by default, so start the data collector set running the start command where <Name> is the name of the data collector set:

```
Logman start <Name>
```

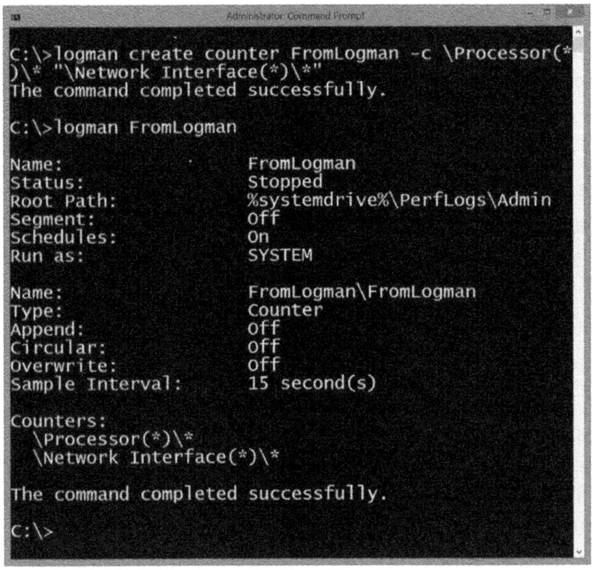

FIGURE 2.23

Using Logman to create and query a data collector set.

In Figure 2.23, I am using Logman to create a performance counter data collector and a data collector set named FromLogman with two counter paths, and then, I am getting the details of the FromLogman data collector set. Notice that I had to enclose the Network Interface counter path within double quotes due to the space in the name.

QUERYING A PERFORMANCE COUNTER DATA COLLECTOR USING LOGMAN

To get details of a data collector set, simply enter the name of the data collector set as an argument to the Logman command. This command is helpful with querying remote computers using the -s parameter.

Use the following syntax to get the details of a data collector set:

```
Logman <Name>
```

COMMONLY USED PARAMETERS OF LOGMAN

The Logman command-line tool is useful for managing the data collector sets on many computer systems. The following is a list of commonly used Logman parameters with descriptions and my own comments from the field. These parameters assume the use of create, update, or import verbs.

Remote Server (-s<Computer>)

This is my favorite parameter of Logman because this executes the command against a remote computer. I commonly use this to manage many computers from a single workstation.

Counter Path (-c<path [path [...]]>)

The counter paths to collect are separated by a space. Any counter paths that have a space in them such as "\Network Interface(*)*" must be enclosed in double quotes. If the list of counter paths is too large for the command prompt to handle, then consider the -cf or -xml parameters to import a list of counters from a file.

File Type (-f<bin|bincirc|csv|tsv|sql>)

The file type specifies the log file format. The default is binary, which I recommend using since it collects all counter instances that come and go. Binary circular (discussed earlier) is also a good format to use since it can be used to create counter log that will not infinitely consume disk space. For more information on counter log file types, see the "Managing the size of counter logs" section earlier in this chapter.

Sample Interval (-si<[[hh:]mm:]ss>)

Specifies the time interval in which counter samples are collected. See the section "Selecting a sample interval" discussed earlier in this chapter for more information about setting an appropriate sample interval.

Begin Time (-b<M/d/yyyy h:mm:ss[AM|PM]>)

Begin the data collector at specified time. This parameter is not necessary unless you want the data collector set to start at a specific time in the future. As a best practice, consider using double quotes due to the space between the date and time:

```
-b "4/13/2013 22:35"
```

Use the appropriate date-time syntax based on your locale. For example, Canada and the United Kingdom use d/M/yyyy. Interesting enough, this parameter accepts the yyyy/M/d as well, which is the date-time format that I prefer.

Also, the hour (h) field accepts 24 h time—meaning you can use 14:00 to indicate 2 PM instead of specifying 02:00 PM.

End Time (-e<M/d/yyyy h:mm:ss[AM|PM]>)

End the data collector at specified time. Specifying a stop time is important when creating a data collector set because it helps prevent the data collector from consuming too much disk space. Use the same considerations as the -b parameter mentioned above.

Output File Path (-o<path!dsn!log>)

It is the path of the output log file or the Data Source Name (DSN) of a database. The default path is '%systemdrive%\PerfLogs\Admin'. When using this parameter against a remote computer, the path is the local path respective to the remote computer. For example, if I execute the command

```
Logman create counter OutputTest -c \Processor(*)\* -s RemoteComputer -o
D:\Perflogs\OutputTest.blg
```

this will create an output file at D:\Perflogs\OutputTest_000001.blg on the remote computer where 000001 is the first serial (sequence) number used by the data collector. This serial number updates each time the data collector set is started.

Counter File (-cf<Filename>)

This is the file path to a text file relative to the local computer where this command is being executed containing a list of counter paths to include in a performance counter data collector. The counter paths must be separated by a line feed and will look something like this:

\Processor(*)*
\Memory*
\Network Interface(*)*

The list is not case-sensitive. The text file must be in ASCII or Unicode encoding. Otherwise, you will get the error "The data is invalid."

Any counter paths that do not exist on the computer such as "\DoesNotExist(*)*" will be included in the data collector's list but will be ignored when collected. On older versions of Windows and Windows Server, the Event Log might show an event indicating it was not able to collect a performance counter.

This parameter does not accept data collector template files (*.xml). Use the "-Import" feature of Logman.exe for data collector template files.

If you are not sure of what counters to collect, then consider using the PAL tool, to create a counter list text file (*.txt) based on the threshold file(s) that you choose in the tool, and the file is intended specifically for the -cf parameter in Logman. The PAL tool is covered in Chapter 12 of this book.

XML Template (-xml<filename>)

The file path to a performance counter data collector template file (*.xml) to import or export. This parameter must be used with the import or export verbs.

If you are not sure of what counters to collect, then consider using the PAL tool, to create a performance counter data collector set template file (*.xml) based on the threshold file(s) that you choose in the tool, and the file is intended for use with the -xml parameter in Logman or in the data collector creation wizard in Performance Monitor. The PAL tool is covered in Chapter 12 of this book.

Maximum File Size (-max<value>)

Maximum log file size in MB or number of records for SQL logs. This parameter is required when creating a binary circular log file because it needs to know how large the file should be until it can overwrite the oldest data.

LODCTR AND UNLODCTR

LODCTR and UNLODCTR are command-line tools that help with installing, uninstalling, and repairing performance counters. They work by updating registry keys related to performance counters. These tools are part of the Windows and Windows Server operating systems dating back to the first version of Windows NT.

DETECTING AND REPAIRING CORRUPTED PERFORMANCE COUNTERS

Counter corruption is very rare but can still happen if the Perflib registry key is inaccessible, corrupted, or deleted. When this happens, Performance Monitor will show a partial list of performance counters, no performance counters, or numeric values where performance counters should be. Figure 2.24 shows what the Add Counters dialog box shows when the Perflib registry key is inaccessible.

If corruption of performance counters is detected, then use the following command to initiate a repair using the current registry settings and backup INI files. This command requires a Command Prompt elevated with administrator rights.

```
LODCTR /R
```

In most cases, this command will fix counter corruption, but if you continue to have counter corruption, then check the permissions on the HKLM\SOFTWARE\Microsoft\ Windows NT\CurrentVersion\Perflib registry key using Regedit. Regedit is a user interface tool that is part of the Windows and Windows Server operating system.

The Perflib registry key will have the following permissions by default:

- Full control to the Administrators group and the SYSTEM account
- Read access to the CREATOR OWNER user account and to the Performance Monitor Users and Performance Log Users security groups

If counter corruption persists, then consider reinstalling specific counters detailed in the next section of this chapter, consider using the Process Monitor tool to detect abnormal file or registry access, or consider opening a support case with Microsoft to address the problem.

The Microsoft Knowledge Base article 2554336 at http://support.microsoft.com/ kb/2554336 has more information regarding rebuilding corrupted performance counters.

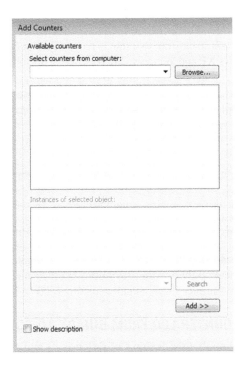

FIGURE 2.24

Corrupted counters on Windows 7.

INSTALLING AND UNINSTALLING PERFORMANCE COUNTERS

To rebuild specific counter objects, including extensible, product-related counter objects, use the LODCTR and UNLODCTR command-line tools. The procedure is relatively simple as long as you have the INI file associated with the counter definitions. These files are commonly packaged with the installation media of the respective product. Therefore, refer to the documentation of the respective product. In regard to Microsoft products, search the Microsoft Knowledge Base for the term "LODCTR" and the product you are interested in. You will most likely find articles referring to files that ship with the installation media of the product.

Once you have the proper INI file, use the following command to rebuild the counters described in the INI file where < INI-FilePath > refers to the location of the INI file:

```
LODCTR /R:<INI-FilePath>
```

For more information on rebuilding extensible performance counters, see the article "How to manually rebuild Performance Counter Library values" at http://support.microsoft.com/kb/300956.

RELOG

Relog.exe is another command-line tool that is part of the operating system and was introduced in Windows XP and Windows Server 2003. This tool creates a new counter log from existing counter logs. It is able to convert counter logs from one type to another such as binary (*.blg) to a CSV (*.csv) file; filter based on counter, type, or time; or merge multiple counter logs into a single counter log. Counter logs used in this way will not be deleted or altered by Relog.

As a best practice, use input files originally created by a data collector and input files that were previously the output of Relog.

WARNING

When Relog converts a counter log with more than 1000 samples, the precision of the data points might be slightly skewed.

Be aware that when using the Relog tool to convert a counter log with more than 1000 samples in it, there might be some deviations in the results. This is another reason to try to keep the samples in the counter logs to 1000 or less.

CONVERTING A COUNTER LOG FROM BINARY TO CSV USING RELOG

One of the most commonly used features of Relog is its ability to convert a binary (*.blg) counter log to a text-based counter log such as a CSV (*.csv) file or a TSV (*.tsv) counter log. As mentioned earlier, recording a counter log in binary is recommended because it is able to collect transient counter instances that come and go, but a binary log (*.blg) is difficult to parse with other tools. Therefore, there is often a need to convert it to a text-based log.

The following example converts the binary (*.blg) counter log DataCollector01.blg to a CSV file logfile.csv:

```
Relog DataCollector01.blg -f csv -o logfile.csv
```

REDUCING THE SIZE OF A COUNTER LOG USING RELOG

Have you ever created a performance counter data collector intending to run it for a few days and then suddenly realize it has been running for a month and it is 2 GB in size? It happens. Unfortunately, counter logs above 500 MB are difficult to load and work with in Performance Monitor simply due to the large size.

When this happens, the Relog command-line tool has many filtering features that you can choose to help with converting it to a more practical size.

Counter Filtering (-c<path [path . . .]>)

Counters to filter from the input log. This option will produce a counter log with only the counter instances that match the counter paths specified as arguments to this parameter. The syntax is identical to the -c parameter in Logman. Each counter path is delimited by a space.

Use the following syntax to filter a counter log using the -c parameter:

```
Relog <Filename> -c <CounterPath [CounterPath ...]> -o <OutputFile>
```

In the following command, I am filtering DataCollector01.blg for counter instances that match **\Processor(*)*** or **\Network Interface(*)*** and producing NewLog.blg:

```
Relog DataCollector01.blg -c \Processor(*)\* "\Network Interface(*)\*" -o
NewLog.blg
```

Counter Filtering with a File (-cf<filename>)

File listing performance counters to filter from the input log. Default is all counters in the original log file. This parameter is identical to the -c parameter where the counter log is filtered by the counter paths provided except that a text file containing a list of counter paths is used instead of listing the counter paths on the command line. Similar to the -cf parameter in Logman, the file must be a text file using ASCII or Unicode encoding where each counter path is delimited by a line feed.

Data Filtering (-t<n>)

Only write every *n*th record into the output file. Default is to write every record.

Time filtering (-b<M/d/yyyy h:mm:ss[AM|PM]> and -e<M/d/yyyy h:mm:ss[AM|PM]>)

These parameters will filter the input file by the time range provided. This option is helpful when you only need a specific time range of a counter log.

FIXING CORRUPTED COUNTER LOGS USING RELOG

In rare cases, a counter log can get corrupted. This can happen if a system is suddenly halted when a performance counter data collector is running. When this happens, Relog might be able to filter the corrupted counter log and produce a good one. This procedure might require using one or more of the filtering options mentioned earlier in this chapter.

MERGING COUNTER LOGS USING RELOG

Relog is able to merge multiple counter log files into a single counter log file. This feature only works with binary log files (*.blg) as input. For best results, use counter logs from the same performance counter data collector with the settings of the data collector unchanged. Otherwise, mixing counter logs of different data collectors or settings can produce unpredictable results.

CONCLUSION

In this chapter, we covered Performance Monitor's common usage and management of performance counter data collectors and introduced Performance Monitor-related tools. As a best practice, always record counter logs in binary format to get the best experience in data collection and analysis and consider "black box" performance counter data collectors for perpetual data gathering on hand when needed.

Twitter handles of Performance Monitor experts

If you have a question that this chapter did not address, then consider reading the blogs or contacting one of the following subject matter experts over Twitter:
Benny Lakunishok

   Twitter: @Lakunishok (https://twitter.com/Lakunishok)

Bruce Adamczak

   Twitter @BruceAdamczak (https://twitter.com/bruceadamczak)

   Blogs: http://blogs.technet.com/b/bruce_adamczak

Chris Davis

   Twitter: @ChrisDavis9z (https://twitter.com/ChrisDavis9z)

   Blog: 9z.com

Clint Huffman

   Twitter: @ClintH (https://twitter.com/clinth)

   Blog: http://blogs.technet.com/clinth

Ewan MacKellar

   Twitter: @EwanMackellar (https://twitter.com/ewanmackellar)

Mark Fugatt

   Twitter: @mfugatt (https://twitter.com/mfugatt)

   Blog: http://blogs.technet.com/mfugatt

Storage

> *Do not offend the testing gods by saying something like we don't need a*
> *backup because it's stored on the SAN.*
> **Robert George (Microsoft Testing Consultant)**

INTRODUCTION

The disk drive is arguably the slowest resource in a computer system. Therefore, the Windows operating system is tuned to avoid it at all costs. Inevitably though, data must be read from or written to disk to persist it before power is removed. The point of this chapter is to help you understand disk-related concepts, bring the concepts together to create an initial indicator formula of a disk performance problem, and introduce various tools that will help you toward the root cause.

This chapter would have normally been titled "Disk," but with the popularity of solid-state storage and virtualization of storage media, I can't rightfully call it "Disk" anymore. With that said, when the words "disk" or "hard drive" are used, they are synonymous with any of these storage mediums.

As I travel the world and learn more about Windows performance analysis, I often find myself comparing disk performance to fast-food restaurants. Orders can be taken (I/O request packets, IRPs) and the respective order fulfilled—not always in a first-in, first-out sequence. The length of the line (the queue) doesn't necessarily reflect how long it will take to get your food. What "really" matters is how fast you are served!

INITIAL INDICATORS OF POOR DISK PERFORMANCE

If I only had one indicator of a disk performance problem, it would be the **\Logical-Disk(*)\Avg. Disk sec/Transfer** performance counter. This counter is the average time, in seconds, of a disk transfer (a read or write operation according to the operating system). In other words, it is the average time that all of the disk transfers waited until served by the disk driver. Unlike other counters, LogicalDisk counters with "Avg" in the name average "all" of the IRPs between each time it is sampled.

This means that if this counter was sampled every 60 s and there were 1000 disk transfers between the samples, then all 1000 disk transfers would be averaged together.

If I only had two indicators of a disk performance problem, I would use **\LogicalDisk(*)\Avg. Disk sec/Read** and **\LogicalDisk(*)\Avg. Disk sec/Write**. These counters are identical to how the sec/Transfer counter works but are simply the reads and writes broken out. Knowing if reads or writes are a problem can help identify problems with disk cache.

Going back to the restaurant analogy, these counters would be like asking each person leaving the restaurant how long it took to get their food after ordering it and then periodically computing an average for that time range. If the average is computed too often, then there might be too much data to manage, but if sampled too infrequently, then it would be difficult to determine the peak lunch hour or peak dinner hour.

Therefore, when sampling the "latency" counters, try to find the "Goldilocks" range of not too often and not too long. A good starting sample interval is 15 seconds (which happens to be the default), but avoid longer than 1 min.

NOTE

The counters of **\LogicalDisk(*)\Avg. Disk sec/Read|Write|Transfer** and **\PhysicalDisk(*)\Avg. Disk sec/Read|Write|Transfer** are often referred to as the disk response times or disk latency. I use these names synonymously throughout this book.

If any of the latency counters are greater than the service times of the storage device on average, then it warrants more investigation. Why? Well, service times are the typical amount of time it should take a storage device to complete an I/O according to the manufacturer. As a matter of fact, this information is typically part of the specifications of the storage device.

The expected service time of most 5400 RPM disk drives is about 17 ms and that of 7200 RPM disk drives is about 13 ms, so the generically accepted threshold (when you don't know the service times of the storage device you are working with) is 15 ms. This means that if the disk drive always had one outstanding I/O request in the queue, then each I/O would be serviced at the average expected service time or less (many factors can significantly improve I/O request completions). When you introduce many outstanding I/O request, then all of them are waiting, adding to their individual latency timers just like customers waiting on their food.

Windows and Windows Server begin the latency timer right when an I/O is placed in the queue (when food is ordered).

If two I/O requests are placed in the queue at the same time, then both requests are queued and start their respective timers. The disk drive tries to service all of the I/O requests as fast as it can. Let's say that it takes a disk drive 8 ms to service each I/O. The first I/O would be serviced in 8 ms, but the second I/O would have to wait in the queue for 8 ms while the first I/O was serviced (assuming that the storage device or disk is only able to handle one IO at a time) and wait another 8 ms for the disk drive to service it. The disk drive is running consistently at 8 ms, but the average "response time" has increased due to the cumulative effect of the I/O requests waiting in the queue. In this case, the average response time to both I/O requests is 12 ms (8 ms + 16 ms) / 2. This means that when a disk is overwhelmed with I/O requests, the more outstanding I/O requests there are, the longer the response times will be.

This is one of the reasons why a high queue length is "generally" considered bad. If the logical disk had 20 outstanding I/O requests in the queue with 1000 physical disk drives behind it, would that change anything? It certainly would. It would be similar to having 1000 checkout registers with only 20 people ready to check out. This is why response times are often a better indicator of disk performance problems than the queue length.

STORAGE HARDWARE AND INDUSTRY TERMINOLOGY

Before I can talk about how to solve performance problems with disk, we need to cover some core concepts of disk hardware and industry terminology.

HARDWARE AND TERMINOLOGY

This is the terminology that I use in this book. This is important because many of these terms can be subjective depending on the hardware and operating systems that you and/or your vendors work with.

I/O Request Packet

First, I/O stands for the input or output of data to or from a device—it is how a computer communicates with the hardware and other logical devices. An IRP is the request structure that Windows and Windows Server use to transfer data to and from devices, but this structure is used for all kinds of I/O such as network and disk. This means that some of the operating system performance counters lump network I/O and disk I/O together, making it difficult to determine what kind of I/O we are working with. I will mention some of these counters later in this chapter when analyzing disk performance with Performance Monitor.

I/Os per Second

This is an industry term describing the number of I/O requests that are fulfilled per second. This term is often used to describe the amount of throughput that a disk or hardware controller can handle, but the measurement doesn't always include other contributing factors such as the size of the I/O and if it is sequential or random I/O, all of which can dramatically affect the number of I/O operations per second (IOPS) the disk can do. Therefore, it is important to specify these conditions when reporting the IOPS of a device. I might say my 7200 RPM disk drive is capable of 90 IOPS when doing 50% random reads, 50% random writes, and I/O sizes of 64 KB, or it can do 260 IOPS when doing sequential reads and writes at the same I/O size.

Disk Transfers/sec is the number of read and write operations completed per second—this is the Windows and Windows Server equivalent of IOPS, but not necessarily the number of IOPS that the hardware is doing. Windows Server could be doing 100 write operations per second, but the hardware RAID1 controller would have to do 200 IOPS (100 I/O operations to two disk drives). The counters **\LogicalDisk(*)\Disk Transfers/sec** and **\PhysicalDisk(*)\Disk Transfers/sec** measure the number of disk transfers per second to the respective logical disk or physical disk.

Hard Disk Drive (spindle)

The ye olde spindle is the spinning magnetic disk still widely used today for disk storage. Most spindles can only handle one I/O at a time. Now, one might think if a disk queue has more than one outstanding I/O on average, then it is overwhelmed; well, that "could" be true, but keep in mind that there are many other considerations like hardware cache built into the disk drive and controller that help dramatically with performance. Even the driver can help the drive to optimize the head position and rotation to read or write many I/Os in a single rotation.

Keep in mind that the performance of a single disk drive will vary greatly depending on the peripheral bus, hardware controller, cache, and revolutions per minute (RPM).

Solid-State Drive

A solid-state drive (SSD) is a data storage device that uses solid-state memory to persist data in the same way as a hard disk drive—meaning the data is retained when power is removed. These drives are based on similar media as USB "thumb" drives, usually use less power than hard disk drives, and often have significantly faster access times than hard disk drives, making them popular in laptops and other mobile devices. There are many types of SSDs, but my intent is to cover them only from a generalized perspective.

The only disadvantage of SSDs that I know of is that it oxidizes the media when it is written to limit the number of times that the media can be written to before it is unusable. This raises concerns about its long-term viability in enterprise environments. In addition, it is currently more expensive than hard disk drives per gigabyte. With that said, I have been using SSDs under constant use for over 6 years now with no problems. As a matter of fact, so far all of my SSDs have out lived my 1 TB spindle hard disk drives bought around the same time.

Another observation that I noticed about the SSD drive in my laptop is that when there is little demand (few, if any, outstanding I/O requests in the queue), then the response times are often higher than 15 ms. This is most likely due to the drive going into a power saving mode. But when under constant load, the SSD runs extremely fast—less than 2 ms on average. This is similar to behavior that I've seen on enterprise-class servers connected to a storage area network (SAN). My point is that when analyzing disk performance, a major consideration is whether or not the disk has constant load or not. This topic is covered in the "Understanding the disk queue" section later in this chapter.

Direct-Attached Storage

Hard drives that are represented to the operating system as a physical disk or logical unit number (LUN) are considered direct-attached storage or DAS. The computer assumes it is a single storage device "directly attached" to the computer. With that said, hardware disk controllers can control many hard drives and represent them as one or more "physical drives" or LUNs to the computer. This means that from a Windows and Windows Server perspective, we really don't know how many physical spindles are really behind any given LUN and we don't know the physical distance to it. With that said, as of Windows 8 and Windows Server 2012 forward, if the system has the SMI-S provider or SMP provider, then it is possible to determine the physical topology of a LUN using Powershell. For more information on SMI-S, see "Getting started with SMI-S on Windows Server 2012" at http://blogs.technet.com/b/filecab/archive/2012/07/06/3507632.aspx.

In any case, my point is that if a disk controller represents a "physical disk" to Windows or Windows Server, then the disks from that hardware are considered "direct-attached."

Just a Bunch of Disks and RAID Types

A just a bunch of disks (JBOD) is an industry term that refers to a physical grouping of disk drives that are not part of a network of drives such as a SAN or network-attached storage (NAS) device. They are simply "JBOD" where every physical disk drive is presented to the operating system (Figure 3.1).

Network-Attached Storage

A NAS is a physical device that emulates a network file system on a TCP/IP network. A NAS can emulate the Server Message Block (SMB) protocol, which is a common protocol that Windows and Windows Server use for network file storage (Figure 3.2).

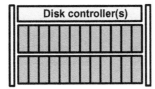

FIGURE 3.1

A diagram of a JBOD.

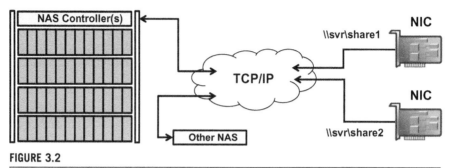

FIGURE 3.2

A network diagram of a NAS device and interface cards.

In regard to performance, a NAS is dependent on the performance of the network interface card (NIC) and the TCP/IP network nodes along the way. Therefore, refer to Chapter 9 "Network" on performance and troubleshooting of network resources.

SAN and Fibre Channel

A SAN is a network of storage devices (such as disk drives or SSDs) and is managed by one or more controllers. The word "network" in the name refers to the network of drives within the enclosure. A SAN can be attached to a computer system through Internet small computer systems interface (iSCSI) or Fibre Channel (FC). FC (also known as the "fabric") is made up of fiber-optic cables and optionally fiber-optic switches. A host bus adapter (HBA) is a physical interface that is installed on computers to access the FC network. The HBA allows the computer to access one or more SANs. The LUNs (a physical disk drive) presented to the operating system are considered "DAS" even though the SAN might be physically located elsewhere (Figure 3.3).

Regarding performance, SANs are often powerful and fast. With that said, in my experience, they are relatively expensive and therefore often become overused and abused. Even the fastest SAN can be overrun with enough I/O demand, so it's

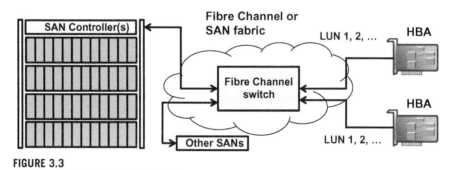

FIGURE 3.3

A diagram of a Fibre Channel network.

important to constantly monitor their performance. Unfortunately, the complexity of this type of environment often makes it difficult to understand where to start.

From my perspective, I start by comparing the SAN-attached LUNs to the performance of a single disk drive—meaning if the SAN cannot beat the performance of my 7200 USB disk drive, then there is something wrong. To be specific, I look for an average disk queue length of at least two to indicate a constant load on the disk and response times greater than 15 ms when working with 64 KB or smaller I/O sizes.

Internet Small Computer Systems Interface

iSCSI connects LUNs from a SAN to a computer just like an FC network but uses commodity NICs and a TCP/IP network. In many cases, this solution is more cost-effective because the I/O can be transferred using relatively inexpensive twisted pair "copper" cables instead of fiber-optic cables.

In regard to performance analysis, I treat these with the same initial indicators and thresholds as SAN-attached LUNs—meaning I look for constant I/O requests (disk queuing), high disk latency, and the I/O sizes (Figure 3.4).

I/O OPERATIONS PER SECOND

IOPS is an industry standard for measuring the throughput of a disk subsystem. The maximum number of IOPS that a storage device can do is often associated with a static number, but the reality is that it changes based on what seems a near infinite number of variables such as I/O size, cache, ratio of reads to writes, and RAID configuration. Therefore, it is important to note when comparing IOPS numbers that they are only relevant when compared with I/Os performed with the same workload, such as the same I/O size, and whether they are random or sequential.

From a Windows and Windows Server perspective, IOPS is the number of IRPs that have been fulfilled per second and change as the I/O demand changes. As the I/O request is passed down through the hardware and then to the physical disk drive, each layer has its own number of IOPS. For example, a RAID1 configuration will need to split a write operation to two disk drives.

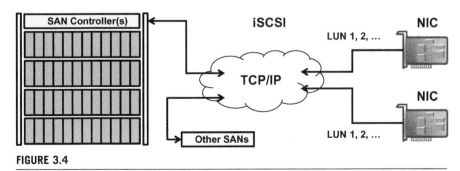

FIGURE 3.4

A diagram of an iSCSI network.

Storage device	IOPS	Service time (ms)
3.5" floppy disk USB drive	1.7	600
5400 RPM hard disk	60	17
7200 RPM hard disk	80	14
10K RPM hard disk	125	11
15K RPM hard disk	200	6
Solid state drive (SSD)	5000	0.2

FIGURE 3.5

The IOPS and service times expected of common storage devices.

Figure 3.5 shows the worst-case, no cache, typical service times for common storage devices. The service times in this chart are referring to the I/O that the device is currently serving—not what is queued.

Use the chart in Figure 3.5 as a very rough indicator of what to expect from storage devices in these categories, but always check with your hardware vendor for a more precise specification. The numbers (IOPS and typical service times) are based on 64 KB I/O sizes and a 50% random read/random write ratio. Storage devices should perform better than the numbers given here simply because most workloads include sequential I/O and smaller I/O sizes, allowing the device to respond to those requests faster. I/O size considerations are discussed later in this chapter.

DEDICATED VERSUS SHARED SPINDLES

Before the arrival of SANs, computers running Windows Server frequently used dedicated disk arrays within close physical proximity. This configuration gave the servers consistent and reliable amounts of IOPS, response times, and transfer rates, but disk drives would often be idle during low system usage.

Figure 3.6 shows three servers with different I/O demands. Server A's I/O demands are high and the drives are 100% utilized, server B's I/O demands are moderate where half of the drives are idle, and server C's I/O demands are low

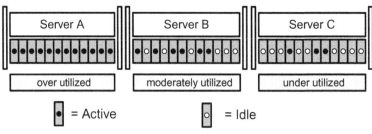

FIGURE 3.6

An example of unbalanced spindle utilization.

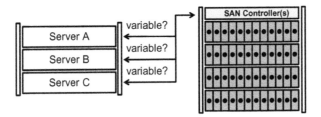

FIGURE 3.7

An example of share disk drives maximizing all disk drives, but at the cost of inconsistent performance.

and most of the disk drives are idle. In addition, this scenario assumes that capacity demands are irrelevant.

In this example, server A clearly needs more disk drives to accommodate the high I/O demand. But when the purchase order is given to the manager, the manager doesn't understand why more disk drives are needed when many of them are idle on server B and server C. It seems a waste of good resources to not be able to utilize the idle drives, but distributing the I/O load to all of the disk drives is impractical when they are in production.

Now that SAN technology has arrived, administrators can share spindles across multiple servers, allowing all of the drives to be used (so they are less likely to be idle) and maximizing the monetary investment in hardware. However, the likelihood of the servers getting consistent and reliable IOPS from the shared disk drives is often unpredictable. Also, if one or more of the servers have a high demand for I/O, then it might negatively affect the performance of the other servers (Figure 3.7).

For example, server B might have had great performance from the SAN a week ago, but now that server A is busy again, it is saturating the SAN and cascading the effects to server B and server C. This can make isolation of the performance problem quite complicated.

Furthermore, if we are load testing an application on server C while server A and server B are in production, then the testing will not be able to get consistent results. Consistent results are vital to load testing because changes to the solution need to be measured with precision. Therefore, I highly recommend using dedicated hard drives in an isolated environment when doing testing.

In summary, SANs are incredible devices that try to maximize the usage of all of the disk drives, but like any other device, they can be overwhelmed.

PHYSICAL DISKS AND LOGICAL DISKS

A physical disk is a Logical Unit Number (LUN) presented to the operating system by a hardware controller. Even though it is presented as a single physical disk, there could be one or more disk drives behind the LUN.

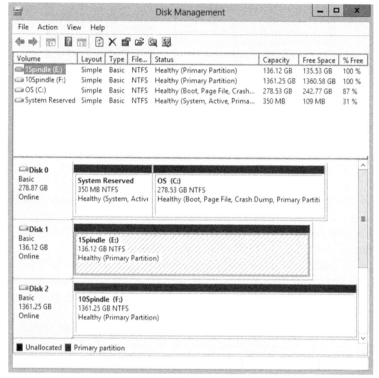

FIGURE 3.8

A sample configuration of Disk Manager.

In Figure 3.8, physical disks are shown in the lower left pane of Disk Manager as Disk 0, Disk 1, and Disk 2. Disk 1 has a single disk drive behind it, but Disk 2 has 10 disk drives (often referred to as spindles) behind it even though it appears as a single physical drive to Windows Server.

In this case, there is a logical disk of C:, E:, and F: respective to each of the physical disks. Logical disks can span multiple physical disks and multiple logical disks can be created on a single physical disk. When logical disks are created across physical disks, it is referred to as software RAID.

DISK CAPACITY

The storage capacity of disk drives must be greater than the current and expected needs of the operating system as well as the expected workloads of applications and services; otherwise, functionality may fail. Special operating system files such as paging files, memory dumps, and shadow copies can quickly consume large amounts of space, so it is important to understand and anticipate these needs. For example, if the computer has 32 GB of physical memory and if the crash dump setting is set to complete memory dump, then one of the page files must be the size of physical memory (32 GB) plus 1 MB (header data) to accommodate the dump. Also, when identifying consumers of hard drive space, consider tools that are aware of hard links, symbolic links, junctions, and compression. Each of these can affect the amount of reported disk usage.

IDENTIFYING LOW STORAGE CAPACITY

Low free space on disk drives can be identified in many ways such as through Windows Explorer, Disk Management, Windows Powershell, WMI, and performance counters.

The LogicalDisk performance counters % Free Space and Free Megabytes can help determine if the disk is low on free space. The thresholds for these counters are relative to the expected needs of your applications or services. % Free Space measures the percentage of total usable space of a logical disk drive. A disk with less than 10% free space might not be significant when working with large capacity disks or RAID sets, so consider the Free Megabytes counter can provide a more precise value. Also, keep in mind that tools such as the disk defragmenter might require a specific percentage of free space (Figure 3.9).

In any case, when disk space is low, it is important to free up space to prevent application or service failures.

FILE SYSTEM ALLOCATION SIZE (BLOCK SIZE) CONSIDERATIONS

The file system allocation or cluster size is commonly referred to as the block size of the disk. If a logical disk is formatted at a 4 KB block size (default on Windows and Windows Server), then a file that is 44 bytes in size will use a 4 KB (4096 bytes) block on disk to store it making the "size on disk" 4 KB. This wastes 4052 bytes of space. Figure 3.10 shows the file properties of test.txt demonstrating this effect.

Now, before you start formatting all of your disks at 512 bytes (the smallest allocation size in the Format dialog box), keep in mind that management of a disk drive is done at the block size level. This means that small block sizes take longer to manage than large block sizes. Would you rather manage a room full of large boxes or a room full of sand? There is certainly a trade-off between storage capacity and management efficiency, so choose a block size that best matches your needs.

Counter	Warning	Critical
% Free Space	< 10%	< 5%

FIGURE 3.9

Thresholds for % Free Space.

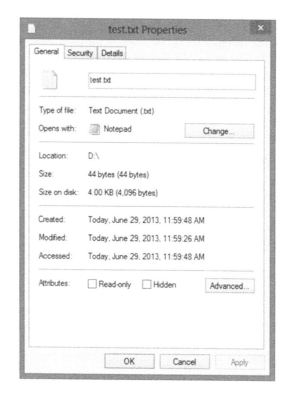

FIGURE 3.10

File properties showing the file size and size on disk.

TROUBLESHOOTING FREE SPACE

There are certainly many tools that can help with identifying the largest consumers of disk space usage and/or assist with freeing up space. Here are a few that are relatively quick and easy to use.

Disk Cleanup Wizard

The Disk Cleanup wizard (part of the Desktop Experience feature) is often overlooked but is quite effective at freeing up disk space by removing files and other items that are no longer needed. Also, it is part of the operating system, so this should be your first tool to consider. It cleans up downloaded programs, temporary Internet files, off-line Web pages, the Recycle Bin, and so on. Probably the best feature is its ability to reduce the Windows component store (%windir%\WinSxS folder) directory that contains backup files of hotfixes and service packs. This feature works best shortly after applying a service pack, allowing it to remove the backup files of hotfixes replaced by the service pack. For more information on cleaning up the Windows component store, see the article "How to address disk space issues that are caused by a large Windows component store (WinSxS) directory" at http://support.microsoft.com/kb/2795190. For more information on the Disk Cleanup wizard, see the article "Delete files using Disk Cleanup" at http://windows.microsoft.com/en-US/windows-vista/Delete-files-using-Disk-Cleanup.

Disk Usage

This command-line tool is part of the Sysinternals suite and is available for free at http://live.sysinternals.com/du.exe. According to the Sysinternals Web site, Du reports the disk space usage for the directory you specify. By default, it recursively enumerates directories to show the total size of a directory and its subdirectories.

WinDirStat (Windows Directory Statistics)

This is a free tool that visually shows the largest directories and files on one or more hard drives. According to the WinDirStat Web site, WinDirStat is a disk usage statistics viewer and cleanup tool for various versions of Microsoft Windows. The tree map represents each file as a colored rectangle, the area of which is proportional to the file's size. For more information on this tool, go to http://windirstat.info/.

Windows Management Instrumentation (WMI)

WMI can be used to get disk free space using the following Powershell command: gwmi win32_logicaldisk | Select Name, FreeSpace | ft -AutoSize.

UNDERSTANDING AND MEASURING DISK PERFORMANCE

This part of the chapter focuses on understanding the initial indicators of poor disk performance, what they are measuring, and how they are measuring it in order to warrant more investigation. Later in this chapter, I will go into various disk analysis tools that can help with identifying the root cause. For a deep dive into analyzing disk performance, consider the "Disk Subsystem Performance Analysis for Windows" document at http://download.microsoft.com/download/e/b/a/eba1050f-a31d-436b-9281-92cdfeae4b45/subsys_perf.doc.

PHYSICALDISK AND LOGICALDISK COUNTER OBJECTS

We (Microsoft Support) are commonly asked if we should use the PhysicalDisk counters or the LogicalDisk counters in Performance Monitor for disk analysis. The question should not be about which counter object is better, but understanding what they measure.

I commonly start with LogicalDisk counters simply because it is the closest measurement to the application creating the I/O demand. What I mean is when Microsoft SQL Server writes to a disk, it writes to a logical disk, so from an application perspective, the performance of the logical disk is more important than the underlying physical disk performance. If I see two or more logical disks performing poorly, I bring up the PhysicalDisk counters to see if they are related to the same physical disk. For reference, the PhysicalDisk object measures the activity at the partition manager and the LogicalDisk object measures the activity at the volume manager.

UNDERSTANDING THE DISK QUEUE

Each logical disk and physical disk has a queue containing IRPs waiting for servicing. This is similar to placing an order for a latte and waiting for it to be filled. There has always been a lot of speculation as to what thresholds we can place on the queue length and what we can derive from it. But a queue is still a queue and I think we can all agree that it isn't how long the queue is, but how fast you get through it. With that in mind, I'll discuss some of the assumptions that have been made in regard to queue depth and their respective thresholds.

Most, spinning hard disk drives can only service one I/O at time, so naturally, performance counters that relate to the disk queue, such as Avg. Disk Queue Length, % Idle Time, and % Disk Time, have been initial indicators in the industry for many years. But there is a common assumption that the I/O requests are evenly distributed across all of the disk drives (spindles) behind a given LUN and that all of the disk drives are dedicated (not shared) to the LUN. This isn't always the case, therefore the queue length shouldn't be the only performance indicator to use.

As an example, if the Avg. Disk Queue Length counter is 2 and there are 10 dedicated spindles behind the LUN, then the LUN should have no problem with handling the load. Right? This is like having 10 checkout lines with an average of only two people wanting to check out. Well, this assumes that there is an equal distribution of those I/O requests to physical spindles (checkout lines), which isn't always the case. Furthermore, the workload (the I/O requests in the queue) of the disk could quickly change from second to second.

In Figure 3.11, the disk queue on the left is a single spindle (disk drive) that is aware of all six I/O requests but can only service one of them at a time. Being aware of all six I/O requests allows the driver to optimize the path that the head takes to improve the response times. The disk queue on the right is no different than the queue on the left except that the hardware (a SAN in this case) can service all of the I/O requests at the same time.

Avg. Disk Queue Length

The Avg. Disk Queue Length counter doesn't actually measure the queue length directly. It is an estimate based on the formula of Avg. Disk sec/Transfer multiplied by Disk Transfers/sec. This means that if there were 100 Disk Transfers/sec and it took 10 ms for each to be serviced, then there must have been one request queued/in-flight on average. The real disk queue length can vary dramatically from second to second, so in many cases, this counter can help provide some stability.

Since a LUN can have many spindles behind it that may or may not be shared with other LUNs and since we cannot assume an equal distribution of IOs across the

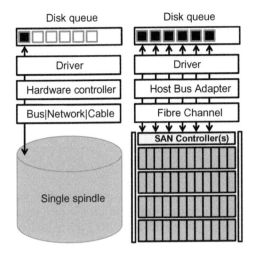

FIGURE 3.11

A diagram of disk queues and related hardware.

spindles, we can't assign a "one-size-fits-all" threshold to this counter. Instead, use this counter as an indicator of average I/O demand and correlate it to the latency counters discussed later in this chapter.

Current Disk Queue Length

The value of Current Disk Queue Length is a "point in time" of how many IRPs are in the disk queue/in-flight at the moment it is sampled. The size of the queue can vary greatly between samples, making it difficult to measure, but keep in mind that the more I/O requests in the queue, the more efficient the disk driver can be. Like the other queue-related counters, correlate this counter with the latency counters discussed later in this chapter.

% Idle Time

The % Idle Time performance counter is a popular counter used in many technical articles. Despite its popularity, be careful about relying on it as the only indicator of performance. % Idle Time reports the percentage of time that the disk queue had nothing in it. This means that if the disk queue had at least one outstanding I/O for the duration of the sampling, then % Idle Time will be zero. This doesn't mean that the disk is overwhelmed—it just means that it had work to do whether it was one outstanding I/O or 1000 outstanding I/Os. Knowing if the disk queue constantly had work to do is important when correlating it with the latency counters such as Avg. Disk sec/Transfer.

If the value of % Idle Time is below 10, then it is worth investigating the latency (response times) of the disk to see if the IRPs are waiting in the queue longer than the average expected service time of the physical media.

DISK TRANSFERS, IOPS, AND READ/WRITE RATIOS

Disk Transfers/sec, Disk Reads/sec, and Disk Writes/sec are performance counters under the LogicalDisk and PhysicalDisk counter objects that measure the number of read and/or write operations on a disk drive per second. Disk Transfers/sec is the closest counter that we have to the number of IOPS on a disk drive, but this is from the operating system's perspective—meaning hardware RAID could be doing more IOPS depending on the RAID type. For example, Disk 2 in Disk Manager might appear as a single physical disk to Windows Server but might have two spindles (disk drives) in a RAID 1 mirror set behind it. In this case, the operating system will do one write operation, but the hardware controller will have to do two operations—one to each disk drive (Figure 3.12).

RAID 5 is popular because it is a good balance between capacity and redundancy, but it is one of the worst RAID types to choose when it comes to small, random, write operations. For every one write operation, RAID 5 has to read the data, read the parity, calculate parity, write the data, and write the parity, making it a 1:4 ratio. Now, this is a generalization that does not take into consideration bulk write operations, but my point is that RAID 5 is not always the best option for write performance.

Many SAN vendors will say that you don't have to worry about the RAID type because the massive amount of cache in front of the SAN will compensate for it and this is probably true in most cases, but keep in mind that some services like Microsoft Exchange Server will do continuous write operations that might eventually overrun the hardware cache. For this reason, it is important to choose a RAID type that best matches the expected I/O patterns and letting the cache make it perform that much better.

THE EFFECTS OF I/O SIZES

It's a common practice to assign a maximum IOPS number to a disk drive based on properties like rotational speed and seek time. With that said, the rotational speed of a drive is just one of the many factors that determine the effective IOPS. Variables such as I/O sizes, read/write ratios, and random/sequential patterns can have a dramatic effect on the throughput.

RAID type	Calculated IOPS formula
RAID 0	(1 x reads) + (1 x writes)
RAID 1	(1 x reads) + (2 x writes)
RAID 5	(1 x reads) + (4 x writes)
RAID 0+1 or RAID 1+0	(1 x reads) + (2 x writes)
RAID 6	(1 x reads) + (6 x writes)

FIGURE 3.12

Calculated IOPS of RAID types.

Ultimately, the only way to accurately gauge performance of a disk is to test it with a real/accurate workload and establish baseline performance metrics.

As an experiment, I tested the effects of increasing I/O sizes on a single 7200 RPM disk drive and measured the throughput in megabytes (MB) and IOPS. This was done using 100% random writes, hardware controller cache disabled, and I/O flagged as write-through forcing the Windows system cache to immediately write the I/O instead of lazy writing it. In addition, the disk drive was formatted at 4 KB block sizes with partition alignment. Partition alignment is not covered in this book. For more information about block sizes and partition alignment, go to "Disk Partition Alignment Best Practices for SQL Server" at http://msdn.microsoft.com/en-us/library/dd758814(v=SQL.100).aspx. Even though this article is specific to Microsoft SQL Server, this practice still applies to similar storage access patterns.

As you can see in Figure 3.13, the 16 KB I/O size averaged at 5 MB/sec data transfer rates at 343 IOPS. When I increased the I/O sizes to 64 KB, the data transfer rate tripled to 16 MB/sec, but the IOPS reduced to 263. Finally, when I increased the I/O sizes to 1 MB (16 times larger than 64 KB), the data transfer rate increased by almost the same multiplier at 72 MB/sec, but the IOPS dropped to 73.

In addition, the I/O sizes have the same effect on the response times of a disk as well. In Figure 3.14, the larger the I/O size, the higher the data transfer rate, but the response times increased significantly as well. This result showed that if response times are high, then it could be due to large I/O sizes. This is an important consideration because response times are often used as the initial indicator of disk problems.

In summary, this experiment showed that the larger the I/O size, the more efficient the disk is at transferring data, but the IOPS and response times will be significantly affected by it.

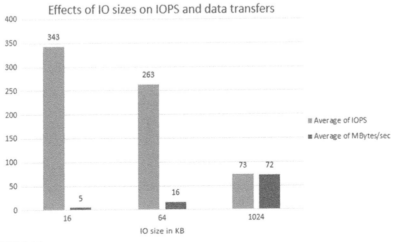

FIGURE 3.13

I/O sizes greatly affect the data throughput and IOPS of a disk.

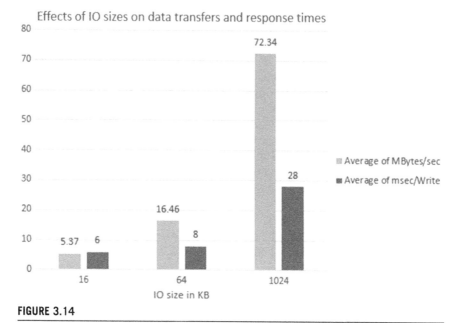

FIGURE 3.14

I/O sizes greatly affect the data throughput and response times of a disk.

Split I/O

When an I/O request is too large, it might be split into smaller sizes to accommodate the underlying hardware or software. Examples of this are when a large I/O is written to a BitLocker encrypted disk drive and when an I/O can't be written to a single contiguous block due to fragmentation (Figure 3.15).

NOTE

The reason the Split IO/sec counter (Figure 3.15) is showing zero is because this counter only measures I/O that is split due to disk fragmentation.

To demonstrate the effects of split I/O (where a single I/O request is split into multiple I/O requests) due to disk encryption, I load tested a 7200 RPM disk drive with 100% 1 MB I/O sizes with a 50% read and 50% write ratio. I used a testing tool to keep two outstanding I/Os in the disk queue. In this case, the write I/Os are split from 1 MB to 64 KB (a 16 times difference), dramatically increasing the number of outstanding I/Os in the disk queue. Likewise, read I/Os are reduced from 1 MB to 256 KB (a 4 times difference), and we see that the respective queue lengths (read and write) show the relative multipliers due to the I/O split in this way. The increase in the outstanding IRPs can significantly increase the average response times of the I/O. In summary, large I/O sizes can certainly increase the amount of data transferred per second, but the underlying hardware or software might need to split it, resulting in more than expected I/O requests queued.

LogicalDisk	D:
% Idle Time	0.000
Avg. Disk Bytes/Read	256,060.519
Avg. Disk Bytes/Write	65,352.670
Avg. Disk Queue Length	15.466
Avg. Disk Read Queue Length	3.982
Avg. Disk sec/Read	0.087
Avg. Disk sec/Write	0.060
Avg. Disk Write Queue Length	11.484
Current Disk Queue Length	15.210
Disk Transfers/sec	237.633
Split IO/Sec	0.000

FIGURE 3.15

Performance counters showing a high disk queue length due to hard drive encryption.

I/O RESPONSE TIMES

Response times are arguably the best indicator of how a disk is performing. This is because when load is put on a disk beyond what it can handle, the I/O requests simply wait longer in the queue, increasing the average response time. A "response time" starts when the I/O request is placed in the disk queue (in-flight) and ends when the I/O request is fulfilled or "transferred." This is not a measurement of the actual transfer times of the disk, but the time that the I/O requests are waiting in a queue until completed (Figure 3.16).

Often referred to as the "response time" or disk latency counters, the Avg. Disk sec/Read, Avg. Disk sec/Write, and Avg. Disk sec/Transfer performance counters are part of the LogicalDisk and PhysicalDisk counter objects. These counters calculate the average amount of time from when the I/O request is placed in the queue until the I/O request is completed in seconds. This means that if there were 1000 disk

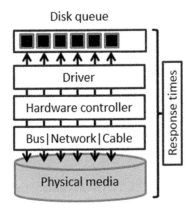

FIGURE 3.16

A diagram showing the measurement of disk response times.

transfers since the last time that the counter was sampled, then all 1000 are averaged producing the counter value.

When the average response time exceeds the average expected, typical, service time (the manufacturer's guarantee of the typical time that it should take to get an I/O from the disk), then it is an indicator that warrants investigation. The reason I don't say "problem" is because the average expected service time is based on relatively small I/O sizes—something often missing from the claim. My assumption is that the claims are based on 64 KB or smaller I/O sizes. Therefore, if the disk queue has outstanding I/O requests, and if the average response time exceeds the average expected service time of the disk, "and" if the I/O sizes are 64 KB or smaller, then the disk may be overwhelmed.

PROCESS I/O OPERATIONS

Earlier in this chapter, we defined that IRPs are used to request I/O from a storage device. Well, IRPs are also used to request I/O to and from NICs and other devices. Unfortunately, when looking at the I/O-related counters under the Process counter object, the values represent all of those devices. With that said, these counters can be used as supplemental evidence, but not as direct evidence related to disk I/O (Table 3.1).

As an experiment, I used a disk load testing tool to induce a "party mix" of read and write load on D: drive to see which I/O-related counters under the Process object will give me a clue as to which process is responsible for the disk I/O. Since the load is issuing data operations to the disk, the I/O Data Operations/sec counter is the most logical to start with (Figure 3.17).

In this case, the process called "Dynamo" has the most sustained number of data operations/sec, giving me indirect evidence that it is likely the one issuing the most I/O requests to disk. The reason it is an indirect evidence is because this I/O could be related to network or other devices. Also, this evidence does not indicate which disk is involved with the data I/O.

The point is that if you see a high number of disk transfers on a disk and if a process is doing a high number of I/O Data Operations/sec, then it "might" be that process. The same can be done when correlating \LogicalDisk(*)\Disk Bytes/sec to \Process(*)\IO Data Bytes/sec.

Finally, to get hard evidence of which processes are causing the most disk I/O and the files involved, you must use tools other than the Performance Monitor. These tools are discussed later in this chapter.

DISK PERFORMANCE ANALYSIS TOOLS

This part of the chapter discusses a few tools that can be used to analyze disk performance problems.

Table 3.1 I/O-Related Process Counter Object Descriptions

Process Counter	Description
I/O Data Bytes/ sec	The rate at which the process is **reading and writing bytes in I/O operations**. This counter counts all I/O activities generated by the process to include file, network, and device I/O
I/O Data Operations/sec	The rate at which the process is **issuing read and write I/O operations**. This counter counts all I/O activities generated by the process to include file, network, and device I/O
I/O Other Bytes/ sec	The rate at which the process is **issuing bytes** to I/O operations **that do not involve data** such as control operations. This counter counts all I/O activities generated by the process to include file, network, and device I/O
I/O Other Operations/sec	The rate at which the process **is issuing I/O operations** that are **neither read nor write operations** (for example, a control function). This counter counts all I/O activities generated by the process to include file, network, and device I/O
I/O Read Bytes/ sec	The rate at which the process is **reading bytes from I/O operations**. This counter counts all I/O activities generated by the process to include file, network, and device I/O
I/O Read Operations/sec	The rate at which the process is **issuing read I/O operations**. This counter counts all I/O activities generated by the process to include file, network, and device I/O
I/O Write Bytes/ sec	The rate at which the process is **writing bytes to I/O operations**. This counter counts all I/O activities generated by the process to include file, network, and device I/O
I/O Write Operations/sec	The rate at which the process is **issuing write I/O operations**. This counter counts all I/O activities generated by the process to include file, network, and device I/O

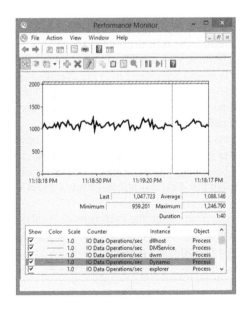

FIGURE 3.17

Performance Monitor with instances of Process I/O Data Operations/sec loaded.

DISK ANALYSIS USING PERFORMANCE MONITOR

Now that we have covered the disk queue, response times, and disk transfers (similar to IOPS), we can bring it all together into a formula that will help identify disk performance problems worthy of investigation.

Performance Monitor will rarely be able to solve disk performance problems, but it can indicate when more investigation is needed or when disk is likely a bottleneck. Now, let's put everything we have learned into a practical formula that can be applied to a single spindle or a large disk array.

Formula: If \LogicalDisk(?)\Avg. Disk Queue Length is greater than 2 (indicating that the disk queue had work do) and **\LogicalDisk(?)\Avg. Disk sec/Transfer** (indicating the average time that an I/O waited in the queue until completed—also popularly known as response times) is greater than the average expected service time of the storage device (for reference, the average expected service time of a common 7200 RPM disk drive is 13 ms) and if **\LogicalDisk(?)\Bytes/Read|Write** is less than 64 KB (the average expected service time of disk hardware is measured at 64 KB or smaller workloads), then the disk is overwhelmed. If **\LogicalDisk(?)\Bytes/Read|Write** is greater than 64 KB, then add 10 ms to the average expected service time as a threshold. The question mark (?) indicates the same respective logical disk is being analyzed.

As an example, my 7200 RPM disk drive has an average expected service time of 13 ms. This means that it should never take more than 13 ms to get a 64 KB or smaller-sized I/O from the disk. If the disk queue constantly has work queued up and if the response times are greater than the seek time (Avg. Disk sec/Transfer greater than 13 ms), then the disk is overwhelmed.

Figure 3.18 shows D: drive with a % Idle Time of less than 10% (any of the disk queue related counters can be used to determine load or no load on the disk), but the response times (Avg. Disk sec/Transfer) are well below the average expected service time of this drive; therefore, the disk is not overwhelmed.

Figure 3.19 shows D: drive with a % Idle Time of less than 10%, but the response times (Avg. Disk sec/Transfer) are greater than the average expected service time of the disk; in this case, 13 ms or less is expected, and the I/O sizes (Avg. Disk Bytes/Transfer) are less than 64 KB (65,536 bytes); therefore, the disk is overwhelmed and warrants more investigation.

If this formula seems too complicated, then a simpler formula is to just look for **Avg. Disk sec/Transfer** greater than 15 ms regardless of the storage media such as a SAN or SSD. This is because a SAN or SSD should always be faster than a single 7200 RPM disk drive, but this more simplified formula doesn't take the I/O size into consideration.

To make this analysis even easier, the Performance Analysis of Logs (PAL) tool can analyze counter logs using the complex formula we just discussed and diagnose when a disk is having a performance problem. Disk analysis using the PAL tool is covered next.

LogicalDisk	**D:**
% Idle Time	0.975
Avg. Disk Queue Length	1.865
Avg. Disk sec/Transfer	0.006
Current Disk Queue Length	1.610

FIGURE 3.18

A screenshot of Performance Monitor showing a disk that is not overwhelmed.

LogicalDisk	**D:**
% Idle Time	0.067
Avg. Disk Bytes/Transfer	13,417.426
Avg. Disk Queue Length	11.877
Avg. Disk sec/Transfer	0.016
Current Disk Queue Length	11.717

FIGURE 3.19

A screenshot of Performance Monitor showing an overwhelmed disk.

DISK ANALYSIS USING THE PAL TOOL

The PAL tool is a free, open-source tool available for download at http://pal.codeplex.com. I wrote and started this project around August 2007 to make the analysis of performance counter logs easier. Today, the tool has grown and many industry leaders have created threshold files to represent most of the enterprise products of Microsoft and a few other products. I encourage you to try it out and see for yourself.

As mentioned earlier in the Disk analysis using Performance Monitor section, the formula to identify disk performance problems can be a bit complicated and the PAL tool has an automated analysis that implements the formula (Figure 3.20).

This PAL tool analysis generates a "fake" performance counter called \LogicalDisk(*)\Disk Overwhelmed. It takes into consideration the workload of the disk queue, the size of the I/O, and the response times to compute a good or bad condition in regard to if the disk is overwhelmed or not. If % Idle Time is less than 10 and response times are greater than 25 ms for I/O sizes of 64 KB or smaller or 35 ms for I/O sizes greater than 64 KB, then the disk is overwhelmed. The reasoning is that the disk has a nearly constant I/O demand and the response times are higher than what it would take a 7200 RPM disk drive to return the appropriate I/O sizes. This analysis requires \LogicalDisk(*)\% Idle Time, \LogicalDisk(*)\Avg. Disk Bytes/Transfer, and \LogicalDisk(*)\Avg. Disk sec/Transfer counters to be in the counter log, and instances of _Total are ignored because they are aggregates of all counter instances.

If the PAL-generated counter of \LogicalDisk(*)\Disk Overwhelmed has a value of one (warning), then it means that the % Idle Time is less than 10% or Avg. Disk Queue Length is greater than 2 and the response times are greater than 15 ms. If this

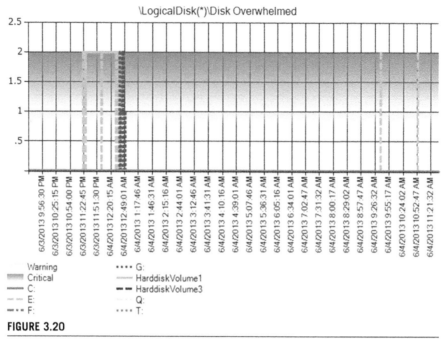

FIGURE 3.20

A PAL tool chart identifying a disk overwhelmed.

counter has a value of 2 (critical), then it means that % Idle Time is less than 10% and the response times are greater than 25 ms for I/O of 64 KB or smaller and 35 ms for I/O sizes greater than 64 KB.

DISK ANALYSIS USING TASK MANAGER AND RESOURCE MONITOR

Task Manager is part of the operating system and has been significantly updated in Windows 8 and Windows Server 2012. Figure 3.21 shows the activity of D: drive in the Performance tab of Task Manager while under high load.

> **NOTE**
>
> Windows Server 2012 does not show disk activity in Task Manager by default. Execute "diskperf-v" in an administrator command prompt to enable disk activity.

In this case, it tells us that the disk is 100% active and it has 6.6 seconds of response times. The data that it shows comes from Event Tracing for Windows (ETW) data, which is not the same source as the LogicalDisk and PhysicalDisk performance counter objects, so the results of Task Manager might not correlate with the data from performance counters. In any case, this kind of load and latency warrants

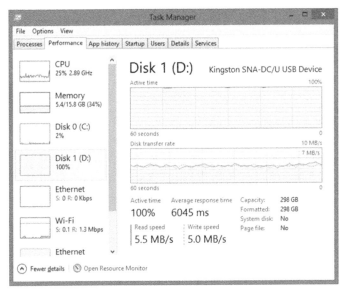

FIGURE 3.21

Task Manager showing disk activity.

more investigation with Resource Monitor, which also ships with Windows 8 and Windows Server 2012.

Microsoft Resource Monitor (Resmon for short) is a performance analysis tool built into Windows and Windows Server. It was first introduced in Windows Vista/Windows Server 2008 and then later improved in Windows 7/Windows Server 2008 R2. It can be launched from the Start menu as "Resmon" or by clicking Open Resource Monitor on the Performance tab of Task Manager. Once open, navigate to the Disk tab for more information on disk performance (Figure 3.22).

In the Disk tab of Resource Monitor (Figure 3.22), we can see that the process (process names are under the Image column) Dynamo.exe is doing the most disk activity—about 10 MB/second of disk activity. When we filter on just Dynamo.exe using the selection box, the Disk Activity pane shows all of the files that Dynamo.exe is accessing. In this case, D:\iobw.tst. It shows us that Dynamo.exe is doing about 10 MB/second of I/O to D:\iobw.tst and the average response time is 15 ms. This level of detail is very helpful when trying to identify the root cause of a disk performance problem. Unfortunately, Resource Monitor is not able to detect the activity of elevated applications, so it might be necessary to use other tools to detect them.

DISK ANALYSIS USING PROCESS MONITOR

Process monitor is a free, Sysinternals tool written by Mark Russinovich and Bryce Cogswell. It captures file system activity, registry key activity, network activity, profiling events, process, and thread activity. In this case, we use it for capturing and

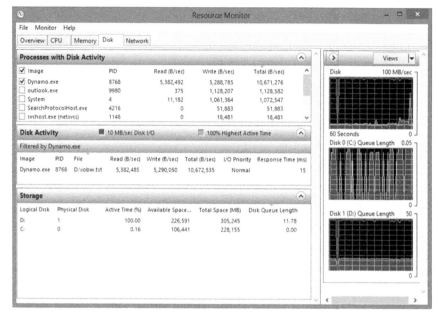

FIGURE 3.22

Resource Monitor showing disk performance information.

analyzing disk I/O. One of its best features is that it doesn't require installation, making it very portable. In addition, Sysinternals tools are owned by Microsoft.

Similar to the other demos, I added load to D: drive. The intent is to use Process Monitor to provide evidence of the processes and files inducing the most disk I/O.

After starting Process Monitor, I set the filter to "Path begins with D:\" and hide all of the events except for file system activity (Figure 3.23).

In this case, it is obvious that Dynamo.exe is inducing the I/O load, but let's assume that it wasn't so obvious. To discover which process is doing the most I/O on D: drive, I clicked on Tools, Process Activity Summary (Figure 3.24).

This view showed me an aggregate of all of the I/O shown in the main display based on the current filter settings and proved that Dynamo.exe induced the most I/O. Next, I used the File Summary view to show an aggregate view of the files most involved in the disk I/O, which happens to be D:\iobw.tst in this case (Figure 3.25).

Alternatively, I could have changed the filter to just show the file I/O related to Dynamo.exe or any other process. Finally, my favorite view is the Stack Summary (Figure 3.26).

The Stack Summary view shows an aggregate view of the thread stacks taken by the I/O. This view is helpful when needing to know the execution path of an application. Also, when looking at the kernel-mode stack, we can see evidence of file system filter drivers that might be unnecessarily processing the I/O such as multiple

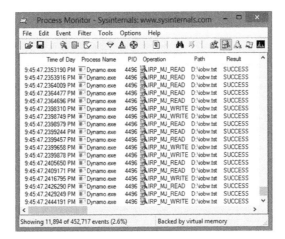

FIGURE 3.23

Process Monitor capturing file I/O.

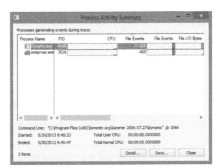

FIGURE 3.24

The Process Activity Summary view of Process Monitor.

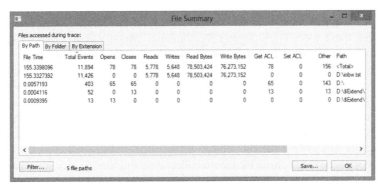

FIGURE 3.25

The File Summary view of Process Monitor.

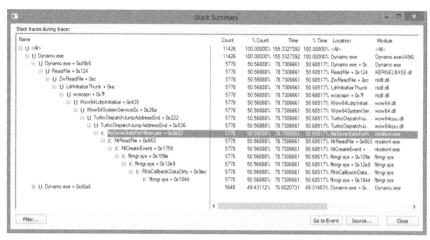

FIGURE 3.26

The Stack Summary view of Process Monitor.

antivirus or anti-intrusion drivers. If you suspect a file system filter driver is causing unnecessary delays, then looking at the Stack Summary is arguably the easiest way to provide evidence of it.

For more information on the Process Monitor tool, go to the Sysinternals Web site at http://technet.microsoft.com/en-us/sysinternals/bb896645. It is also explained in detail in Chapter 4 of the "Windows Sysinternals Administrator's Reference" book (http://technet.microsoft.com/en-us/sysinternals/hh290819).

DISK ANALYSIS USING WINDOWS PERFORMANCE ANALYZER

The Windows Performance Recorder (WPR) and Windows Performance Analyzer (WPA) tools are free, ETW tools from Microsoft that offer deep diagnostic information allowing you to find the root cause to performance problems. They are similar to Performance Monitor where data is collected and then analyzed by you (no automated analysis), but uses ETW data instead of performance counters. Some argue that these tools might replace Performance Monitor, but I like to think of these tools as the "microscope" to performance analysis and Perfmon as the high-level view. You certainly wouldn't go walking around with microscope on your eyes. With that said, a lot of effort went into the data collection to ensure that it is as nonimpactful to the system as possible and safe for production use while gathering a large amount of data. My suggestion is to use Performance Monitor to get an idea of the resources that you are dealing with and then use WPR/WPA to dig in and find the root cause.

First, we need to use the WPR tool to collect disk and file I/O activity as shown in Figure 3.27 and then click the Start button to begin collecting data in real time. Once

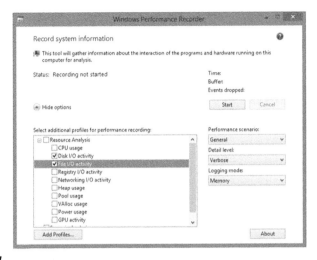

FIGURE 3.27

The Windows Performance Recorder tool with disk and file I/O activity selected.

you feel that enough data is collected, save the trace and then open the resulting ETL file with the WPA tool.

In the WPA tool, we can expand the Storage category in Graph Explorer and expand Disk Usage to look at disk usage by physical disk, process, I/O time, service time, and many other measurements. Figure 3.28 shows that Disk 1 is 100% utilized, the Dynamo.exe process is consuming the most I/O, and the file being read from and written to the most is D:\iobw.txt.

This level of detail is very helpful in showing many aspects of disk and file I/O in Windows and Windows Server allowing us to have hard evidence of the processes and files involved in the disk I/O—something that Performance Monitor is unable to provide.

Similar to Process Monitor WPA can also show evidence of poorly performing file system filter drivers and which function (assuming symbols are available) the stack is spending most of its time. In this case, I brought up the File I/O Size by Process, Stack chart, and then removed all columns except for Process, Stack, and Duration aggregated by Process and Stack (left of the golden bar) (Figure 3.29).

This view shows me the call stack most commonly taken by the System process. Look for a significant difference in the Duration field.

If evidence is needed to prove if the storage hardware is performing poorly, then consider using Storport tracing discussed later in this chapter. Tools provided by the hardware vendor are needed when performance analysis is needed below the Storport driver. This is because the Storport driver is the last bit of software that hands the I/O request to the hardware.

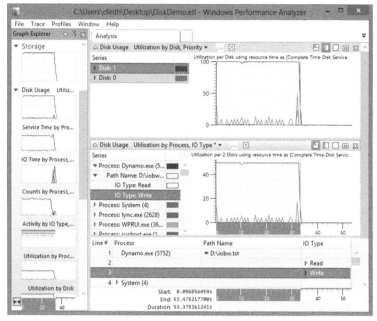

FIGURE 3.28

The Windows Performance Analyzer tool with disk-related charts.

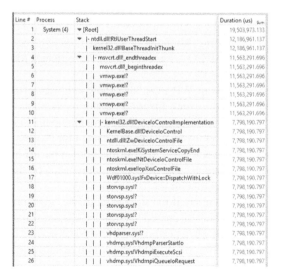

FIGURE 3.29

Windows Performance Analyzer (WPA) shows the most common thread stacks.

COMMON CAUSES, RECOMMENDATIONS FOR POORLY PERFORMING DISKS, AND BEST PRACTICES

Now that we have covered how to detect and analyze poor disk performance, it is only natural to cover the common causes and resolutions.

TOO MUCH SHARING

By far the most common cause of disk performance problems that I have dealt with over the years is over shared disk drives attached to a SAN. SANs are great devices, but they can become overwhelmed just like any other device.

If the LUN provided to your system is not adequate in regard to response times, IOPS, or capacity, then measure the performance and discuss these concerns with your SAN administrator. For more information, see the "Load testing disk performance and how to speak SAN-ish" section later in this chapter.

TOO MUCH I/O DEMAND

Whether you have an enterprise, 1000 spindle disk group, or a single hard drive in your laptop, too much I/O demand can overwhelm any storage device. Use tools like Resource Monitor (built into Windows and Windows Server) or Process Monitor to trace the processes and files doing the most disk I/O. Once you understand where the demand is coming from, then you can make a decision on which is necessary and disable or stop the unnecessary I/O demand.

HIGH DISK FRAGMENTATION

Disk fragmentation is a condition in which the portions of one or more files are stored at various locations on a disk. The NTFS file system tries to keep files contiguous on disk so that when the files are read, the disk can read the file sequentially optimizing the read speed of the disk. If the file is highly fragmented, then the disk has to move the head to each location, which can take longer. The most common cause of disk fragmentation is lack of contiguous blocks of free space when a file is being written. If the file cannot be completely written to a single block of free space, then the file must be broken up into small pieces on the disk.

Just like regular disk drives, SSDs can become fragmented, but since data on an SSD can be read from any location at the same speed, there is no benefit from defragmenting it. As a matter of fact, as of Windows 8 and Windows Server 2012, SSDs are trimmed as a scheduled task instead of defragmentation.

NOTE

Solid-state drives are immune to disk fragmentation because file data can be read from any location on the disk at the same speed.

If you suspect high disk fragmentation or are just curious about it, then run the Disk Defragmenter tool on Windows and Windows Server in analysis mode. It can generate a report to show which files are most fragmented on disk. Knowing which files are most fragmented can greatly help with determining if running the tool is beneficial. For example, frequently accessed files should be defragmented as much as reasonable. On the other hand, files such as Microsoft SQL Server data files might have clustered indexes (indexes that sort the data by disk location) and not recommended to be defragmented.

When working with specialized storage hardware such as a SAN, disk defragmentation might be unnecessary due to how the disk is "virtualized" across the SAN. Therefore, consult with your storage administrator or vendor on if a disk should be defragmented by Windows or Windows Server.

HARDWARE FAILURE

Windows and Windows Server can sometimes detect disk hardware failures and will report on these failures in the system event logs. For a list of system event log errors that indicate possible I/O problems, go to the article "Windows System Event Log Errors that indicate possible I/O problems can be associated with database inconsistency or performance problems for SQL Server" at http://support.microsoft.com/kb/2091098.

In addition, some disk hardware features include a fault light of when the disk is failing or suspected to fail, so consider physically walking by the server to look for these warning lights.

CHKDSK

ChkDsk is a command-line utility that checks the integrity of the file system and the physical sectors on the disk. It was updated in Windows 8 and Windows Server 2012, making it significantly faster and more efficient with detecting and fixing disk problems.

In Windows 8, ChkDsk is capable of determining problems prior to a system reboot and then fixing these known problems during start (called a spotfix), so that system downtime is greatly decreased.

FC TROUBLESHOOTING

In regard to FC (Fibre Channel) networks and other specialized storage hardware, the vendor can usually provide tools and/or assistance to identify faulty parts.

LOAD TESTING DISK PERFORMANCE AND HOW TO SPEAK SAN-ISH

Before going into production with a given disk, JBOD, SAN drive, or just about anything that presents itself as a disk to Windows, it's important to load test it to see what it is capable of. This is especially important when a disk has been provided by an unknown source such as an outsourced SAN department.

So, a system administrator walks into a bar, asks the SAN administrator for a 300 GB LUN, and walks out of the room. The SAN administrator finishes his beer, grins, and says to himself, "He didn't say how fast it needs to be. I hope he likes floppy drive speeds."

The unfortunate reality in the industry is that disk capacity is a premium in the enterprise and we tend to focus on the immediate need for storage capacity and not thinking of the actual performance needs of the drive such as response times and IOPS. Just asking for a disk with 300 GB of capacity and nothing else leaves the SAN administrator with the problem of filling in the gaps. When requesting a disk from a SAN administrator, provide the following information to help fill in these gaps.

Capacity

How much disk space do you predict that your solution will need? If you have an existing solution, then use the **\LogicalDisk(*)\Free Megabytes** counter and run disk capacity tools mentioned earlier in this chapter to determine if all of the files on the existing disk are necessary.

I/O Sizes

What will be the most common I/O size? Most applications use 4 KB and 8 KB I/O sizes, so disk drives formatted at these sizes will run just fine. With that said, services like Microsoft SQL Server will often use 32 KB and 64 KB I/O sizes. Knowing your application's common I/O sizes will help the SAN administrator with partitioning and formatting of the disk group and the LUN. As mentioned earlier in this chapter, I/O sizes can be measured using the **\LogicalDisk(*)\Avg. Bytes/Read|Write| Transfer** counters.

IOPS

As mentioned earlier in this chapter, IOPS can vary greatly with the service times of a disk drive, I/O sizes, sequential I/O, and random I/O. Therefore, when asking for a sustained number of IOPS from the SAN administrator, discuss the kind of hardware that will be used, the expected services times, and how it should perform when under the various conditions above.

The counter **\LogicalDisk(*)\Disk Transfers/sec** is the counter to use to measure the total number of read and write operations per second. While this technically might not be the number of IOPS that the hardware is doing (due to the RAID type), it is the logical IOPS from Windows and Windows Server perspectives.

DISK PERFORMANCE WHEN LOAD TESTING

I used to be a testing consultant with the Microsoft Services Labs. The first step during the execution of the load testing lab is to establish a baseline run and confirm the baseline run. Its purpose is to confirm that when no changes are made to the solution, there are consistent results. If you do the same run twice under the same conditions yet get significantly different results, then that means that you can't make the measurable changes and therefore cannot do a proper load test.

In my experience, the most common cause of high variance between runs is due to virtual disks running off of a SAN. SANs are incredible devices, but they also introduce a lot of complexity. And with complexity comes an increasing risk of unknown and variance. Therefore, my recommendation is to use dedicated hardware that is completely separate from all other variables such as JBODs or other non-SAN-attached disks for best results.

FILE SYSTEM FILTER DRIVERS

Filter drivers are optional drivers that can load above or below a device driver and can modify the behavior of the device. Antivirus and antimalware software commonly install one or more file system filter drivers in order to scan incoming and outgoing I/O. This means that the response times reported by the disk latency counters mentioned earlier can be effected by filter drivers before the I/O request is sent to the hardware device. For example, if the response times of PhysicalDisk 2 (E: drive) is 30 ms, but yet the hardware hosting this device is responding in 5 ms, then the 25 ms delays might be caused by one or more filter drivers.

A relatively quick way of seeing the registered filter drivers is to run the tool "Fltmc." Fltmc is a command-line tool that is part of the operating system. To show the filter drivers registered in the system, run the following command from an administrator command prompt:

Fltmc

In Figure 3.30, I ran Fltmc on my laptop and it shows the file system filter drivers registered on my system. Each filter name corresponds to a driver and most drivers are located in the %windir%\system32\drivers folder.

Each filter name can be looked up using the following WMI query example:

gwmi -Query 'SELECT * FROM Win32_SystemDriver WHERE Name = "mpfilter"'

Just replace the name value in the WMI query to be the filter name you are interested in (Figure 3.31).

In this case, MpFilter.sys is the Microsoft Malware Protection Driver that is part of Microsoft System Center Endpoint Protection software.

If evidence is needed on the performance impact of a file system filter driver, then consider using WPA or Sysinternals Process Monitor. These tools are described in more detail in the "Disk performance analysis tools" section earlier in this chapter.

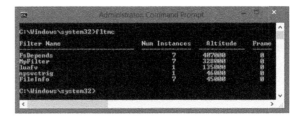

FIGURE 3.30

Fltmc showing the filter drivers related to disk.

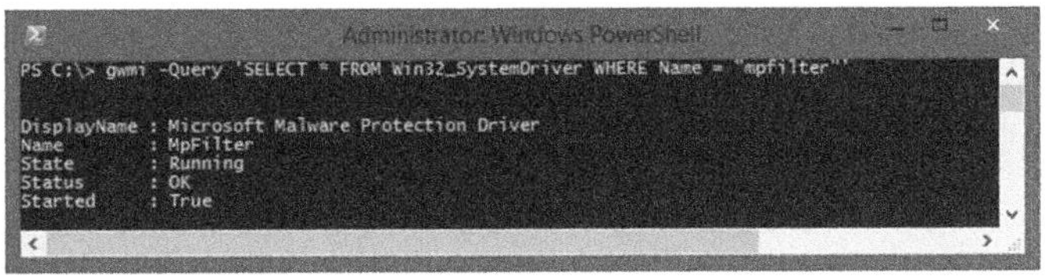

FIGURE 3.31

Powershell looking up the details of MpFilter.sys.

For more information on file system filter drivers, see the article "Load Order Groups and Altitudes for Minifilter Drivers" at http://msdn.microsoft.com/library/windows/hardware/ff549689(v=vs.85).aspx.

STORPORT TRACING

When evidence is needed that software related to Windows Server is not at fault, Storport tracing can provide that proof. The Storport.sys driver is the last bit of software running under Windows Server that deals with IRPs before they are passed on to the SAN hardware for servicing, making this an important place to measure performance. This level of tracing is rarely needed, but available if storage administrators are unable to isolate the problem between the drivers and the SAN hardware.

Like many of the other tools we've talked about, Storport tracing also uses ETW data as its source and Performance Monitor can be leveraged to gather this data. At the time of this writing, Storport tracing might be a bit difficult to implement; therefore, I recommend searching the Internet for "Storport tracing" articles and tools and contacting Microsoft Support to assist with this kind of tracing.

CONCLUSION

In this chapter, we covered the basic concepts of storage hardware and terminology, the identification of disk performance problems and how to do deeper analysis using various tools, and common causes of poor disk performance.

DISK PERFORMANCE ANALYSIS EXPERTS

If you have a question that this chapter did not address, then consider reading the blogs or contacting one of the following subject matter experts:
Moti Bani

Moti.ba@hotmail.com

Robert Smith

sandude@outlook.com

Process memory

PROCESS VIRTUAL ADDRESS SPACE

The operating system and applications have three major ways to run out of memory: virtual address space, committed memory, and physical memory (RAM). The purpose of this chapter is to introduce process virtual address space concepts and how to identify and troubleshoot process memory leaks.

NOTE

In the context of this book, the term "application" refers to the user-mode side of a process. An application might not have a user interface such as a Windows service.

Each application is presented with a virtual world of memory depending on the architecture of the operating system. The memory presented in this way is private to this application and cannot be exceeded. An ideal condition is when an application is presented with far more virtual address space than what could be possibly used. This is generally true with x64 (64-bit) applications which are presented with 8 TB of virtual address space. As of this writing, it is unlikely for an application to consume all 8 TB, and the operating system only provides physical resources to the application when it is actually used (Figure 4.1).

WHAT YOU NEED TO KNOW ABOUT AN APPLICATION'S VIRTUAL ADDRESS SPACE

In short, there is little concern about 64-bit ($\times$64) applications because each process gets its own private 8 TB of virtual address space or 128 TB in the case of Windows 8.1 and Windows Server 2012 R2. The idea is to have far more virtual address space than physical memory, so that applications never run out of memory—at least in "their" virtual world. 32-bit applications have a far smaller virtual address space that ranges from 2 GB to 4 GB depending on the combination of application and system settings. While this seems like a limitation today, it was unimaginably large back in 1993 when most systems had 8 MB—yes 8 MB of RAM. See "The concept and advantages of virtual memory" later in this chapter to learn why virtual memory is much more efficient than direct access to physical memory.

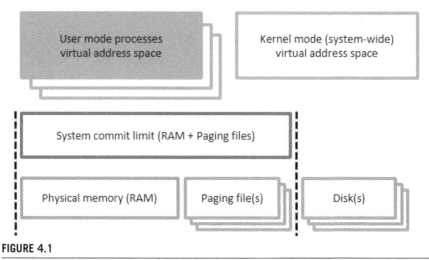

FIGURE 4.1

Overall memory layout with the user-mode virtual address space highlighted.

Regardless of the amount of physical memory and paging files in a system, the amount of virtual address space presented to an application will be the same. This memory is private and "fake"—meaning that the operating system can give out a near infinite amount of these environments to applications and each application is alone in the space provided. This is similar to presenting a dynamically expanding 120 GB virtual hard drive to a virtual computer where the physical impact of the VHD's file size (roughly 4 GB) is quite small compared to what was presented to the VM.

The chart in Figure 4.2 shows the amount of virtual address space presented to applications. As you can see, the amount of virtual address space presented to applications is based on the architecture of the system and the architecture of the application. This is the "sand box" that each application is presented and applications cannot exceed it.

Application architecture	Operating system architecture			
	32-bit (x86)	32-bit (x86) with IncreaseUserVA	64-bit (x64)	64-bit (x64) Windows 8.1 and Windows Server 2012 R2
32-bit (x86)	2 GB	2 GB	2 GB	2 GB
32-bit (x86) with large address aware	2 GB	Size of setting between 2 GB and 3 GB	4 GB	4 GB
64-bit (x64)	N/A	N/A	8 TB	128 TB

FIGURE 4.2

The amount of virtual address space presented to applications.

For the record, applications are "supposed" to have an unimaginably large amount of virtual address space such as the case with x64 at 8 TB, but modern hardware has exceeded the 32-bit address space. For a long-drawn-out story about how this happened, check out "The concept and advantages of virtual memory" later in this chapter.

IDENTIFYING APPLICATIONS THAT RUN OUT OF VIRTUAL ADDRESS SPACE

It is actually quite difficult to scientifically determine if an application is truly out of virtual address space because memory allocation failures can occur for many reasons. Applications are more likely to be out of virtual address space when they are using more than 75% of their address space. This is because there is an assumption that most of the memory is fragmented, which commonly happens in memory-intensive applications.

When an application runs out of virtual address space, it will receive an out of memory error depending on the memory manager, the size of the allocation request, and if the allocation must be contiguous. This would be similar to being unable to put your car in the garage. . . but the toolbox still fits! Therefore, an out of memory condition could mean that the application is just unable to do the current requested allocation of virtual address space and/or unable to get committed memory (discussed later), but smaller requests might still work. Most applications don't handle this condition, and it commonly results in a fatal crash of the application. Therefore, it is very important to monitor the virtual memory usage of an application to prevent this condition.

This section of the book focuses on the lack of virtual address space condition. Committed memory failures are covered in Chapter 6 "System Committed Memory."

HOW TO DETERMINE THE MAXIMUM VIRTUAL ADDRESS SPACE FOR AN APPLICATION

It is important to know if an application is close to running out of virtual address space. Therefore, use the techniques in this section to determine the maximum amount of virtual address space an application has and compare it to the virtual address space usage (Virtual Bytes) of the application. When an application is out of virtual address space, it will receive an out of memory condition, which can lead to the application crashing if not handled.

As stated earlier, applications are presented with a private virtual address space that cannot be exceeded. Think of this as its "sand box." The amount of virtual address space given to an application is dependent on the memory architecture—not by the amount of physical memory or paging files (Figure 4.3).

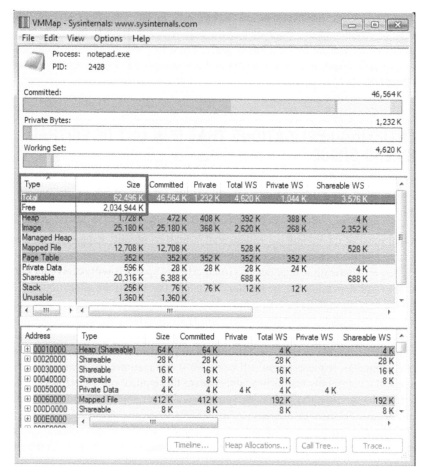

FIGURE 4.3

The Sysinternals VMMap tool shows that the 32-bit version of Notepad has 2 GB of virtual address space.

VMMap (a free Sysinternals tool) is arguably the best and easiest tool to investigate the virtual memory usage of an application. When I attach VMMap to an x86 (32-bit) instance of Notepad.exe and add up the Free memory and Total (all nonfree) memory, I end up with 2,097,440 KB, which is roughly 2 GB. This is the maximum amount of virtual address space that this instance of Notepad can address regardless of the amount of physical memory and page file sizes.

The maximum amount of address space presented to a 32-bit (×86) application can become complicated when the 32-bit address space is adjusted or when running on a 64-bit (×64) version of Windows or Windows Server. For this reason, attaching VMMap to the process and adding up the Total memory and Free memory is a reliable way of determining the maximum address space of an application. If it is not

	Operating system architecture			
Application architecture	32-bit (x86)	32-bit (x86) with IncreaseUserVA	64-bit (x64)	64-bit (x64) Windows 8.1 and Windows Server 2012 R2
32-bit (x86)	2 GB	2 GB	2 GB	2 GB
32-bit (x86) with large address aware	2 GB	Size of setting between 2 GB and 3 GB	4 GB	4 GB
64-bit (x64)	N/A	N/A	8 TB	128 TB

FIGURE 4.4

The maximum virtual address space of applications.

possible or practical to use VMMap, then the chart in Figure 4.4 can help to estimate the maximum sizes.

CAN THE MAXIMUM VIRTUAL ADDRESS SPACE OF AN APPLICATION BE RETRIEVED REMOTELY USING WINDOWS MANAGEMENT INSTRUMENTATION?

Not for Windows 8, Windows Server 2012, and earlier. On Windows 8.1 and Windows Server 2012 R2, the method call "GetAvailableVirtualSize()" was added to the Win32_Process Windows Management Instrumentation (WMI) class. This came about when Jeffrey Snover (inventor of Powershell) sent a message on Twitter that his team was looking for feedback on WMI and I responded with this need.

The "GetAvailableVirtualSize()" method call gets the amount of free virtual address space from the process instance effectively showing us if any of the processes are running low on virtual address space.

Here is an example of a Powershell script that is able to get the amount of available virtual address space from all processes either locally or remotely (from another computer):

```
$oProcesses=Get-WmiObject -Class Win32_Process
$aObjects=@()
ForEach($oProcess in $oProcesses)
{
    $oMem=$oProcess.GetAvailableVirtualSize()
    $oObject=New-Object pscustomobject
    Add-Member -InputObject $oObject -MemberType NoteProperty -Name
'Name' -Value $($oProcess.Name)
    Add-Member -InputObject $oObject -MemberType NoteProperty -Name
'AvailableVirtualSize' -Value $($oMem.AvailableVirtualSize)
    $aObjects+=@($oObject)
}
$aObjects | Sort-Object AvailableVirtualSize -Descending | ft -AutoSize
```

On earlier systems, use VMMap interactively at the console to attach to a target process. VMMap is noninvasive and safe to use on any process but should still be tested before using in a production environment.

The default user-mode (application) architecture can be queried on earlier systems, but this is not process-specific—meaning that it always reports the native size.

From a command prompt, execute the following command:

```
C:\>wmic PATH Win32_OperatingSystem GET MaxProcessMemorySize
```

From a Powershell session, execute the following command:

```
PS>Get-WmiObject  -Class  Win32_OperatingSystem  |  Select  MaxProcess
MemorySize
```

> **NOTE**
>
> Keep in mind that the application architecture might not be the same for all applications. 64-bit ($\times$ 64) versions of Windows and Windows Server will return 8 TB or 128 TB depending on the operating system version, but 32-bit applications running on these computers will have 2 GB or 4 GB of maximum virtual address spaces.

IDENTIFYING APPLICATION VIRTUAL ADDRESS SPACE PROBLEMS USING PERFORMANCE MONITOR AND THE APPLICATION EVENT LOG

This procedure requires administrator rights to use Performance Monitor and the application event logs (both are part of the operating system) and either access to the desktop to run Performance Monitor interactively or DCOM network connectivity to gather performance counters from another computer. This procedure provides a small amount of information about the memory usage of an application but can serve as an initial indicator that warrants more investigation since performance counters are relatively easy to monitor. For more information on using Performance Monitor, see Chapter 2 "Performance Monitor."

The following performance counters are needed to identify when an application might be out of virtual address space:

\Process(*)\Virtual Bytes

\Process(*)\ID Process

The counter \Process(*)\Virtual Bytes measures all of the reserved and committed memory usage of each process. Both reserved memory and committed memory take up space inside an application's virtual address space.

Use the chart in Figure 4.4 to determine the virtual address space size of applications (processes), and then compare it respectively to the Virtual Bytes of the application. If the value of Virtual Bytes is greater than 75% of the virtual address space of the application, then it might run out of memory soon. For example, if the application is 32-bit, not large address aware, and running on a 32-bit version of Windows or Windows Server, then it has a 2 GB address space. If the value of Virtual Bytes

Counter	Warning	Critical
\Process(*)\Virtual Bytes	> 75% of process's address space	< 90% of process's address space

FIGURE 4.5

Thresholds for the Virtual Bytes performance counter.

of the application/process is close to 2 GB, then the application is at risk of running out (Figure 4.5).

In Figure 4.6, the Virtual Bytes performance counter shows that the counter instance of BTSNTSvc#12 goes above 1.5 GB and the process ID changes for the counter instance. This happens to be a 32-bit application on a 32-bit version of Windows Server 2003, so it has a 2 GB virtual address space. This suggests that a BTSNTSvc.exe process that was bound to the BTSNTSvc#12 counter instance exited and another BTSNTSvc.exe instance came up assuming the same counter instance. This is not direct evidence of an application out of memory condition, but it strongly suggests it. The evidence in this case was correlating the PID changes with System.OutOfMemoryException events in the application event log.

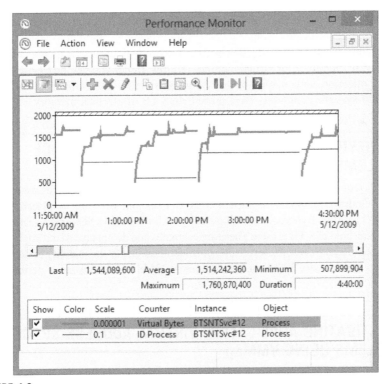

FIGURE 4.6

Virtual Bytes and ID Process suggest an application running out of memory.

Please keep in mind that the chart in Figure 4.4 is an estimate of the virtual address space size for applications. If you need to know for sure, then attach the Sysinternals tool VMMap to the application/process.

Each instance of a process (application) is given a unique identifier called a PID for the lifetime of the process, and it cannot be changed. Performance Monitor instance names are often reused such as svchost#12. The value of the counter "ID Process" is the PID of that process instance, so if "ID Process" changes its value when Virtual Bytes is more than 75% of its virtual address space, then the application exited and restarted. This could be due to a lack of virtual address space, but it could have also been a normal restart of the application. Therefore, it's important to use other means such as the application event logs to confirm if the application exited due to a lack of address space such as a System.OutOfMemoryException.

NOTE

Keep in mind that there are exceptions to this guidance. For example, 32-bit SQL Server would commonly consume all of its virtual address space as a normal behavior.

There is no clear way to know if an application truly ran out of virtual address space using Performance Monitor alone, but correlating the counter \Process(*) \Virtual Bytes with the chart in Figure 4.4 and watching for changes in the process ID of a process instances using \Process(*)\ID Process are enough to warrant more investigation. To know for sure, discuss the concern with the application's vendor to learn how to monitor it for virtual memory failures. Better yet, get the 64-bit version of the application, so you don't even have to consider virtual memory limitations at least until systems commonly have more than 8 TB of physical memory.

IDENTIFYING APPLICATION VIRTUAL ADDRESS SPACE PROBLEMS USING THE PAL TOOL

The PAL tool is limited to using performance counters and input from the user. When 32-bit Windows Server is selected a 1.5 GB threshold of 2 GB is placed on the \Process(*)\Virtual Bytes counter. Likewise, if 64-bit Windows Server is selected, then a 7 TB threshold of 8 TB is used. These are estimates and do not take 32-bit applications running on 64-bit Windows Server into consideration due to the inability to determine which applications are 32-bit and which ones are 64-bit when only using performance counters.

INVESTIGATING APPLICATION VIRTUAL ADDRESS SPACE PROBLEMS USING VMMap

This procedure requires access to the desktop (interactive log-in) and Internet access (only to download a tool). Use this procedure if basic information is needed of an application's memory usage.

The easiest way to determine if an application is nearly running out of its virtual address space and the largest contiguous block of free space is to use the Sysinternals tool, VMMap. Browse http://live.sysinternals.com/vmmap.exe to download it directly from the Sysinternals website, and then run it (no installation required). It can only be attached to one application (process) at a time, so attach it to an application that you suspect may be running out of virtual address space.

In VMMap, select the Free row and sort the items in the lower pane by size (largest to smallest). Scroll to the top. This shows the largest contiguous blocks of free memory in the application's virtual address space. If it is less than 25% of the application's virtual address space size (see Figure 4.7) or if there are only relatively small free blocks left (dependent on how the application's memory

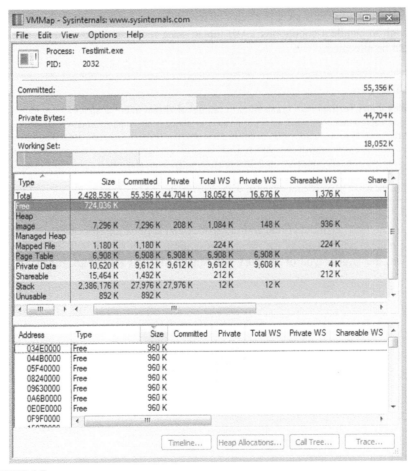

FIGURE 4.7

VMMap showing 724,036 KB free but only small (960 KB) free blocks.

manager allocates memory), then the application is likely running out of virtual address space. "Relatively small free blocks" is based on the contiguous memory block needs of the application's memory manager—this is unique to each application.

Figure 4.7 shows VMMap attached to a 32-bit instance of Testlimit.exe (a memory testing tool from Sysinternals), which has a 2 GB address space in this case. Testlimit created as many threads (1 MB contiguous memory allocations) as it could and then ran out of memory (ran out of virtual address space). It has 707 MB (724,036 KB) of free space, yet it cannot allocate another 1 MB thread stack. This is because the address space is highly fragmented and the largest contiguous block of free memory is 960 KB, which is not large enough to handle a 1 MB thread stack. This is why it is important to know the free contiguous memory blocks of 32-bit applications.

Figure 4.8 shows a visualization of the 2 GB address space of 32-bit Testlimit. exe. The white spaces are the blocks of free memory, but none of them are large enough to handle a contiguous 1 MB thread stack reservation, so no more threads could be allocated.

NOTE

Why didn't Testlimit.exe crash when it ran out of virtual address space?
Most applications crash when an out of memory condition is hit. Application developers have to write code to handle errors this condition. Most developers don't expect an application to run out of memory, and when it does, the developer would have to figure out what memory to deallocate, which can take time and resources even if done correctly. So, sometimes, it's just easier to let the application crash (wipes the application's memory clean) and start over. In this case, Testlimit handled the out of memory error condition and it didn't crash.

When looking at the virtual address space of an application (process) in VMMap, take note of which type of memory is using up the most space. In Testlimit's case above, the largest type of memory was stack, which is related to threads. If the

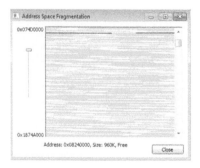

FIGURE 4.8

Address space fragmentation of 32-bit Testlimit.exe.

managed heap is the most used memory, then it is related to the Microsoft .NET Framework. Click on the category to get details of that memory in the lower pane. Show this data to the developer or vendor of the application, and it should give them clues to the memory usage. For more information about VMMap and the memory types, see Chapter 7 of the Windows Sysinternals Administrator's Reference book.

Periodically refresh (F5 or View, Refresh) VMMap to get another scan of the application's memory usage especially when there is a significant amount of memory usage difference. VMMap will enable the Timeline button at the bottom that shows the difference in memory usage between each refresh. This can help determine where memory usage is increasing over time. Research the category of memory usage and consult with the developer of the application on these findings. Further investigation might be needed using debugging tools like DebugDiag or WinDBG. Out of memory conditions can only be truly fixed by changing the application's code. This is why the developer of the application is needed. With that said, increasing the application's virtual address space can treat the symptoms, but this may still require that the application's executable (EXE) be modified.

ABOUT DebugDiag

The Debug Diagnostic Tool (DebugDiag) is a free tool offered by Microsoft (written by my friends, Wade Mascia and Mourad Lagdas) that assists in troubleshooting application issues such as hangs, slow performance, memory leaks, and crashes. It is available for download at http://www.microsoft.com/en-us/download/details.aspx?id=26798. It requires installation, but it is designed to run in a production environment and no reboot required. For more information on how to use DebugDiag, check out the whitepaper at http://www.microsoft.com/en-us/download/confirmation.aspx?id=23521.

PREPARING FOR A CALL WITH MICROSOFT SUPPORT

This procedure requires administrator rights and interactive access to the desktop in order to capture performance counters and install tools. Internet access is optional but can help with resolving symbols. This procedure can provide a very high level of detail about the memory usage of an application. The procedures discussed earlier in this chapter are provided as self-help and might not be enough to solve why an application is running out of virtual address space. The Microsoft Support services have a wealth of experience with investigating application memory problems. This procedure helps you prepare data that will likely help Microsoft Support professionals toward solving your application's memory problems. Please keep in mind that troubleshooting procedures used by Microsoft Support professionals can change without notice.

CAPTURE A PERFORMANCE COUNTER LOG OF WHEN THE APPLICATION(S) RAN OUT OF MEMORY

Capture the following performance counters into a binary (*.blg) performance counter log:

\Memory*, \Process(*)\Virtual Bytes, \Process(*)\Private Bytes, \Process(*)\Working Set, \Process(*)\ID Process, \Process(*)\Thread Count, and \Process(*)\Handle Count

Indicate which process names and process IDs are suspected of running out of memory, provide information about the application architecture, the system architecture such as 32-bit or 64-bit, if PAE is used, if large address aware is set on the applications, and if IncreaseUserVa is used.

The operating system version, architecture, and PAEEnabled setting can be queried using this Powershell command:

gwmi Win32_OperatingSystem | Select OSArchitecture, Caption, PAEEnabled

The default user virtual address space setting can be queried using this Powershell command:

gwmi Win32_OperatingSystem | % {$_.MaxProcessMemorySize / 1MB}

Offer any memory dump files and/or ETL traces if you have them. Please be aware that memory dumps (*.dmp) and event tracing for Windows trace files (*.etl) might contain personal and/or sensitive information, so protect them as needed.

WARNING

Many memory-related files such as memory dumps (*.dmp) and traces (*.etl) often contain sensitive information. Always use encryption when transferring these files over nonsecure networks.

OFFER SYMBOLS FILES

Request the symbol files from the application's developer. Symbols are used by debugging tools to map memory offsets of an EXE or DLL to the function calls within those files. This dramatically helps with isolating problematic code. I like to think of symbols as being similar to reverse DNS where a number is converted into a meaningful name.

Symbols must be created at the time the application was compiled and are unique to the build. For more information on debug symbols, see Appendix C "Debug Symbols."

DEALING WITH 32-BIT APPLICATIONS THAT RUN OUT OF VIRTUAL ADDRESS SPACE

Modern 32-bit applications need to be lean on memory usage; otherwise, they might crash due to a lack of virtual address space. The largest number that can be represented by 32 bits is 4 GB. This is calculated as 2 to the power of 32 (2^{32}). The address space is divided among the kernel at 2 GB and each process at 2 GB (Figure 4.9).

If you suspect that a 32-bit application is running out of virtual address space on a regular basis, then consider the next few sections for potential solutions.

ADDING PHYSICAL MEMORY OR INCREASING PAGING FILES HAS NO EFFECT

As mentioned earlier and contrary to popular belief, adding physical memory or increasing the paging file will not increase the amount of virtual address space presented to an application. Changes to the architecture of the system and/or the application are necessary. If the virtual address space of an application is increased through IncreaseUserVA or by running it on a 64-bit version of the operating system, then it allows the application to use more virtual address space. Availability of more virtual address space is not a direct correlation to physical memory or committed memory usage.

ANALYZE MEMORY USAGE AND FIX THE CODE

The proper way to deal with 32-bit applications that run out of virtual address space is to identify how memory is being used, fix the code, and then redeploy the application. This solution requires tools like VMMap (Sysinternals) or DebugDiag and access to the source code and build environment. Fixing the code can range from a one-line fix, to a full redesign of the application. Consider using Microsoft Support to assist with this effort. Otherwise, consider treating the symptoms by following the next steps.

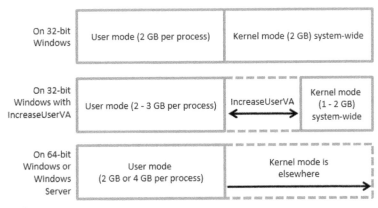

FIGURE 4.9

Diagrams of the ×86 (32-bit) virtual address space layouts.

RECOMPILE THE 32-BIT APPLICATION TO 64-BIT

If possible, the ideal solution is to recompile the application to 64-bit ($\times$64) and run it on a 64-bit ($\times$64) version of Windows or Windows Server. This presents the application with 8 TB of virtual address space (or 128 TB on x64 versions of Windows 8.1 and Windows Server 2012 R2), which should be enough at the time of this writing. Recompilation requires access to the source code and full testing to ensure proper functionality. In addition, if the application is dependent on 32-bit hardware or software components, then 64-bit versions of these dependencies will be required. These requirements can make going to go to 64-bit difficult. If unable to obtain a 64-bit ($\times$64) version of the application and dependencies, then try the next step.

If this solution is implemented, the 32-bit application will go from a 2 GB address space to 8 TB or more.

RUN THE 32-BIT APPLICATION ON A 64-BIT VERSION OF WINDOWS OR WINDOWS SERVER

32-bit ($\times$86) applications running on a 64-bit ($\times$64) version of Windows or Windows Server are still presented with 2 GB of virtual address space. But, if the application has a large address aware flag (discussed later in this chapter), then it can address up to 4 GB of virtual address space. This assumes that the application was developed with a memory manager (heap allocator) that can address more than 2 GB of virtual address space when it is available. In my experience, I haven't seen any application that couldn't address the extra memory yet. The large address aware flag is part of the application's executable (EXE) header and can be enabled with tools like Dumpbin or Imagecfg.

If this solution is implemented, the 32-bit application will go from a 2 GB address space to 4 GB of virtual address space.

CONSIDER IncreaseUserVA WITH CAUTION

The IncreaseUserVA setting is only effective on 32-bit versions of Windows 7 and Windows 8, and Windows 8.1. This is because 64-bit versions of Windows and Windows Server already have vastly more virtual address space to work with. IncreaseUserVA modifies the 4 GB balance between user-mode (application) virtual address space and kernel-mode virtual address space.

In my professional opinion, this solution should not be considered other than as a last resort because if this is not managed properly, then it can contribute toward the system running out of kernel resources, which is arguably worse than the application running out of virtual address space. Please read through the kernel-mode part of this chapter and/or consult with an expert in this area before considering this option.

Virtual address space was never intended to be a limiting factor, so if your only resort is using this setting, then this should be a red flag that the applications need to be migrated to 64-bit as soon as possible. 64-bit provides at least 8 TB or more of virtual address space for the kernel and for each application (Figure 4.4).

The IncreaseUserVa setting is implemented through BCDEdit and takes effect after a reboot.

Bcdedit /set IncreaseUserVa xxxx

Where xxxx is the number in megabytes between 2048 MB and 3072 MB as the divider between user mode and kernel mode. The kernel-mode space becomes the value of 4096 MB (4 GB) minus the value set by IncreaseUserVa. Attemp this procedure "only" if there is more than 50,000 Free System PTEs (\Memory\Free System Page Table Entries) and if Pool Paged and Pool NonPaged are using less than 50% of their respective virtual address space. See Chapter 5 "Kernel Memory" for more information (Figure 4.10).

If this solution is implemented, the 32-bit application will go from a 2 GB address space to the value of IncreaseUserVa (in MB) up to 3 GB.

FIGURE 4.10

Using BCDEdit to set IncreaseUserVa.

DISTRIBUTE THE COMPONENTS OF THE 32-BIT APPLICATION ACROSS MORE PROCESSES

If it is not possible to migrate to 64-bit or use a 64-bit version of the operating system, then consider distributing the components of the application across multiple processes. Each 32-bit application is presented with its own private virtual address space. Therefore, if the highest memory-consuming components are placed in their own process space, then this could allow the application to "scale out."

IDENTIFYING AND ADDING LARGE ADDRESS AWARE

The large address aware flag is part of the application's executable (EXE), and it allows a 32-bit application to access virtual address space larger than 2 GB, but not more than 4 GB since 32-bit cannot mathematically go beyond 4 GB. This change should be enabled by the developer of the application to ensure functionality after changed. If the developer of the application or the source code is not available, then tools like Imagecfg can be used to modify the executable to be large address aware (Figure 4.11).

Making an executable large address aware is relatively safe and easy to do; keep in mind that in rare cases, an application's memory manager might not recognize the additional address space.

The imagcfg.exe tool is very old and difficult to find. Therefore, I have placed it on my Microsoft OneDrive at http://aka.ms/clinth, and then go to the Tools folder.

FIGURE 4.11

Using Imagecfg.exe to make an executable large address aware.

THE CONCEPT AND ADVANTAGES OF VIRTUAL MEMORY

Years ago when my cousin, Jimmy, and I wanted to play Doom 2 on a computer running Microsoft DOS 6.22, we had to have about 600 KB of the 640 KB of physical memory (RAM) freed up in order to get Doom 2 up and running. These are the times when a mouse was a convenience, so we often had to "REM out" the mouse and reboot for the extra RAM space. Furthermore, once Doom 2 had the 600 KB of memory, it was completely up to it to manage that memory.

Now, imagine an operating system that manages a lot more applications running at the same time. If the operating system simply gave away all of the physical memory that the applications want, then who knows if those application will use the memory efficiently and if the operating system even has that much memory to go around.

Windows and Windows Server use virtual memory to "trick" applications into thinking that they have more memory than they will ever need. Furthermore, instead of just giving applications the memory they want, the operating system only places the memory that the application actually uses into physical memory. This allows the operating system to use physical memory much more efficiently.

The private "virtual world" that an application is given is similar to you stepping into a holodeck on the Starship Enterprise. The holodeck allows you to do things with the physical limitations of the real world removed. To you, the world is now unimaginably vast. Yet, physically, you are still contained in a small room.

While in the holodeck simulation, you decide to visit the Great Wall of China. Certainly, it would never physically be able to fit in the hull of the ship, but virtually, it is real to you. You see the wall stretch to the horizon and touch it. You feel the texture of the bricks as you walk along the path. The experience is as real as being there, but in reality, the ship's computer is making the matter under your foot falls and the bricks that you touch temporarily physical and then taking away portions of the physical object when no longer needed. If the ship's computer is low on matter (physical resources), then it might be more aggressive at removing the least frequently touched matter.

This scenario provided you with a private, virtual experience well beyond the physical limitations of the ship, yet you experienced it, and the ship's computer only had to provide you with the physical resources you actually touched. The memory management of Windows and Windows Server behaves in the same way as the ship's computer, and this is the benefit of virtual memory—a full experience with a high efficiency of physical resource usage.

32-BIT (×86) VIRTUAL ADDRESS SPACE

Windows NT 3.1 was released in 1993 as a 32-bit operating system. The largest number that can be represented by 32 bits is 4 GB. This is calculated as 2 to the power of 32 (2^32). The address space was divided among the kernel and each process—2 GB for the kernel space and 2 GB of address space private for each process. This means

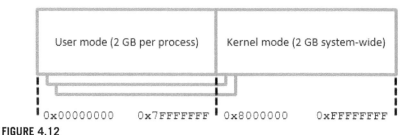

FIGURE 4.12

A diagram of the x86 (32-bit) virtual address space layout.

that each application has its own, private, 2 GB of virtual memory. At the time, 2 GB of virtual address space for each process was considered unimaginably large considering most systems had about 16 MB of RAM (Figure 4.12).

Even though the 2 GB of virtual address space for each process was more than sufficient for applications of that time, modern enterprise applications commonly needed more. Unfortunately, it cannot be increased without changing the underlying architecture such as modifying the user-mode and kernel-mode spaces or recompiling the application to 64-bit.

Generally speaking, there is no relationship between virtual address space and physical memory (RAM) other than through a system page table entry (PTE), which maps a virtual memory page (a 4 KB memory unit) to a physical memory page. In other words, the amount of physical memory installed on a system has no impact on the amount of virtual address space presented to an application. For example, I often explain to my customers that their 32-bit web applications on 32-bit Windows Server 2008 with 32 GB of RAM are still each given a 2 GB virtual address space. Busy or poorly written 32-bit web applications often crash with a System.OutOfMemoryException condition because they ran out of the 2 GB of virtual address space even though the system often has plenty of physical memory available.

NOTE

Paging files are often referred to as "virtual memory" because they allow the system to back more virtual memory allocations than what is normally possible with physical memory alone. With that said, like physical memory, the amount and size of paging files have no impact on the amount of virtual address space presented to an application.

In summary, no matter how much physical memory is installed and no matter how large the paging files are, 32-bit applications are presented with a 2 GB address space by default. Applications that need more than 2 GB must either modify the 4 GB address space between user mode and kernel mode (discussed later in this chapter) or be recompiled to run in a 64-bit environment.

64-BIT (×64) VIRTUAL ADDRESS SPACE

The largest number that can be represented by 64 bits is 16 EB (exabytes)—calculated as 2 to the power of 64 (2^64) bytes. Advanced Micro Devices created the ×64 processor architecture, which allows memory access of up to 256 TB of virtual address space.

According to the Windows Internals sixth edition book, the ×64 architecture did not implement the essential CMPXCHG16B instruction limiting Windows and Windows Server to address up to 44 bits of memory, which calculates to 16 TB. This space is further divided into a user-mode space of 8 TB and a kernel-mode space of 8 TB. This means that applications running on ×64 versions of Windows and Windows Server have a virtual address space of 8 TB (Figure 4.13).

64-bit versions of Windows 8.1 and Windows Server 2012 R2 now support the full 256 TB in ×64 giving each process a 128 TB virtual address space and the kernel 128 TB of virtual address space.

NOTE

Windows Server 2012 does not support the 64-bit (IA64) Itanium architecture.

When I attach Windows Sysinternals VMMap to an ×64 instance of Notepad, the sum of Free memory and Total memory is roughly 8 TB (Figure 4.14). This means that Notepad is running in a private address space of 8 TB.

MANY PROCESSES, ONE KERNEL

The user-mode and kernel-mode diagram (Figure 4.13) often used in other technical books unintentionally gives the impression that there is an instance of the kernel in every process. In actuality, there is simply a reference to the same kernel space in each process. This means that there is only one instance of the kernel that is referenced by all of the processes (Figure 4.15).

This should also reinforce that each process is presented with a private virtual address space—they are not pooled together.

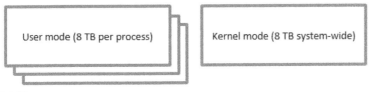

FIGURE 4.13

A diagram of the x64 (64-bit) virtual address space layout.

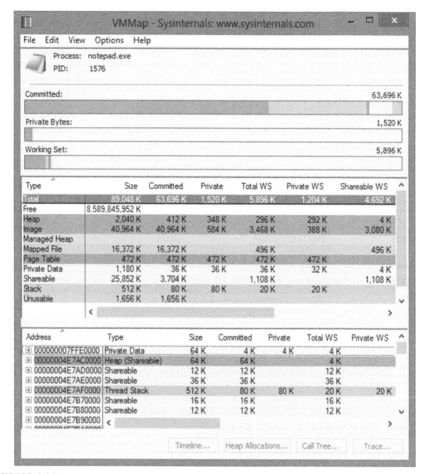

FIGURE 4.14

The Sysinternals VMMap tool shows that the x64 version of Notepad has 8 TB of virtual address space.

HOW CAN EACH APPLICATION HAVE A PRIVATE 8 TB ON A SYSTEM WITH 4 GB OF PHYSICAL MEMORY?

On ×64 (64-bit) versions of Windows and Windows Server, each application is presented with 8 TB of virtual address space. This is the world that the application runs in. The virtual memory manager of Windows and Windows Server simply provides for the needs of an application as it uses memory.

This concept is very similar to a dynamically expanding virtual hard drive file (*.vhd). I can give a virtual machine (VM) a 120 GB virtual hard drive. The virtual machine is presented a 120 GB hard drive, but the VHD file on the host system might only be 10 GB size. I can keep giving out as many 120 GB virtual hard drives as

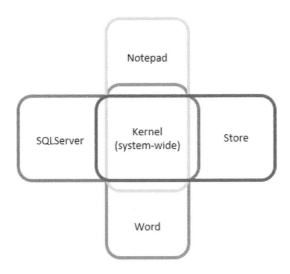

FIGURE 4.15

A hub and spoke diagram of how kernel-mode memory is referenced by each process.

I want even though the physical hard drive on the host doesn't have the capacity to handle it. The assumption is that many of the VMs will not actually use all of the space presented to them resulting in a hardware savings.

The virtual address space of a process works the same way. The virtual memory manager of the operating system can present an application with a fake 8 TB of virtual space and keep doing nearly indefinitely.

To learn more about the memory needs of an application that require to be backed by physical resources, go to the "Reserved, committed, and free memory" section later in this chapter.

VIRTUAL MEMORY AND PAGING FILES

Paging files are often referred to as "virtual memory" because they allow the system to back more virtual memory allocations than what is normally possible with physical memory alone. Figure 4.16 is the setting for paging files and has a title of "Virtual Memory." Likewise, the virtual address space presented to processes is also referred to as "virtual memory." While both terms are correct, they are referring to different aspects of it, which can be confusing, so I will try to clarify.

The amount and size of paging files have no impact on the amount of virtual address space presented to an application (user mode) or the virtual address space presented to the kernel. With that said, the amount of physical memory and paging file sizes determine the amount of virtual memory that can be committed across all processes.

The relationship between virtual address space and physical resources is covered later in this chapter in the "Reserved, committed, and free memory" section.

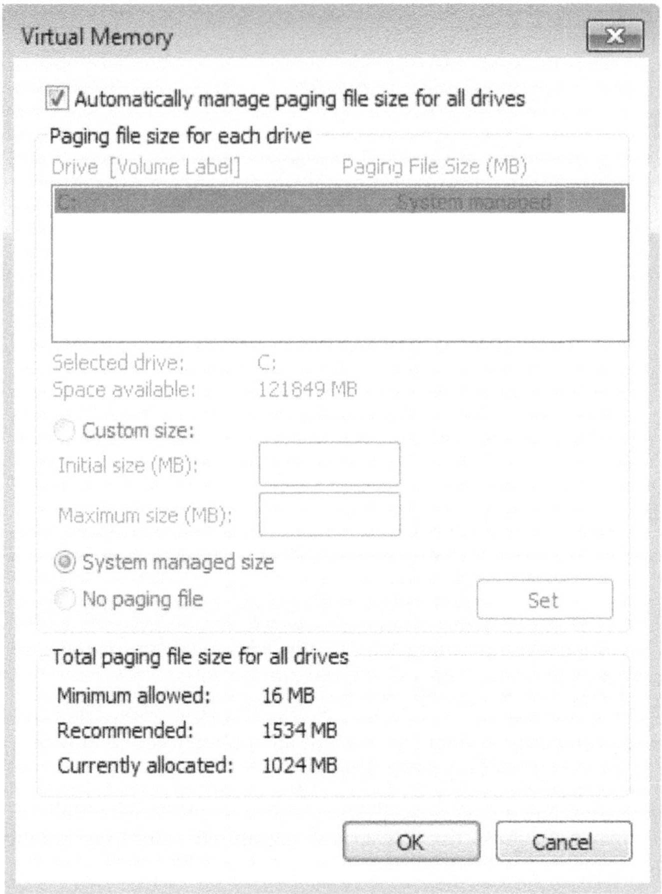

FIGURE 4.16

The page file properties page is titled "Virtual Memory."

RESERVED, COMMITTED, AND FREE MEMORY

A page is the unit by which Windows and Windows Server manage memory. It is for both virtual memory and physical memory management. Pages are 4 KB in size on all ×86 and ×64 versions of Windows and Windows Server—Itanium (IA64) systems have an 8 KB page size.

It's important to know the state of the virtual memory pages of an application because it determines how much impact it has on physical resources of the operating system. Keep in mind that applications can have dramatically different memory usage patterns depending on how the application is used and the amount of load on it.

FREE MEMORY

A page of memory that has never been used or is no longer in use is considered free. A process begins with all memory pages free. It is not backed by physical memory or a paging file.

RESERVED MEMORY

It is a page of memory that might be used and is cordoned off to protect the memory from other memory allocations within the process. For example, a thread stack reserves a 1 MB contiguous block of memory just in case it might need it. This is because a thread operates by moving a memory pointer. This is similar to reserving an entire floor at a hotel just in case you might need the space. If/when the thread stack actually needs the space, it already has it reserved and it is already contiguous (Figure 4.17).

A memory reservation is not backed by physical memory or a paging file other than the amount of memory needed to describe the reservation—this is called a virtual address descriptor (VAD). Think of a VAD as the entry into the hotel's paper book used to reserve the entire floor of rooms. It is a trivial amount of physical resources needed for the hotel to describe the reservation on a piece of paper similar to a VAD describing memory reservations. With that said, if the hotel received billions of reservations, then the paper used to record the reservations would become significant. When I reserved 1 TB of memory, it used 2 MB of system committed memory to describe it. This is a trivial ratio, and so we often consider memory reservations at practically no significant impact on the system.

In Figure 4.18, Process Explorer (Sysinternals) shows that an instance of 32-bit Testlimit.exe has reserved nearly all of its 2 GB (2,097,152 KB) of address space based on its virtual size. Yet, only about 5 MB of physical resources (physical memory and paging files) has been committed for this process to function. Furthermore, only about 1.7 MB of physical memory (touched memory) is needed for this process

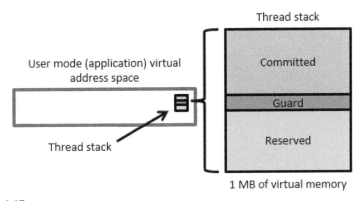

FIGURE 4.17

A thread stack reserves 1 MB just in case it might need it all.

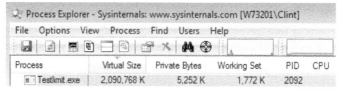

FIGURE 4.18

Process Explorer (Sysinternals) shows the memory usage of Testlimit.exe.

to operate based on its working set. This is a condition where the operating system is saving nearly 2 GB of physical resources by only putting the touched memory of this process into physical memory versus its wants (reserved memory and committed memory) turning this memory-hungry application into a trivial amount of overhead.

Figure 4.19 shows that Testlimit.exe consumed its entire 2 GB of virtual address space, so it is out of virtual address space, but it only committed about 5 MB.

Extreme cases of reserved memory usage typically result in an application out of memory condition where the application is out of virtual address space. For more information on this topic, see the "Identifying application out of virtual address space conditions" section later in this chapter.

PROCESS COMMITTED MEMORY

A page of memory in virtual address space that is backed by system committed memory (made up of physical memory and all page files) is considered committed. When a committed memory allocation is requested by an application, the memory manager

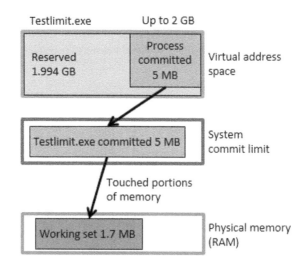

FIGURE 4.19

Testlimit.exe's impact on memory.

checks if it has enough system committed memory to back the request. Once the memory manager has granted the committed memory request (committed to the request), the system commit charge increases by the same amount in acknowledgement "promising" that the physical resources will back the request when needed. The commitment to back the allocation is not an actual consumption of resources until the memory is referenced (actually written to or "touched"). For this reason, it is possible for the system to reach its commit limit (sum of physical memory and all page files) and still have plenty of available physical memory. This condition is covered in more detail in Chapter 6 "System committed memory".

TOUCHED MEMORY

It is a page of memory that has been referenced as in written to or "touched." "Touched" is not a state of an application's virtual address space—pages within an application's address space can be free, reserved, or committed. From the application's perspective, the memory is committed and hasn't changed state, but from the operating system's perspective, physical resources are now in use versus just committed.

Once touched, a virtual memory page in the application's address space is mapped to a physical memory page through a system PTE. The act of touching memory causes it to be put in the process' working set, which resides in physical memory. This is the point at which physical memory is actually used.

IDENTIFYING APPLICATION OUT OF VIRTUAL ADDRESS SPACE CONDITIONS

Generally speaking, an application can be "out of memory" in two ways: out of virtual address space or unable to commit memory. This section of the book focuses on the first one—out of virtual address space. The out of committed memory condition is covered in Chapter 6 "System Committed Memory" (Figure 4.20).

When an application is out of virtual address space, it really means that it is unable to make a memory allocation within its virtual address space. This most often occurs when the memory allocation requires a modest amount of contiguous space. For example, when the Microsoft .NET Framework tries to allocate a 64 MB contiguous address space for the next Gen0 heap, smaller allocations such as a 128 KB allocation might still succeed. This would be similar to being unable to put a car in your garage, but a toolbox fits just fine.

When an application is unable to allocate memory, it receives an error condition—this is considered a first chance exception. If the error is not handled—meaning that the developer did not put in code to do something when this error occurs—then it becomes a second chance exception. Second chance exceptions are fatal to the application—meaning that the application's crash is imminent, but if a

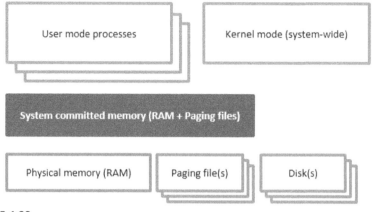

FIGURE 4.20

Memory diagram with system committed memory highlighted/filled solid.

debugger is attached, then it has a chance to do something such as creating a dump file of the memory of the application before the application actually crashes.

Identifying an application that is crashing due to out of virtual address space is difficult simply because it depends on how the application handles the condition. This could be writing to a specialized log, writing to an event log, or just nothing at all.

SYSTEM.OutOfMemoryException ERRORS

When a .NET application fails to allocate virtual address space and the developer doesn't handle the error condition, then the application will crash and in most cases report the error in the user interface and write an entry in the application event log.

READ THIS IF YOU ARE CONSIDERING /3GB OR INCREASEUSERVA

The simple answer is that if you have a system with more than 2 GB of physical memory, then don't use /3GB or IncreaseUserVa. It's just too risky on modern systems. Is it much better to run 32-bit applications on a 64-bit version of Windows or Windows Server, so that the kernel has plenty of virtual address space and the 32-bit applications enjoy the full 4 GB (their maximum possible). Let me explain.

Mathematically, the largest number that can be represented by 32 bits is 4 GB, so if your application needs more than 4 GB, then you must go to 64 bits, which will provide 8 TB of virtual address space. Years ago, when /3GB was first introduced, most systems had 1 GB or less physical memory. The kernel must track all of the physical memory pages, so it needs virtual address space to manage the physical memory.

The boundary between user-mode (process) space and kernel-mode space can be changed. This can provide more virtual address space to applications that are large address aware, but the cost is taking the same amount of virtual address space from the kernel. In PAE mode, 28 bytes represents each 4 KB page of physical memory—this is a ratio of 146:1. This means that roughly 6 MB or 7 MB is needed in the Page Frame Number (PFN) database, which is resident in kernel virtual address space to describe each 1 GB of physical memory. This might not sound like much, but if you have a 32-bit system with 16 GB of physical memory, then it requires about 112 MB of the 2 GB of kernel virtual address space just to address the RAM. In many cases, this is just too large to fit in the kernel's reduced 32-bit virtual address space.

NOTE

There is of course Address Windowing Extensions (AWE), which cheats by locking physical memory for direct use for an application, but it is difficult to implement and likely just easier to go to 64-bit.

For more information on the PFN database, check out my public wiki article at http://social.technet.microsoft.com/wiki/contents/articles/15259.page-frame-number-pfn-database.aspx.

IDENTIFYING PROCESSES LEAKING SYSTEM COMMITTED MEMORY

The most common type of memory leak is one or more processes leaking memory that affects the system-wide system committed memory. This is a limited (limited by the size of physical memory and the maximum size of page files), system-wide, resource that can be consumed by user-mode or kernel-mode virtual memory depending on how the memory is allocated. If the system runs out of system committed memory, then it can result in application and/or system hangs.

The most common cause of the system running out of system committed memory is processes. Therefore, it's important to be able to identify processes that use a large amount of system committed memory. For more information about system committed memory and other consumers of this kind of memory, go to Chapter 6 "System Committed Memory."

System committed memory is provided to a process when it is granted by the virtual memory manager as process committed memory. The code of an application can request a memory allocation to become committed, which means that the system will back/support the request with physical memory or page file if the system has enough to fulfill the request. This is a commitment/promise that the system is making to the process and is charged against the system commit charge. This is similar to checking into a hotel with the key card in hand where the hotel has

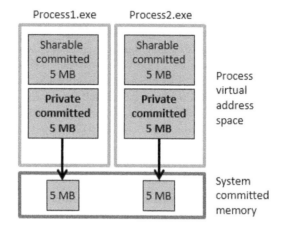

FIGURE 4.21

Only the private committed memory of a process is charged against the system commit charge.

committed/promised a room, but you are not physically occupying the room. Once the memory is actually used by the process (occupying your hotel room), it becomes mapped to physical memory. This is the difference between committed memory and touched memory.

A process has sharable committed memory and private committed memory. The shareable committed memory consists of portions of DLLs and EXEs that can be retrieved from a disk at any time (this is why you might get a sharing violation if you try to delete a DLL or EXE); therefore, it does not need to be backed by physical memory or a page file and does not count toward the system commit charge. This means that the size of the application's DLLs and EXEs does not directly impact the system commit charge. Only the private committed memory of a process is charged against the system commit charge since these data is not already on the disk. This is a cumulative effect meaning that the private committed memory of all processes is added to the system commit charge. Typically, one or two processes are to blame for leaking memory, but there are certainly plenty of "death by a thousand cuts" situations (Figure 4.21).

SOME TOOLS FOR MEASURING PROCESS PRIVATE COMMITTED MEMORY

- **Microsoft Performance Monitor** using the counters **\Process(*)\Private Bytes** or **\Process(*)\Page File Bytes**.
- **Microsoft Task Manager** using the Commit Size column on the Details tab. On older versions of Windows or Windows Server, it will be either the **Memory— Commit Size (Commit Size)** column or the **Virtual Memory Size (VM Size)** column under the Processes tab. These columns might need to be added.

- **Microsoft Resource Monitor** using the **Commit (KB)** column on the **Memory** tab or grouping.
- **Windows Sysinternals Process Explorer** using the **Private Bytes** column under **Process Memory**.
- **Microsoft Windows Management Instrumentation (WMI)** using the Win32_Process.PageFileUsage property.

TIP

Most tools refer to process, private, committed memory as Private Bytes.

WHEN IS IT CONSIDERED A LEAK?

A memory leak is a condition where a process is increasing in size and retaining unnecessary memory over time. When a process initially starts and does work, it needs memory to operate, so it is normal for a busy process to use a significant amount of memory. But, when the process returns to an idle state, it should release unneeded memory. The idle state of a process (if it exists) may not be easily identified, so it is important to monitor the process over a long period of time.

For example, the performance counter log shown in Figure 4.22, which shows the combined private committed memory of all of the processes on the system (**Process (_Total)\Private Bytes**) (bold black line) over a seven-day period, is slowly leaking system committed memory. The system commit charge (**Memory\Committed Bytes**) is the red line.

Each valley in both Figures 4.22 and 4.23 represents the end of each workday. Ideally, the memory usage should return to the same amount, but we see a progressive increase compared to the end of the previous day. The process names of this application are censored due to customer privacy.

Given enough time, the system will eventually run out of system committed memory. Therefore, troubleshooting is needed. Performance analysis is like Seattle traffic—you can get where you want to go so long as you put in enough time and effort. Do you tackle the root of the problem with an unpredictable amount of time and effort or just limp along by just restarting the processes? The choice is yours.

Be aware that in order to fix a memory leak, the code must be changed. If you do not have the ability to change and recompile the leaky application, then go to "Treating the symptoms of process committed memory leaks" later in this chapter. Otherwise, continue toward troubleshooting it.

Finally, if you are dealing with a process working set leak, which is the physical memory usage of a process, then be aware that working set size is generally managed by the operating system, but there are exceptions. For more information, see "Process working sets" in Chapter 8 "Physical Memory."

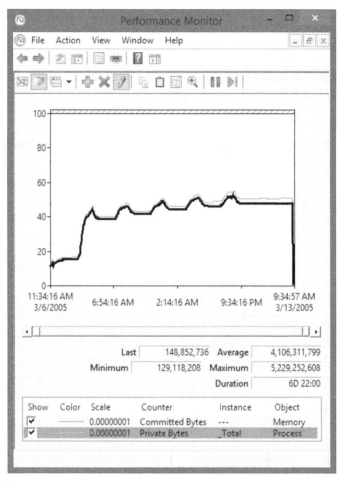

FIGURE 4.22

Committed Bytes is slowly increasing due to one or more processes private bytes.

TROUBLESHOOTING PROCESSES LEAKING SYSTEM COMMITTED MEMORY USING SYSINTERNALS VMMap

Once you have identified one or more processes that are leaking memory using the steps discussed above in "Identifying processes leaking system committed memory," a relatively quick and easy analysis tool is the Windows Sysinternals VMMap tool. This tool is great for getting a general idea of the type of committed memory that is in use and for visually seeing the memory allocation pattern.

According to the Windows Sysinternals Web site at http://technet.microsoft.com/sysinternals/dd535533.aspx, VMMap is a process virtual and physical memory

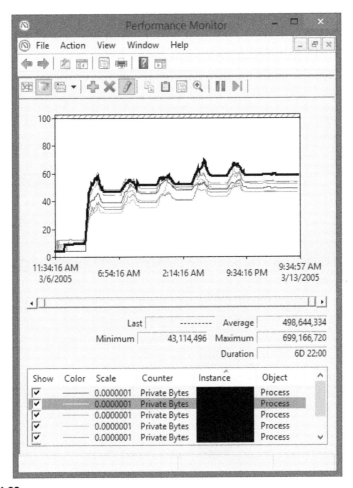

FIGURE 4.23

An example of several processes leaking private committed memory.

analysis utility. It shows a breakdown of a process' committed virtual memory types and the amount of physical memory (working set) assigned by the operating system to those types. Besides graphic representations of memory usage, VMMap also shows summary information and a detailed process memory map. Powerful filtering and refresh capabilities allow you to identify the sources of process memory usage and the memory cost of application features.

VMMap is a "quick" tool simply because it can be easily downloaded from http://live.sysinternals.com/vmmap.exe, it does not require installation, and it is noninvasive—meaning that it is relatively safe to use in production environments though it is still important to test it in a testing environment first.

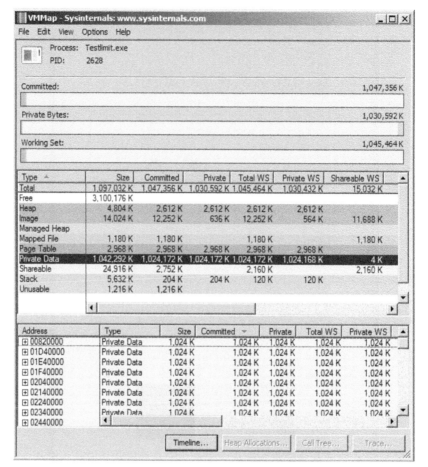

FIGURE 4.24

VMMap showing a 1 GB of private committed memory usage in Testlimit.exe.

In this case, VMMap shows Testlimit.exe that has committed 1 GB of memory. When Private Data is selected, it shows details of the data in the lower pane showing that the 1 GB of private data is actually a large number of 1 MB (1024 KB) allocations (Figure 4.24).

The Fragmentation view of VMMap (Figure 4.25) shows that the 1 MB allocations are contiguous. This is important when dealing with virtual address space fragmentation discussed earlier in this chapter. Also, the Fragmentation View is only for 32-bit processes.

To help identify which area of the memory is increasing over time, use VMMap to attach to the leaky process (can only attach to one process at a time).

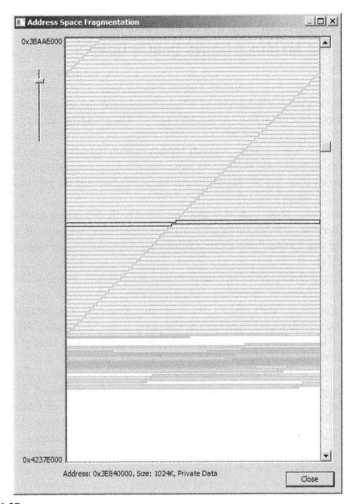

FIGURE 4.25

Fragmentation view of VMMap.

After the related application has finished its "warm-up," refresh VMMap by clicking View, Refresh or by pressing the F5 key. Once refreshed, the Timeline button will enable. The Timeline view shows the relative difference of memory resources for each refresh. With enough time, a pattern of increased memory usage should emerge.

For more information on how to use the features of VMMap, consider reading the "Windows Sysinternals Administrator's Reference" book by Mark Russinovich and Aaron Margosis at http://technet.microsoft.com/sysinternals/hh290819.aspx.

TROUBLESHOOTING PROCESSES LEAKING SYSTEM COMMITTED MEMORY USING DEBUG DUMPS

The "ye olde," yet still actively used, method of solving memory leaks is to collect process memory dumps (*.dmp files). In all honesty, there is no "secret" tool or procedure to debugging—it just requires a high degree of Windows architecture understanding to navigate through it. As a matter of fact, Microsoft regularly offers several training workshops on the subject. I have personally taken the Advanced User-Mode Debugging workshop six times, and I still consider myself a novice—not because it's too difficult, but because it is all about experience and pattern matching. This is why it is often best just to get the dump files to Microsoft Support for analysis—they do this stuff every day.

There are many tools available that can assist with debugging analysis without needing a deep knowledge of Windows architecture. See Appendix B "Collecting Process Memory Dumps" for more information on various tools that can be used to collect them.

It is beyond the scope of the book to discuss how the memory leak analysis using process memory dumps is actually done, but I will cover the basic concepts. For more information on how to debug process memory dumps, see the books "Advanced Windows Debugging" and "Advanced .NET Debugging" by Mario Hewardt (Twitter @MarioHewardt) and Daniel Pravat at http://www.advancedwindowsdebugging.com/index.html.

First, when collecting process memory dumps, always use the tool and settings that the person who will be debugging the application has requested. This is commonly a Microsoft Support professional, but the debugging tools are free and public, so this could be anyone. Again, see Appendix B "Collecting Memory Dumps" for more information on various ways to collect process memory dumps.

Once the dumps (*.dmp files) are collected (three consecutive dumps are typically requested), the person who is doing the debugging will typically compare memory structures in each to form a pattern of correlation such as a pattern of 20 strings and 10 integers allocated with 19 strings and 10 integers later deallocated. This would indicate that one of the strings of the related structure is not being deallocated and could result in a memory leak. Free tools such as DebugDiag can automate this comparison and produce a report showing the heaps that are growing and associated modules that are likely related to it.

According to "Debug Diagnostics Tool v2.0" at http://www.microsoft.com/download/details.aspx?id=40336, the Debug Diagnostic Tool (DebugDiag) is designed to assist in troubleshooting issues such as hangs, slow performance, memory leaks or fragmentation, and crashes in any user-mode process. The tool includes additional debugging scripts focused on Internet Information Services (IIS) applications, web data access components, COM+, and related Microsoft technologies.

TREATING THE SYMPTOMS OF PROCESS COMMITTED MEMORY LEAKS

If you do not have the ability to change the source code of an application and recompile it, then it is unlikely to truly fix the committed memory leak in the application.

In any case, there are several ways to "treat the symptoms" of memory leaks without changing the code:

- *Forcibly restart the leaky application*: When an application is restarted, it loses all of its memory structures in its respective processes. This is a relatively easy technique but can result in data corruption if the processes are not "gracefully" shut down. Therefore, discuss this option with the original developer or vendor who wrote the application. A forced restart is the killing of the associated process of the application and then running it again. There are many tools that can be used to kill a process such as navigating to the Details tab in Task Manager, selecting the target process, right-clicking on it, and selecting End Task. Products such as the Microsoft IIS have recycling features that restart the associated worker process when it reaches a specified amount of memory usage (virtual memory or committed memory).
- *Increase the system commit limit*: Restarting an application during high-activity hours can be difficult especially if the application is critical. If the system commit limit is increased, then it can allow the application to operate for a longer period of time depending on the rate of the memory leak and the size of physical memory and the page files, which determine the size of the system commit limit. Therefore, consider adding more physical memory (preferred due to the speed), increasing the size the page files, and/or creating more page files. If the physical memory cannot be added to the system and the page files have to be increased, then see "Systems with a low amount of physical memory" in Chapter 7 "Page Files" for more information on where to place them and why.

As a reminder, increasing the system commit limit is not a solution for a memory leak since given enough time, a leaky application will eventually run the system out of committed memory.

CONCLUSION

This chapter introduced process virtual address space concepts and memory leak analysis tools. Keep in mind that processes can run out of virtual address space before the system runs out of resources and vice versa.

Kernel memory

5

INTRODUCTION

Similar to applications, the kernel operates in virtual address space and has limits based on the available virtual address space, the system committed memory, and the amount of physical memory of the system. Figure 5.1 highlights the kernel-mode virtual address space. This chapter discusses how to detect and investigate problems with kernel virtual address space and how it relates to system committed memory and physical memory.

WHAT YOU NEED TO KNOW ABOUT KERNEL (SYSTEM) MEMORY

When the kernel resource runs out of memory, then it will be unable to allocate memory within that resource. This can quickly result in system-wide hangs and/or applications unable to operate. This is why it is important to know how to detect when the kernel is low on resources.

WARNING

A lack of kernel resources can result in system-wide hangs and/or applications unable to operate.

There are three primary kernel memory resources that need to be monitored for potential problems. They are Pool Paged, Pool Nonpaged, and system page table entries (PTEs).

POOL PAGED

Pool Paged kernel memory is an area of kernel virtual address space used for memory allocations that can be written to the disk. This is the pageable memory that drivers can use.

Windows Performance Analysis Field Guide. http://dx.doi.org/10.1016/B978-0-12-416701-8.00005-3

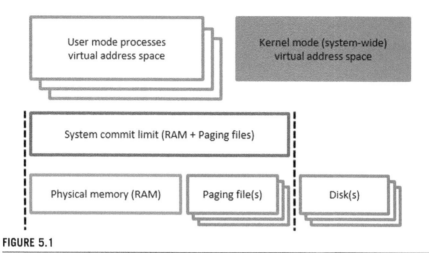

FIGURE 5.1

Overall Windows memory layout with the kernel mode highlighted.

POOL NONPAGED

Pool Nonpaged kernel memory is an area of kernel virtual address space used for memory allocations that cannot be written to the disk and must remain in physical memory. This is the nonpageable memory that drivers can use.

SYSTEM PAGE TABLE ENTRIES

PTEs are kernel resources that map virtual address space to physical memory. They use the remainder of the available kernel virtual address space after all other memory structures are established, so a lack of free PTEs is really a lack of available kernel virtual address space. When there is not enough free system PTEs, the system is unable to map virtual address space pages to physical memory pages. This can lead to application or system hangs.

NOTE

64-bit (x64) versions of Windows and Windows Server are unlikely to run out of kernel virtual address space due to the 8 TB or 128 TB of space depending on the version of Windows or Windows Server and are more likely to run out of physical memory or system committed memory first.

INITIAL INDICATORS OF POOL PAGED AND POOL NONPAGED KERNEL MEMORY

This procedure requires administrator rights and either desktop access or DCOM network connectivity.

WHAT TO LOOK FOR

Getting straight to the point, if **\Memory\System Page Table Entries** is less than 20,000, then the system is low on kernel virtual address space. PTEs are covered in more detail later in this chapter.

In addition, if you are using a 32-bit version of Windows or Windows Server, then another "canary in the coal mine" that should tell you that you need to seriously look at this is Event ID 2019 or 2020 in the system event logs. It is a clear indicator that the system is running out of these resources.

TIP

Figure 5.2 shows the virtual address space limits of the respective kernel pools. The "real" pool maximum sizes are based on available kernel virtual address space, available system committed memory, and available physical memory. This means that just because Pool Nonpaged memory has a virtual address space the size of 75% of RAM, it is still limited to the amount of available physical memory.

The Performance tab of Task Manager (Ctrl+Shift+Esc) (and then the Memory group on Windows 8 and Windows Server 2012 and later) shows the amount

Operating system (OS)	Pool type	Maximum on 32-bit	Maximum on 64-bit
Windows 7 and Windows Server 2008 R2	Nonpaged	75% of RAM or 2 GB* whichever is smaller	75% of RAM or 128 GB, whichever is smaller
Windows 7 and Windows Server 2008 R2	Paged	2 GB* or system commit limit, whichever is smaller	128 GB or system commit limit, whichever is smaller
Windows 8 and Windows Server 2012	Nonpaged	75% of RAM or 2 GB*, whichever is smaller	2 × RAM** or 128 GB, whichever is smaller
Windows 8 and Windows Server 2012	Paged	2 GB* or system commit limit, whichever is smaller	384 GB or system commit limit, whichever is smaller
Windows 8.1 and Windows Server 2012 R2	Nonpaged	75% of RAM or 2 GB*, whichever is smaller	2 × RAM** or 16 TB, whichever is smaller
Windows 8.1 and Windows Server 2012 R2	Paged	2 GB* or system commit limit, whichever is smaller	15.5 TB or system commit limit, whichever is smaller

*2 GB or 4 GB minus the size of IncreaseUserVa, whichever is smaller.
**The virtual address space limit is 2 × RAM, but the actual usage cannot be larger than 1 × RAM.

FIGURE 5.2

The estimated virtual address space limits of Pool Paged and Pool Nonpaged kernel memory.

of Pool Paged and Pool Nonpaged usage. Unfortunately, it doesn't provide the maximum size of the respective pools, so the chart in Figure 5.2 provides an estimate. If the usage is over 75% of their respective maximum sizes, then it is an indicator that warrants more investigation.

NOTE

The kernel virtual address space of 32-bit versions of Windows Vista and Windows Server 2008 is limited to 2 GB or (4 GB minus the size of IncreaseUserVa), whichever is smaller. For example, a system with 2 GB of kernel-mode virtual address space could potentially have a Pool Paged size of up to 2 GB minus other kernel resources. This means that both Pool Paged and Pool Nonpaged cannot both occupy 2 GB at the same time.

On 32-bit versions of Windows Vista and Windows 2008 or later, the sum of Pool Paged and Pool Nonpaged cannot be larger than 2 GB or (4 GB minus the size of IncreaseUserVa), whichever is smaller, minus all of the other kernel-mode memory usage (Figure 5.3). This is due to the mathematical limitation of 32 bits and another reason to go to 64-bit versions of Windows and Windows Server. This is a "huge" improvement from 32-bit versions of Windows XP and Windows Server 2003, which were more limited.

TIP

On the 32-bit version of Windows Vista, 32-bit version of Windows Server 2008, 32-bit version of Windows 7, 32-bit version of Windows 8, and 32-bit version of Windows 8.1, the easiest way to indicate a potential 32-bit kernel-mode virtual address space problem is to monitor free system PTEs (**\Memory\Free System Page Table Entries**). Free system PTEs are counted by the amount of pages that are free in kernel virtual address space. Since Pool Paged or Pool Nonpaged can potentially use this space, it represents how much memory is potentially left over for system PTEs. Therefore, a lack of free system PTEs (look for values of less than 20,000) can indicate a potential kernel pool leak.

Be aware that 32-bit versions of Windows XP and Windows Server 2003 and older are far different in the behavior of kernel virtual address space and are beyond the scope of this book simply due to the complexities of the problem.

The pool counters can be monitored enterprise-wide using the performance counters **\Memory\Pool Paged Bytes** and **\Memory\Pool Nonpaged Bytes** (Figure 5.4). See Chapter 2 "Performance Monitor" for more information on various ways to collect these counters.

WHAT TO DO

If the pool usage of either pool is larger than 75% of its respective maximum (maximum defined as its respective virtual address space, physical memory, or system committed memory, whichever is the smallest), then look at the committed and

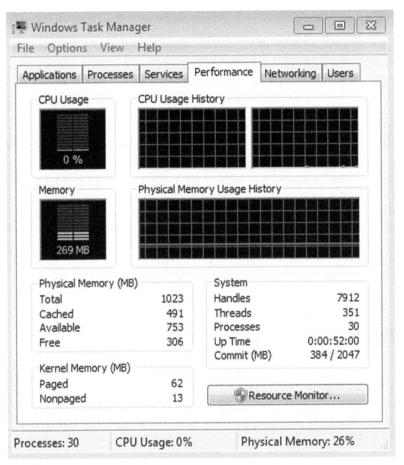

FIGURE 5.3

The Performance tab of Task Manager on a 32-bit (x86) version of Windows 7.

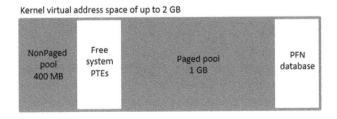

FIGURE 5.4

32-bit kernel virtual address space showing potential Pool Paged and Pool Nonpaged usage.

working set memory usage of the processes on the system. Leaks in kernel memory pools are often associated to leaks in applications/processes. Committed memory and working set memory of processes are covered in more detail in the next chapter. In any case, if more details are needed of the memory usage of the kernel pools, then see the "analyzing" sections later in this chapter.

64-BIT (X64) VERSIONS OF WINDOWS AND WINDOWS SERVER

It is unlikely to have a kernel memory problem on 64-bit versions of Windows or Windows Server. This is because of the 8 TB or 128 TB (depending on the operating system) of virtual address space given to the kernel. Since physical memory sizes are significantly smaller than the virtual address space, it is more likely to run out of physical memory or system committed memory. This is why it is important to monitor physical memory usage and system committed memory usage and to consider kernel memory in your investigations. Physical memory usage is covered in Chapter 8, and system committed memory usage is covered in Chapter 6 (Figure 5.5).

TROUBLESHOOTING A LACK OF PTEs

PTEs map virtual address space pages to physical memory pages. They are allocated out of the available kernel virtual address space. Unlike other kernel resources, system PTEs don't get a designated area of the kernel virtual address space—they get the leftovers—meaning that any kernel virtual address space that is not predesigned already allocated is potential memory that can be used and counted as free system PTEs.

WHAT ARE PTEs?

System PTEs map virtual address space pages to physical memory pages. A lack of system PTEs means an inability to map virtual address space to physical memory, which means that applications could be waiting/hanging on this resource.

WHAT TO LOOK FOR

The only way that I know to monitor for a lack of system PTEs is the **Memory**\ **System Page Table Entries** performance counter other than debugging the kernel. Look for values of less than 20,000. When below 20,000, the system may begin to fail to accommodate memory allocations. When lower than 15,000, memory allocation may fail more frequently. An example of this is Notepad simply failing to start. Every application and every driver behave differently to this condition and might even report unrelated errors.

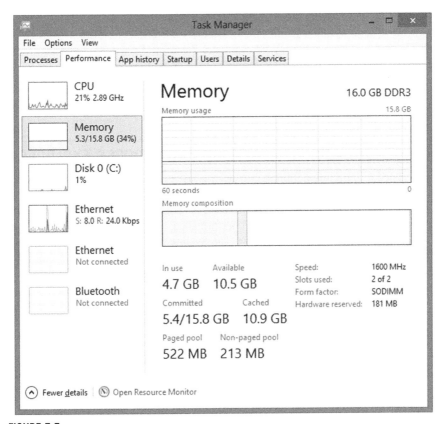

FIGURE 5.5

The Performance tab of Task Manager on a 64-bit (x64) version of Windows 8.

WHAT TO DO

On 32-bit versions of Windows and Windows Server, determine if Pool Paged (**\Memory\Pool Paged Bytes**) and Pool Nonpaged (**\Memory\Pool Nonpaged Bytes**) are greater than 500 MB or a significant amount based on the system settings. Next, determine if this system is using IncreaseUserVa (previously known as /3GB). At an administrator command prompt, run BCDEdit.exe and look for an entry of IncreaseUserVa. If so, consider reducing the value for this setting. Keep in mind that when IncreaseUserVa is reduced, it will re-adjust the virtual address space between user-mode processes (applications) and the kernel. Look at the performance counter **\Process(*)\Virtual Bytes** to determine if any process is using more than 1.5 GB (assuming a moderate level of virtual address space fragmentation); otherwise, reduce or remove the IncreaseUserVa setting. If one or more processes are using more than 2 GB of virtual address space, then try to readjust the IncreaseUserVa to balance the needs of the applications with the needs of the kernel. If this balance cannot be achieved, then seriously consider moving the application(s) to a 64-bit version of Windows or Windows Server because this will allow the kernel to have 8 TB of virtual address space (or 128 TB on 64-bit versions of Windows 8 and Windows Server 2012 and later) and allow the applications that need more than 2 GB of address space the ability to go up to 4 GB—only 3 GB is possible for applications running on a 32-bit version of Windows and Windows Server.

MONITORING KERNEL MEMORY USING PROCESS EXPLORER

This procedure requires administrator access, access to the desktop, and Internet access to download tools and symbol files.

So far, we have only estimated the sizes of the paged and nonpaged kernel memory pools and used Task Manager and performance counters to determine if we are close to the respective maximum sizes. The Sysinternals tool Process Explorer has the ability to query the kernel for the maximum size of these pools, but be mindful that the maximum size is the virtual address space size for the kernel pools which may be further limited by physical memory or system committed memory.

DOWNLOAD PROCESS EXPLORER

First, download the latest version of Process Explorer from http://live.sysinternals. com/procexp.exe. No installation is required—it just runs as a standalone executable.

DOWNLOAD AND INSTALL THE DEBUGGING TOOLS FOR WINDOWS

Process Explorer can certainly run by itself, but in order for it to query the kernel to determine the maximum sizes of kernel pools, it needs the files of the Debugging Tools for Windows. The download location and packaging of it change often. As of this writing, it is bundled with the Windows Software Development Kit (SDK) and with the Windows Assessment and Deployment Kit (ADK). There is no need to install these rather large kits. Start the installation, and uncheck all options except for the Debugging Tools for Windows.

TIP
If the installation of tools is prohibited in a production environment, then consider installing the Debugging Tools for Windows on another computer of the same architecture and copy the installation directory to the target computer.

CONFIGURE THE SYMBOL PATH

Once the files of the Debugging Tools for Windows are on the computer, run Process Explorer. Click Options, and select Configure Symbols (Figure 5.6).

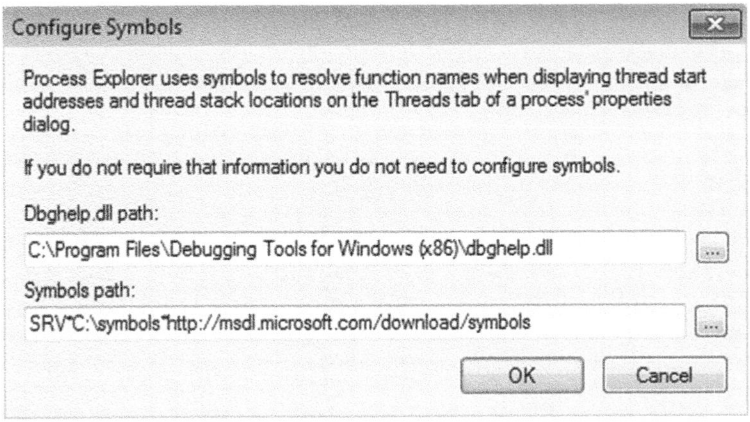

Configure Symbols

Process Explorer uses symbols to resolve function names when displaying thread start addresses and thread stack locations on the Threads tab of a process' properties dialog.

If you do not require that information you do not need to configure symbols.

Dbghelp.dll path:

C:\Program Files\Debugging Tools for Windows (x86)\dbghelp.dll

Symbols path:

SRV*C:\symbols*http://msdl.microsoft.com/download/symbols

OK   Cancel

FIGURE 5.6

The Configure Symbols dialog box of Process Explorer.

Set the Dbghelp.dll path installation directory of the Debugging Tools for Windows. The Dgbhelp.dll file should be in that directory. Set the Symbols path to (without the double quotes) "SRV*C:\symbols*http://msdl.microsoft.com/download/symbols" where C:\symbols can be any directory on the local computer that can be written to. The URL in the path points to Microsoft's symbol server. It is a nonbrowsable address but designed for debuggers. Click OK when done.

NOTE

Configuring Process Explorer and installation or copy of Debugging Tools for Windows is only needed to be done once.

For more information on symbol paths, see Appendix C Debug Symbols.

RUN AS ADMINISTRATOR

If Process Explorer is still running, then close it. Run Process Explorer with administrator rights. Running Process Explorer as administrator is required in order for it to show the maximum sizes of the kernel pools.

VIEW SYSTEM INFORMATION

Click View, and select System Information. Select the Memory tab (Figure 5.7).

Locate the section labeled "Kernel Memory (K)." Paged Limit and Nonpaged Limit are the virtual address space maximum sizes of the respective kernel memory pools.

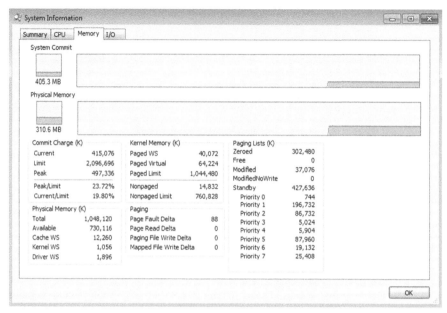

FIGURE 5.7

The System Information dialog box of Process Explorer.

If "No symbols" shows as the value for these fields, then it means that one of the steps mentioned above was missed or the system is not able to access the Microsoft Symbol Server at http://msdl.microsoft.com/download/symbols. Internet access is required.

NOTE

The Microsoft Symbol Server URL is not intended for Internet browsers. Browsing to it might not return anything. Consider checking connectivity to it by running the following command:

```
PsPing msdl.microsoft.com:80
```

PsPing is a command-line tool from Sysinternals downloadable from http://live.sysinternals.com/psping.exe.

In the case of Figure 5.10, it is a 32-bit version of Windows 7 computer with IncreaseUserVa set to 3072 (3 GB) giving applications up to 3 GB of virtual address space but reducing kernel address space to 1 GB. This is why it shows the Paged Limit to be 1 GB.

If the values of Paged Virtual or Nonpaged are near their respective limits, then follow the steps in "Analyzing kernel memory using WPA" to identify the drivers consuming the most memory.

ANALYZING KERNEL MEMORY USING WPA

This procedure requires administrator access to install a tool, access to the desktop, Internet access to download files, and installation of the latest version of the Microsoft .NET Framework (only if analyzing the data with WPA), and a reboot might be required. Use this procedure to provide details of memory usage of kernel memory pools only if you suspect kernel resource problems. The Windows Performance Toolkit works on all versions of Windows 7, Windows 8, Windows Server 2008 R2, and Windows Server 2012.

DOWNLOAD AND INSTALL THE WINDOWS PERFORMANCE TOOLKIT

The WPA tool is part of the Windows Performance Toolkit, which is part of the ADK. As of this writing, the Windows ADK can be downloaded from http://www.microsoft.com/download/details.aspx?id=30652. During installation, only the Windows Performance Toolkit is needed for this procedure—optionally uncheck all other features and finish the installation wizard.

CAPTURE DATA

Once the Windows Performance Toolkit is installed, run the Windows Performance Recorder (WPR) with administrator rights and expand "More options" if not already expanded.

NOTE

It is best to run the WPR tool shortly after a reboot and just before the behavior that results in significant kernel memory usage.

In the select profiles section, clear all options and select "Pool usage." Click Start when ready to collect data (Figure 5.8).

Even though WPR collects a significant amount of data, it actually has a low amount of overhead. It is designed to run in a production environment. By default, it collects data in a circular memory buffer, so it can run indefinitely. Simply stop collecting data after one minute or more by clicking the Save button and following the prompts.

ANALYZE IN WPA

Once the ETL file is saved, open the file in WPA. Once the ETL file is opened, navigate to the left pane and expand the Memory chart, and then double-click Pool Graphs. The Pool Graphs chart will appear in the right pane.

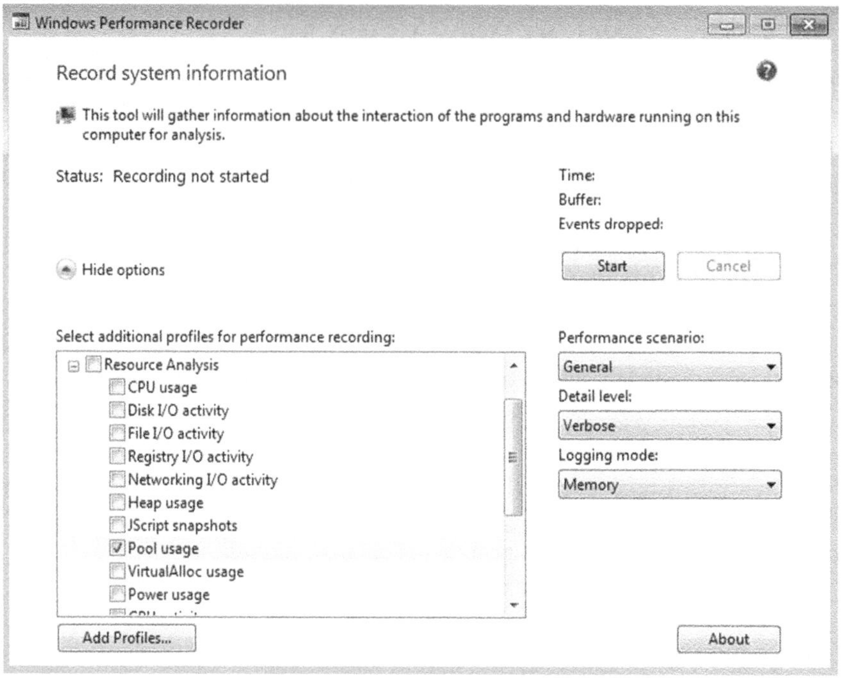

FIGURE 5.8

Windows Performance Recorder (WPR) ready for collecting pool usage.

In the pool chart, double-click on the line that is consuming the most memory or with the most significant increasing trend. In this case, the driver tag consuming the most Pool Paged memory (shown in Figure 5.9) is "Leak." "Leak" is the drive tag of the Sysinternals NotMyFault tool, which is designed to leak kernel pool memory on demand for demonstration purposes.

If you do not recognize the driver tag, then consider searching the drivers on the computer for one that matches the tag. This can be done by running the following command:

strings %systemroot%\System32\Drivers* | findstr Leak

where "Leak" is the pool tag you are searching for.

Strings is a Sysinternals command-line tool that can be downloaded from http://live.sysinternals.com/strings.exe.

Keep in mind that drivers that are using the most memory might not be leaking memory. Busy drivers need memory to function, so consider this procedure only if the system is regularly low on kernel virtual address space, committed memory, or physical memory due to the pool memory usage.

Once the driver or drivers are matched to the pool tag, contact the vendor of the driver to see if there are memory fixes or optimizations in the latest version of the driver. If not, consider opening a support case with the vendor.

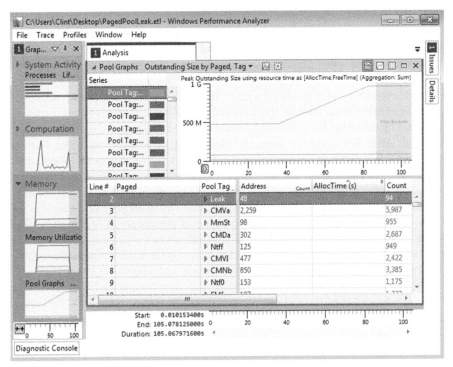

FIGURE 5.9

Windows Performance Analyzer showing pool usage.

For more information on troubleshooting kernel memory pools, consider reading Mark Russinovich's blog post on the subject at http://blogs.technet.com/b/markrussinovich/archive/2009/03/26/3211216.aspx?wa=wsignin1.0. It is relatively old, but much of it still applies to modern versions of Windows and Windows Server.

ANALYZING KERNEL MEMORY USING POOLMON.EXE

The following procedure must be done at the desktop of the computer and requires administrator rights. No installation required.

Poolmon.exe is a free Microsoft tool that provides the number of allocations and data currently allocated to Pool Paged or Pool Nonpaged and the respective pool tags associated with the allocations. A pool tag represents a named memory allocation from a driver and a driver can have more than one pool tag.

Currently, Poolmon.exe can only be downloaded from the Windows XP Service Pack 2 Support Tools on the Microsoft Web site at http://www.microsoft.com/en-us/download/details.aspx?id=18546. If you are not running the Windows XP operating system, extract the file using a zip-based tool such as 7-zip from 7-zip.org. Locate support.cab and extract it in the same way. Poolmon.exe should be one of the extracted files. With the support of Windows XP ending, it is likely that this download will no longer work. Therefore, I have placed it on my personal Microsoft OneDrive account at http://aka.ms/clinth, and then, go to Tools. You should see Poolmon.exe and other performance-related tools. Poolmon.exe is the only file needed.

A 32-bit version of Windows 7 with 4 GB of physical memory has a potential of 2 GB of kernel virtual address space shared with other system resources assuming that the IncreaseUserVa (previously known as the /3GB switch) feature is not enabled. After following the steps in "Monitoring kernel memory using Process Explorer," Windows Sysinternals Process Explorer shows that both Paged Limit and Nonpaged Limit are 2 GB. This is the virtual address space limit, which means that these pools might be limited by other system resources such as system committed memory and/or physical memory. Again, this virtual address space limit is not associated in any way to the physical resources of the system. It is a mathematical limit of 32 bits. This is another case of physical hardware exceeding the intent of virtual address space. Ideally, there should always be far more virtual address space than physical resources, and this is another reason to be on 64-bit if possible.

I induced a driver leak using the Sysinternals NotMyFault tool, and now, Task Manager shows 1662 MB of usage in Paged (Pool) shown in Figure 5.11. This memory must be backed by system committed memory (also known as "page file backed"), and so, the system commit charge must be larger than 1662. In this case, it is at 2178 MB.

At this point, Pool Paged could fail at any time simply due to fragmentation of the system virtual address space and other system resources within the 2 GB. There are plenty of system committed memory and plenty of available physical memory, so only virtual address space is the limiting factor (Figure 5.12).

I was right; as soon as I tried to leak a bit more, it reached 1666 MB (4 MB more) and was unable to allocate any more. The system is unable to allocate any more memory from Pool Paged. This doesn't make the system unstable. It just means that the drivers are now unable to get their memory requests approved. The system doesn't crash because it is expecting this to be a temporary condition where a driver will deallocate some memory allowing the system to operate normally again.

When in this state, odd things may happen. For example, when I tried to open Notepad, I received the dialog box shown in Figure 5.13.

Kernel Memory (K)	
Paged WS	71,196
Paged Virtual	79,424
Paged Limit	2,037,760
Nonpaged	18,240
Nonpaged Limit	2,036,592

FIGURE 5.10

Kernel pool information from Sysinternals Process Explorer.

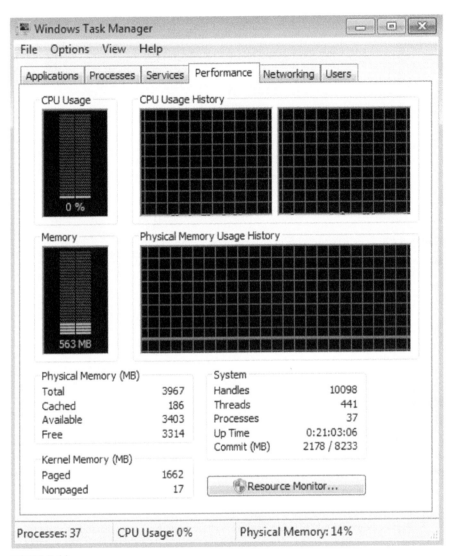

FIGURE 5.11

The Performance tab of Task Manager on Windows 7.

At an administrator command prompt, I ran Poolmon.exe and pressed the "b" button to sort by the tag with the largest amount of bytes. In this case, the pool tag is "Leak"— this is the pool tag associated with the Sysinternals NotMyFault tool (Figure 5.14).

Driver tags are strings inside of a driver file (*.sys). Therefore, the findstr command-line tool (built into Windows and Windows Server) can be used to search the contents of the driver files for the string of the pool tag (Figure 5.15).

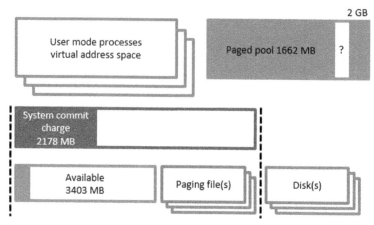

FIGURE 5.12

Diagram of a Pool Paged leak example.

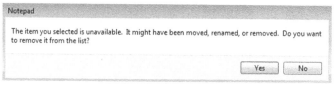

FIGURE 5.13

Notepad is unable to start due to a lack of Pool Paged kernel memory.

Use the following command to search the drivers directory for the pool tag "Leak" in all files that end with ".sys":

Findstr /m /l Leak *.sys

Replace the word "Leak" (it is case-sensitive) with the respective pool tag that you are interested in identifying. The argument "/m" is to display only the filename of the string match. The argument "/l" ("l" as in lima) is to do a literal search making the string match case-sensitive.

Keep in mind that not all drivers reside in %windir%\System32\drivers, so a full file system search might be necessary.

Alternatively, the Windows Sysinternals tool Strings can be used to search for the drivers associated with a pool tag.

Open an Administrator command prompt and change directory to the %windir%\System32\Drivers directory and then execute the following command:

Strings * | findstr Leak

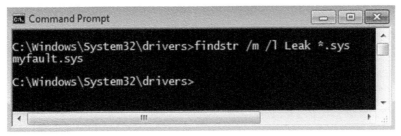

FIGURE 5.14

Poolmon.exe showing the pool tags with the largest number of bytes.

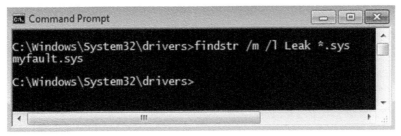

FIGURE 5.15

Findstr is helpful with finding drivers associated with a pool tag.

where "Leak" is the driver tag to look up.

According to Mark Russinovich's (creator of the Sysinternals tools) "Pushing the Limits of Windows: Pool Paged and Pool Nonpaged" at http://blogs.technet.com/b/markrussinovich/archive/2009/03/26/3211216.aspx, after you've found a match, you can dump the driver's version information with the Sysinternals Sigcheck utility. This tool is helpful in determining if the driver has a valid digital signature, which is an important validation step since drivers have privileged access to the system. According to the Sysinternals Sigcheck Web site, Sigcheck is a command-line utility that shows file version number, timestamp information, and digital signature details, including certificate chains. It also includes an option to check a file's status on VirusTotal (http://www.virustotal.com/), a site that performs automated file scanning against over 40 antivirus engines and an option to upload a file for scanning.

For more information on the Sysinternals Sigcheck tool, go to http://technet.microsoft.com/sysinternals/bb897441.aspx.

INSTALLING A KERNEL DEBUGGER

Performance Monitor is only able to provide the current size of the kernel pools using **\Memory\Pool Paged Bytes** and **\Memory\Pool Nonpaged Bytes**. It is not able to tell us the maximum sizes for comparison. This is why the estimated maximum sizes of the kernel pools are provided in Figure 5.2. A kernel debugger is able to provide the maximum virtual address space sizes and other data virtual memory-related resources. With that said, the estimated maximum size chart and the output from a kernel debugger will only show the maximum virtual address space sizes. Keep in mind that system committed memory limits and physical memory limits must also be considered.

The kernel debuggers that I'm familiar with are WinDBG, KD.exe, and Sysinternals LiveKD. WinDBG (GUI interface) and KD.exe (command-line interface) are a part of the Debugging Tools for Windows and require the system to be booted with the /debug boot option (debug mode).

Warning before using debug mode!

Be aware that Sysinternals LiveKD is able to do kernel-level troubleshooting without the need of the system to be in debug mode. With that said, if you still need kernel debugging enabled, then continue reading.

Before you enable kernel debugging on all of your systems, be aware of the following:

- *Temporarily suspend Bitlocker drive encryption*: Temporarily suspend Bitlocker drive encryption before enabling the debug mode; otherwise, the Bitlocker recovery key will be required during boot. Make sure you have a backup of your Bitlocker recovery key; otherwise, all data on the drive could be lost.
- *DRM-protected content will fail*: In addition, Digital Rights Management (DRM)-protected media (and applications dependent on the content) will fail to function when the system is in the debug mode.

This is not a complete list. For example, one of my old PC games failed to function until I disabled the debug mode and rebooted. I doubt that it had anything to do with DRM-protected content. In any case, be sure to remove a production system out of production and test it in debug mode before putting it back in production.

According to the Windows Sysinternals Administrator's Reference book, Sysinternals LiveKD allows you to use kernel debuggers to examine a snapshot of a live system **without booting the system in debug mode**. This can be useful when kernel-level troubleshooting is required on a machine that wasn't booted in debug mode. With that in mind, the Debugging Tools for Windows files are still required for LiveKD to function.

LiveKD can be downloaded from http://live.sysinternals.com/livekd.exe. No installation required. When running LiveKD, it needs to know the location of KD. exe, which is part of the Debugging Tools for Windows. This is done using the "k" parameter. For example, the Debugging Tools for Windows is installed to %ProgramFiles(x86)%\Windows Kits\8.1\Debuggers\x64; therefore, I use the following command to start LiveKD:LiveKD -k "%ProgramFiles(x86)%\Windows Kits. \8.1\Debuggers\x64\KD.exe."

NOTE

As of this writing, if the "-k" parameter is not used, then LiveKD looks for KD.exe at "\Program Files\Microsoft\Debugging Tools for Windows," which is where older versions of the Debugging Tools for Windows are installed to by default. This might change in future versions of LiveKD. Alternatively, copy LiveKD.exe to the installation directory of the debugging tools and run LiveKD from there with no arguments.

THE DEBUGGING TOOLS FOR WINDOWS ON PRODUCTION SYSTEMS

The Debugging Tools for Windows is part of the SDK. If you want to download only the Debugging Tools for Windows, install the Windows SDK (http://go.microsoft.com/fwlink/p?LinkID=271979), and during the installation, select Debugging Tools for Windows box and clear all the other boxes.

The Debugging Tools for Windows does not require installation. A simple file copy of the directory contents to the production system is all that is needed. This is effectively what the installer is doing. Consider installing the tools on another system of the same version of Windows or Windows Server and of the same architecture (x86, x64, IA64, and so on), and then, copy the installation directory to the production system.

TIP

I generally recommend that the Debugging Tools for Windows be available to all production systems. You never know when you might need them in a hurry to get a crash dump or hang dump. They do not alter the system in any way when copied or installed to the system.

The Windows Debugging Tools are explained in more detail in "Windows Debugging" at http://msdn.microsoft.com/library/windows/hardware/ff551063.aspx. For your convenience, I created a shorted URL http://aka.ms/debuggingtools to get you to the Windows Debugging Web site.

NOTE

The aka.ms domain is owned by Microsoft, and only authorized Microsoft employees, partners, and vendors can create a shortened URL from it.

ANALYZING KERNEL MEMORY WITH A KERNEL DEBUGGER

The following procedure requires interactive access to the desktop of the system with administrator rights and Internet connectivity in order to download the symbols.

Once you have a kernel debugger running (this can be done in a production environment noninvasively—see "Installing a kernel debugger" earlier in this chapter) on a system, use the command "!vm" without the double quotes. This command displays information about the virtual memory of the system that is generally not available anywhere else.

Figure 5.16 shows the output of "!vm" on my 64-bit Windows 8.1 laptop. In this case, I used Sysinternals LiveKD to avoid the need to set the system in the debug mode.

```
0: kd> !vm

*** Virtual Memory Usage ***
        Physical Memory:          4147941 (    16591764 Kb)

************ NO PAGING FILE ***********************
        Available Pages:           2069638 (      8278552 Kb)
        ResAvail Pages:            3347290 (     13389160 Kb)
        Locked IO Pages:                 0 (            0 Kb)
        Free System PTEs:       4294606134 (  17178424536 Kb)
        Modified Pages:             115799 (       463196 Kb)
        Modified PF Pages:          115772 (       463088 Kb)
        NonPagedPool Usage:           3024 (        12096 Kb)
        NonPagedPoolNx Usage:        40774 (       163096 Kb)
        NonPagedPool Max:          7980619 (     31922476 Kb)
        PagedPool 0 Usage:          108561 (       434244 Kb)
        PagedPool 1 Usage:           19142 (        76568 Kb)
        PagedPool 2 Usage:           11850 (        47400 Kb)
        PagedPool 3 Usage:           11782 (        47128 Kb)
        PagedPool 4 Usage:           11930 (        47720 Kb)
        PagedPool Usage:            163265 (       653060 Kb)
        PagedPool Maximum:      4160749568 (  16642998272 Kb)
        Session Commit:              13579 (        54316 Kb)
        Shared Commit:              277092 (      1108368 Kb)
        Special Pool:                    0 (            0 Kb)
        Shared Process:              13601 (        54404 Kb)
        Pages For MDLs:             546015 (      2184060 Kb)
        PagedPool Commit:           169990 (       679960 Kb)
        Driver Commit:               13744 (        54976 Kb)
        Committed pages:           2334556 (      9338224 Kb)
        Commit limit:              4147941 (     16591764 Kb)

        Total Private:             1039241 (      4156964 Kb)
         0488 svchost.exe            82989 (       331956 Kb)
         28fc iexplore.exe           50641 (       202564 Kb)
         26ac iexplore.exe           45843 (       183372 Kb)
```

FIGURE 5.16

Sample output of the "!vm" kernel debugging command.

- *Physical memory*: This is the amount of usable physical memory (RAM) installed.
- *Available pages*: The total size and number of available pages in physical memory. The sum of the pages on the Zero, Free, and Standby page lists.
- *ResAvail pages*: Resident available memory is not a subset of available memory as I originally thought. It is memory that can be used for code or data that might become nonpageable. A lack of resident available memory when it is needed can result in application or system-wide hangs.

    According to "Pushing the Limits of Windows: Processes and Threads" at http://blogs.technet.com/b/markrussinovich/archive/2009/07/08/3261309.aspx by Mark Russinovich, resident available memory is the physical memory that can be assigned to data or code that must be kept in physical memory.

    According to Pavel Lebedynskiy and other members of the Windows product team, kernel stacks are a good illustration why resident available memory is necessary. Kernel stacks can be paged out, but only if the thread is in a "user-mode" wait. If it waits by specifying the "kernel-mode" wait option, then the stack is nonpageable. Now, imagine an app that creates a large number of threads that all enter user-mode waits. Because their kernel stacks can be paged out, the total size of the stacks could exceed the total physical memory (assuming there is enough system committed memory). But then, if the threads are awoken (by setting an event for example) and then blocked again, this time specifying a kernel-mode wait, there will not be enough physical pages to keep all stacks resident. So, to avoid running out of physical memory, the OS keeps track of how many nonpageable or potentially nonpageable pages have been allocated. MmResidentAvailablePages is how this is implemented. This variable is initialized to the amount of available pages at boot, and then, whenever we allocate memory that is nonpageable or can potentially become nonpageable (like a kernel stack), we subtract the size of that allocation from MmResidentAvailablePages. When the value approaches zero, we start failing allocations.

- *Locked IO pages*: This is the number of pages locked for IO using MmProbeAndLockPages and generally only used in checked/debug builds of Windows and Windows Server.
- *Free system PTEs*: This is the number of PTEs that are available to be used to map a virtual memory page to a physical memory page. This is also the amount of unused free space in the system's (kernel-mode) virtual address space if multiplied by the standard page size.
- *Modified pages*: The total size and number of modified pages in physical memory.
- *Modified PF pages*: This is the number of pages on the modified page list that are destined for a page file (as opposed to regular files). Use in correlation to the **\Paging File(*)\% Usage** performance counter.
- *Pool Nonpaged usage*: This is the amount of system (kernel-mode) virtual address space usage of nonpageable pool memory. The "Nx" represents "No execute" pages which prevent the data from being executed as a security precaution.
- *Pool Nonpaged maximum*: This is the maximum amount of system (kernel-mode) virtual address space usage of nonpageable pool memory. This is also limited by the amount of available physical memory.
- *Pool Paged usage*: This is the amount of system (kernel-mode) virtual address space usage of Pool Paged.
- *Pool Paged maximum*: This is the maximum amount of system (kernel-mode) virtual address space usage. This is also limited by the amount of system committed memory.
- *Session commit*: This is the portion of the system commit charge associated with session pool and drivers. "!vm 4" prints more details about this.
- *Shared commit*: This is the sum of all of the system committed backed shared memory. Shared memory can be created by any process. This memory counts toward the system commit charge, but is not owned or tracked back to that process. Therefore, this is one of the few ways to identify this kind of memory usage.

- *Special pool*: This is the amount of memory in use for a driver placed in a special pool. Special pool is used for isolating the memory usage of a driver generally for troubleshooting purposes.
- *Shared process*: This is MmProcessCommit. It's a mostly redundant counter that includes things like kernel stacks.
- *Pages for MDLs*: This is the number of pages allocated using MmAllocatePagesForMdl(Ex). MDLs are structures that describe a set of locked physical pages that may or may not be mapped somewhere in the virtual address space. They are most commonly used to describe IO buffers, in which case they are built using MmProbeAndLockPages and then destroyed when the IO completes. MmAllocatePagesForMdl on the other hand is a general purpose API for allocating physical pages. It uses MDLs to represent these pages to make it easier to interact with other APIs that handle MDLs.
- *Pool Paged commit*: The total number of pages and combined size of the portion of Pool Paged memory charged against the system commit charge. All of these pages cannot be assumed to be "touched"—meaning not all of the pages will be in physical memory.
- *Driver commit*: The total amount of driver-related memory in Pool Paged and Pool Nonpaged that is charged against the system commit charge.
- *Committed pages*: The number of pages and combined size of the system commit charge.
- *Commit limit*: The maximum number of pages and maximum combined size of the current system commit limit.
- *Total private*: This is the total of all of the private committed memory in use by processes. This is the equivalent of the performance counter **Process(_Total)**\ **Private Bytes**.

If you receive an error about a symbol load failure for LiveKD.exe [TBD—need to confirm the file name], then it can be safely ignored. The "NO PAGING FILE" message is just the current configuration of my laptop. My laptop has plenty of RAM (16 GB) and the solid-state drive has limited capacity, so I opted to not run a page file. See Chapter 7 "Page Files" for more information about page files.

THE PAGE FRAME NUMBER DATABASE, PHYSICAL MEMORY, AND VIRTUAL ADDRESS SPACE

If the size of the system (kernel-mode) virtual address space is relatively small such as the case with 32-bit versions of Windows and Windows Server, then adding too much physical memory can actually hinder the system. This is because all of the pages of the physical memory are managed by the Page Frame Number (PFN) database, which resides in kernel virtual address space. The more physical memory installed, the larger the PFN database has to be.

The PFN database contains lists that represent the physical memory pages of the system. The kernel uses these lists to track which pages are "in use" (allocated to a working set), free, available, and so on. This allows the operating system to know which pages of memory are the best to use or reuse. For example, if a page is needed for a process working set, then the kernel can get a page from its zero or free list.

It's important to note that the PFN database resides in kernel virtual address space and the more physical memory (RAM) that a system has, the larger the PFN database must be, which means less virtual address space for other resources. In non-PAE mode, 24 bytes in the PFN database represents each 4 KB page of physical memory—this is a ratio of 170:1. In PAE mode, 28 bytes represents each 4 KB page of physical memory—this is a ratio of 146:1. This means that roughly 6 MB or 7 MB is needed in the PFN database to describe each 1 GB of physical memory. This might not sound like much, but if you have a 32-bit system with 16 GB of physical memory, then it requires about 112 MB of the 2 GB of kernel virtual address space just to address the RAM. This is another reason why systems with 16 GB of physical memory or more will not allow the 3GB mode (also known as IncreaseUserVA), which increases the user virtual address space to 3 GB and decreases the kernel virtual address space to 1 GB on 32-bit systems.

NOTE

The x64 (64-bit) architecture has 8 TB of virtual address space (or 128 TB on Windows 8.1 and Windows Server 2012 R2), so this should be plenty of space to accommodate a large PFN database for systems with large amounts of physical memory.

The PFN database consists of many page lists. For the scope of this book, I will only mention the ones that are commonly used in troubleshooting:

- *Active list*: The page is "in use" by a working set, which could be a process working set, a session working set, or a system working set. This is the same as the "In use" field in the Performance tab of the Task Manager. In Performance Monitor, this would be the physical memory installed minus **Memory**\ **Available MBytes**.
- *Standby list*: The page is no longer "in use" or active and contains data that was once in a working set or read from disk by the prefetcher. The data in the page is backed by disk. This means that if the data on the disk is needed again, then they can be retrieved from physical memory avoiding the need to read from the disk. Ultimately, this means that the larger the standby list, the less often the disk must be accessed. This is why the more physical memory a system has, the less often the disk must be accessed. Also, since the page is already backed by the disk, it means that the page itself can be emptied and reused without incurring a disk IO. This is the same value as the Standby field on the Memory tab of the Resource Monitor. Most of the memory on this list will be a part of the performance counter **Memory****Standby Cache Normal Priority Bytes**.

- *Modified list*: The page was once in a working set but was removed, and the data it contains is not backed by the disk because it was created or modified in some way. This means that the page itself cannot be reused until the data it contains has been backed by disk. If the system needs to reuse a page on the modified list, then it must write the data to disk before it can be reused. For example, the data destined for a page file are queued here until written to a page file.
- *Free list*: The page is no longer "in use" and has been freed. This could have happened from a process specifically freeing the memory or indirectly freed when a process has exited. The page likely contains data that was private to the process; therefore, it must be "cleaned" by writing all zeroes (0) to the page before it can be reused.
- *Zero list*: The page is free and has all zeroes (0) in it. These pages are immediately available for use.

The sum of the Free list and the Zero list is commonly referred to as "Free" memory. The sum of the Free, Zero, and Standby page lists is commonly referred to as "Available" memory because all of the pages on those lists can be reused without incurring a disk IO to back it up.

For more information on this topic, see Chapter 8 "Physical Memory" in this book and consider Chapter 10 "Memory Management" in the Windows Internals, 6th edition, Part 2 book.

HOT-ADD MEMORY

According to "Hot-add memory support in Windows Server" at http://msdn.microsoft.com/en-us/windows/hardware/gg487553.aspx, on x86-based and x64-based platforms, some Windows Server editions support hot-add memory, which allows ranges of physical memory to be added to a running operating system without requiring a system reboot.

In other words, a RAM module can be added to a running system when it is still powered on. I certainly wouldn't want to be the person who does this due to the high potential of getting shocked, but hey, the hardware supports it.

The PFN database assumes that the full amount of RAM that the system supports could be added at any time. This means that the PFN database size is already fully expanded. On systems where kernel virtual address space is limited such as 32-bit systems, the excessive size of the PFN database can take up a significant amount of space that might be better used for other kernel resources such as Pool Paged.

To reduce the PFN database, consider disabling hot-add memory in the BIOS or create the DynamicMemory registry key and set it to one. The value is in gigabytes, and since the system likely has more than 1 GB of RAM installed, this becomes an invalid entry and the system reverts the size of the PFN database to the size of RAM currently installed.

The DynamicMemory registry key is a DWORD value that can be added at HKEY_LOCAL_MACHINE\SYSTEM\CurrentControlSet\Control\Session Manager \Memory Management in the registry. For more information on reducing the PFN database, see "Decreased performance, driver load failures, or system instability may occur on Hot-Add Memory systems that are running Windows Server 2003" at http://support.microsoft.com/kb/913568.

READ THIS IF CONSIDERING THE /3GB SWITCH OR IncreaseUserVa

32-bit versions of Windows and Windows Server are limited to a 4 GB virtual address space simply because 4 GB is the largest number that can be represented by 32 bits. By default, each process (application) is limited to own private 2 GB and the kernel (system-wide) has its own private 2 GB. This means that regardless the amount of physical memory (RAM) installed and page file sizes, no single process can exceed 2 GB unless the virtual address space architecture is changed.

The /3GB and /USERVA switches on 32-bit versions of Windows XP and Windows Server 2003 and earlier and the IncreaseUserVa (32-bit versions of Windows Vista and Windows Server 2008 and later) setting alter the 32-bit virtual address space so that the process address space (user-mode address space) is set to a size between 2 GB and 3 GB and the kernel address space gets the remainder of the 4 GB of total space. This means that the kernel virtual address space is reduced to a range between 1 GB and 2 GB.

TIP

Avoid using the /3GB switch or IncreaseUserVa setting on 32-bit versions of Windows and Windows Server on systems with more than 2 GB of physical memory. This is due to the reduction of the kernel address space and the size of the PFN database managing physical memory. It is best to go to a 64-bit version of Windows or Windows Server.

As mentioned earlier in this chapter, systems with a large amount of physical memory require a large PFN database, which uses kernel virtual address space. This means that when the kernel virtual address space is reduced, then there is a higher likelihood that the system will run out of Pool Paged, Pool Nonpaged, or free system PTEs. In general, I discourage using /3GB or IncreaseUserVa on systems with more than 2 GB of physical memory. It is best to run the 32-bit applications on a 64-bit version of Windows or Windows Server, so that they have the potential of using up to 4 GB of virtual address space since the 64-bit kernel is elsewhere in an 8 TB address space.

Recently, I had a customer running 32-bit Windows Server 2003 R2 with a single 32-bit web application. The application crashed often with a System.

OutOfMemoryException, which means that the application ran out of its personal 2 GB of virtual address space. The system had 12 GB of physical memory installed, so the customer wondered if they had to add more physical memory or increase page files, but I reminded them that this condition has nothing to do with the amount of physical memory and page files—it's a problem where the memory needs of the application have outgrown its architecture.

The only way to increase the address space is to change the architecture. This can be done by altering the 32-bit address space using the /3GB and /USERVA boot.ini switches (not recommended due to the large amount of physical memory installed), running the web application on a 64-bit version of Windows Server (it will have 4 GB of virtual address space), or recompiling the application as x64 (64 bits) and running on a 64-bit version of Windows Server (this will give it 8 TB of virtual address space).

CONCLUSION

In short, virtual address space was never intended to be a limiting factor; therefore, ensure that the system has plenty of virtual address space for the amount of load expected on it. If the 32-bit address space is too small, then consider using a 64-bit device or 64-bit computer to avoid these limits. If it is impractical to move to a 64-bit device or 64-bit computer, then use the advice given throughout this chapter to learn about other possible solutions.

TWITTER HANDLES OF KERNEL MEMORY ANALYSIS EXPERTS

If you have a question that this chapter did not address, then consider reading the blogs or contacting one of the following subject matter experts over Twitter.

Bhumit Shah

> Twitter @bhumitps (https://twitter.com/bhumitps)
> Email: bhumits@live.com

Clint Huffman

> Twitter @ClintH (https://twitter.com/clinth)

System committed memory

6

INTRODUCTION

Windows and Windows Server can run out of memory in various ways, each with their own symptoms. This chapter covers what you need to know about system committed memory, how to monitor this resource, and how to troubleshoot it.

NOTE

Physical memory (RAM) and page files are also discussed in this chapter since they are closely related to system committed memory.

If you have ever seen a pop-up message that says the system is low on "virtual" memory, then it means that the system is unable to back any further memory demands with physical memory and page files. When the system is in this condition, committed memory allocations are more likely to fail resulting in applications failing to start and services, applications, and drivers that are already running may begin to malfunction. Therefore, it is very important to track system committed memory usage.

The system commit limit is the sum of physical memory and the size of all of the page files combined on the system. It is a factitious resource that prevents the system from overcommitting or "overpromising" physical memory and page files. Therefore, it represents the maximum amount of physical resources that the system can use to back committed memory requests from applications, services, drivers, and various other parts of the operating system. Even though it is a fake resource, it serves as an accounting system for the operating system that when exhausted is unable to function (Figure 6.1).

The system commit charge is the total amount of memory used/committed by the operating system and all processes running on the computer. This memory is considered "in use," but does not mean that the memory has been written to or "touched." This means that it is possible that the system commit charge can reach the system commit limit but still have plenty of available physical memory and plenty of free space on the paging files.

Figure 6.2 shows all of the areas of memory that the system can run out of. This chapter of the book focuses on system committed memory.

FIGURE 6.1

A Windows 7 dialog box indicating it is out of system committed memory.

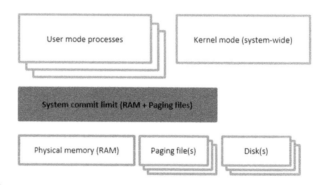

FIGURE 6.2

The areas of memory that the operating system can run out of. System committed memory is highlighted.

THE SYSTEM COMMIT LIMIT

As mentioned earlier, the system commit limit is a factitious resource that is the sum of physical memory and all paging files on the system. It prevents the system from overcommitted or "overpromising" physical memory and the page files. Therefore, when the system is out of system committed memory, it cannot back any more committed memory requests until the system commit limit has increased or until some of the committed memory has been released back to the system. Running out can result in application and/or system hangs. Therefore, it is important to keep the system commit limit higher than the system commit charge.

WARNING

The system and applications will likely hang when the system commit limit is reached.

If you have seen one of the messages shown in Figure 6.3, Figure 6.4, Figure 6.5, or Figure 6.6, then this indicates that the system commit charge has reached the system commit limit and the commit limit is unable to increase.

Check the System Event Logs for Event ID: 2004 on Windows 7 and Windows Server 2008 systems (Figure 6.5).

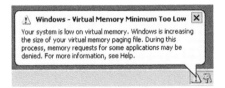

FIGURE 6.3

Virtual Memory Minimum Too Low balloon on Windows Server 2003.

FIGURE 6.4

Close programs to prevent information loss dialog box on Windows 8.

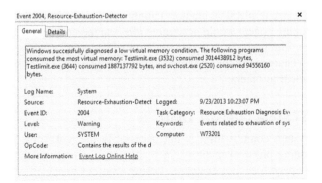

FIGURE 6.5

Event 2004 indicating the system is low on system committed memory.

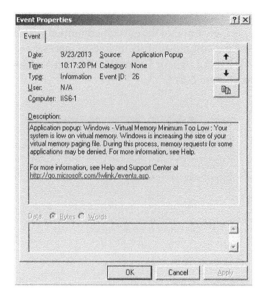

FIGURE 6.6

Event ID 26 indicating a low system committed memory condition.

HOW MUCH IS ENOUGH AND HOW MUCH IS TOO MUCH?

Much of this discussion directly relates to page file sizing. There are three considerations to page file sizing (discussed in more detail in Chapter 7 "Page Files") and making the system commit limit large enough to accommodate the peak, or expected system commit charge is one of those considerations. This is because the size of all of the page files combined plus physical memory is the system commit limit—meaning the larger the page file, the larger the commit limit.

Having a massive amount of physical memory such as 128 GB and an even larger page file such as 160 GB is certainly fine, but if the system commit charge is never larger than 4 GB, then it's a waste of physical memory and disk space for the page file. Likewise, running without a page file (a system commit limit that is slightly smaller than the size of physical memory) might seem lucrative from a performance perspective, but the system would need more physical memory than the peak system commit charge. The problem is that there is no way to predict the peak size of the system commit charge until the system is actually being used. This is true even if the system is identical to others.

THE TRUE SYSTEM COMMIT LIMIT

The current system commit limit is not necessarily the real limit. The limit can increase by adding physical memory, increasing one or more of the paging files, or adding more page files. For example, if using a system-managed paging file (discussed next), then the page file will automatically attempt to grow when the system commit charge nears the system commit limit. The real system commit limit depends on the following:

- *The potential addition of physical memory.* Windows Server supports "hot-add" dynamic memory allowing highly available systems to have physical memory (RAM) added while it is powered on. Microsoft Hyper-V uses this feature (also called "dynamic memory") to add physical memory to virtual machines.
- *The maximum size of page file(s).* Paging files can be set with a minimum value and a maximum value. This means that it can change its size as needed within the confines of these parameters. Also, a system-managed paging file can increase up to three times physical memory or 4 GB whichever is larger.
- *The free space of the disk hosting a page file.* Even if a paging file is set to a large size, it can only grow so long as there is enough free space on the disk. This is likely one of the reasons why page files are often set to the same minimum setting and maximum setting that automatically set the page file to claim the free space. Just make sure that the maximum setting is large enough to accommodate the system commit charge peak.

SYSTEM-MANAGED BY DEFAULT

By default, the page file is system-managed. This means that the page file will grow and shrink based on many factors, one of which is accommodating the system commit charge. When the system commit charge is roughly over 90% of the system commit limit, then the page file will be increased to accommodate it. This will continue to happen until the page file has reached three times the size of physical memory or 4 GB whichever is larger. This all assumes that the system partition on disk is large enough to accommodate a page file of that size.

TIP

Monitor the system commit charge over time to determine its peak usage. This helps with proper physical memory and page file sizing.

MONITORING SYSTEM COMMITTED MEMORY WITH TASK MANAGER

Task Manager is built-in to the operating system and it provides quick access to the values of the system commit charge and the system commit limit. Just press Ctrl+Shift+Esc and Task Manager is there (Figure 6.7).

The current values of the system commit charge and the system commit limit (9.2 GB and 15.8 GB, respectively, in the case of Figure 6.8) can be quickly accessed through the Performance tab of Task Manager. Figures 6.7 and 6.8 show these values in Task Manager in Windows 7 and Task Manager in Windows 8, respectively.

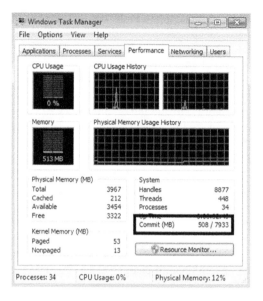

FIGURE 6.7

System committed memory in Windows 7 Task Manager.

FIGURE 6.8

The Performance tab of the Windows 8 Task Manager.

NOTE

Task Manager in Windows 7 is identical to Task Manager in Windows Server 2008 R2. Task Manager in Windows 8 is identical to Task Manager in Windows Server 2012.

Finally, the system commit charge/usage field name in Task Manager has changed over the years. Here is the list of fields that actually refer to the system commit charge/usage:

- Windows XP and Windows Server 2003 are labeled "PF Usage."
- Windows Vista and Windows Server 2008 are labeled "Page File."
- Windows 7 and Windows Server 2008 R2 are labeled "Commit."
- Windows 8 and Windows Server 2012 are labeled "Committed."

MONITORING SYSTEM COMMITTED MEMORY WITH PERFORMANCE MONITOR

If you are analyzing a performance counter log, monitoring a remote Windows or Windows Server computer, or collecting system committed data throughout an enterprise environment, then using performance counters is probably the most convenient way to check the system committed memory.

Performance Monitor has three counters related to system committed memory, **\Memory\Commit Limit**, **\Memory\Committed Bytes**, and **\Memory\% Committed Bytes In Use**. Figure 6.9 shows these counters in report view.

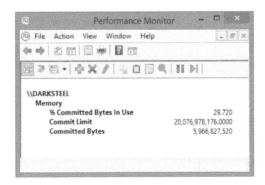

FIGURE 6.9

Performance Monitor with system committed memory counters loaded.

Counter	Warning	Critical
\Memory\% Committed Bytes In Use	> 75	< 90

FIGURE 6.10

Threshold for the \Memory\% Committed Bytes In Use performance counter.

The initial indicator to warrant more investigation into system committed memory is to look for a value of greater than 75 for the counter **\Memory\% Committed Bytes In Use** counter (Figure 6.10). When it breaks this threshold, go to "Where did all of the system committed memory go?" section later in this chapter.

\MEMORY\% COMMITTED BYTES IN USE

This counter is the ratio of **\Memory\Committed Bytes** to **\Memory\Commit Limit**. Committed Bytes is the amount of committed virtual memory that the operating system is backing with physical memory and paging files. Commit Limit is the amount of committed virtual memory that the operating system can back with physical memory and paging files. Committed Bytes cannot exceed Commit Limit. This counter displays the current percentage value only; it is not an average.

\MEMORY\COMMIT LIMIT

This counter measures the system commit limit in bytes. The system commit limit is equal to the size of physical memory and the size of all paging files combined. If physical memory or paging file(s) are increased, then this limit increases accordingly. This counter displays the last observed value only; it is not an average.

\MEMORY\COMMITTED BYTES

This counter measures the system commit charge in bytes. The system commit charge is the amount of committed virtual memory that the operating system is backing with physical memory and paging files. It cannot exceed the system commit limit (**\Memory\Commit Limit**). This counter displays the last observed value only; it is not an average.

MONITORING SYSTEM COMMITTED MEMORY WITH SYSINTERNALS PROCESS EXPLORER

Sysinternals Process Explorer (Procexp) is a free tool that provides detailed information about actively running processes and provides helpful data on system memory that other tools don't. Like most Sysinternals tools, Procexp does not require

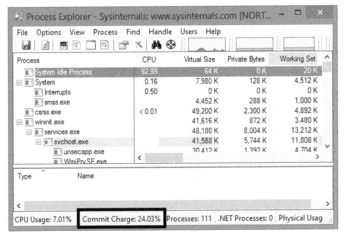

FIGURE 6.11

The main window of Process Explorer with the system commit charge percentage highlighted.

installation. It can be copied and ran on just about any computer running Windows or Windows Server except devices running with the ARM architecture such as the Microsoft Surface devices.

The system commit charge and system commit limit can be measured in two places in Process Explorer—in the main application window and in the System Information window. On the main window, the ratio of the system commit charge is compared to the system commit limit and shown as a percentage on the status bar. See Figure 6.11 for the exact location.

For more details, click View, System Information, or Ctrl+I and select the Memory tab. The details of system committed memory are on the left (Figure 6.11).

The following is the description of this section of Procexp according to the "Windows® Sysinternals Administrator's Reference (p. 94)."

Commit Charge (K): The current commit charge, the limit at which no more private bytes can be allocated without increasing pagefile size, and the peak commit charge incurred on the system since its last boot. This group also shows the percentage of peak commit vs. the limit and the current charge vs. the limit.

The following descriptions are current as of Process Explorer v15.40 (Figure 6.12).

CURRENT

This is the current system commit charge. The system commit charge is the amount of committed virtual memory that the operating system is backing with physical memory and paging files. It cannot exceed the system commit limit.

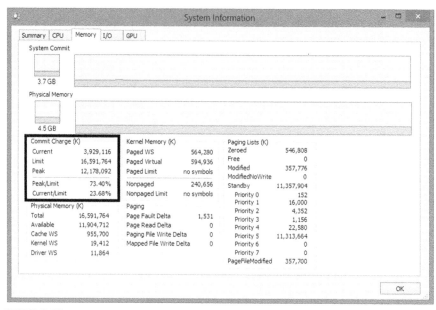

FIGURE 6.12

The System Information window of Process Explorer with system committed memory highlighted.

LIMIT

This is the system commit limit. The system commit limit is the amount of committed virtual memory that the operating system can back with physical memory and paging files. It is equal to the size of physical memory and the size of all paging files combined. If physical memory or paging file(s) is increased, then this limit increases accordingly.

PEAK

This is the peak size of the system commit charge since the last reboot.

Process Explorer is likely the only tool left that still shows the peak usage of the system commit charge—Task Manager of Windows XP used to show it. Even though the system commit charge peak does not directly indicate actual physical memory usage, the peak usage of the system commit charge is helpful for balancing the size of physical memory and page files that make up the system commit limit. For example, if the system commit charge peak is always smaller than the amount of physical memory installed, then it would mean that a page file would not be required to back the committed memory.

TIP

The system commit charge peak can be used as a good starting point for sizing physical memory and the system commit limit.

PEAK/LIMIT

This is the peak of the ratio of the system commit charge to the system commit limit since the last reboot. The system commit limit can increase if the system commit charge is near the system commit limit. The limit can be increased if the size of physical memory is increased, if the size of an existing page file is increased, or if a page file is added. By default, a system-managed paging file can increase up to three times the size of physical memory or 4 GB whichever is larger.

CURRENT/LIMIT

This is the ratio of the current value of the system commit charge compared to the current value of the system commit limit.

MONITORING SYSTEM COMMITTED MEMORY WITH WINDOWS MANAGEMENT INSTRUMENTATION

Windows Management Instrumentation (WMI) is a core service of Windows and Windows Server that provides a repository to query the computer's hardware, operating system, applications, and so on. When needing to monitor hundreds or thousands of computer systems, WMI is arguably the easiest way to collect the data.

WMI can be queried by just about any language and most services such as Microsoft System Center Operations Manager use it extensively for data gathering. In this case, I will use a Powershell command to get system committed memory data from a remote computer called "darksteel."

```
PS  C:\>  Get-WmiObject  -Query  "SELECT  TotalVirtualMemorySize,
FreeVirtualMemory FROM Win32_OperatingSystem" -ComputerName
    darksteel | Select TotalVirtualMemorySize, FreeVirtualMemory
```

IMPORTANT

To query a remote computer via WMI, DCOM connectivity and administrator rights are required by default.

FREEVIRTUALMEMORY

This is a property of the Win32_OperatingSystem class and is the amount, in kilobytes, of system committed memory that is currently unused and available.

TOTALVIRTUALMEMORY

This is a property of the Win32_OperatingSystem class and is the system commit limit, in kilobytes.

WMI does not provide a system commit charge property, but it can be calculated by taking TotalVirtualMemory minus FreeVirtualMemory. The following example shows how to use PowerShell to do the calculation for you. The end result is the current system commit charge in gigabytes.

```
gwmi win32_operatingsystem | Select @{L='System Commit Charge in GB';E=
{($_.totalvirtualmemorysize-$_.freevirtualmemory)*1KB/1GB}}
```

This code was provided by Ed Wilson "The Scripting Guy."

DID YOU KNOW?

System committed memory is often referred to as "virtual memory." Unfortunately, "virtual memory" is also used to describe virtual address space and page files that have no association with each other.

In summary, the Win32_OperatingSystem.TotalVirtualMemorySize is the system commit limit and the system commit charge can be calculated by taking Win32_OperatingSystem.FreeVirtualMemory minus Win32_OperatingSystem.TotalVirtualMemorySize.

WHERE DID ALL OF THE SYSTEM COMMITTED MEMORY GO?

As mentioned earlier, if the system commit charge has reached the system commit limit, then the system and applications will likely hang. This is a situation that is best to avoid. In any case, let's assume that the system commit charge is approaching the real system commit limit and the system is still functional for now. The real system commit limit is discussed earlier in this chapter. This part of the book identifies the most common consumers of system committed memory.

When the system grants system committed memory, the system checks if the system commit charge can increase by the amount requested and still fit within the system commit limit. If the request is granted, the system has "promised" to back the request with physical resources—namely, physical memory and disk. Memory backed in this way cannot be reclaimed by the system unless the owner of the memory willingly frees the memory or if the owning process is ended such as when Microsoft Internet Information Services (IIS) recycles a worker process.

THE USUAL SUSPECTS

The following is a list of the usual suspects that can consume system committed memory. Each is addressed in detail following this list.

1. Process private memory including Address Windowing Extensions (AWE) memory usage
2. Kernel pool memory
3. Driver locked memory
4. System committed backed shared memory

For a full list of system committed memory usage, use a noninvasive kernel debugger such as LiveKD with the "!vm" command. Figure 6.13 shows the output

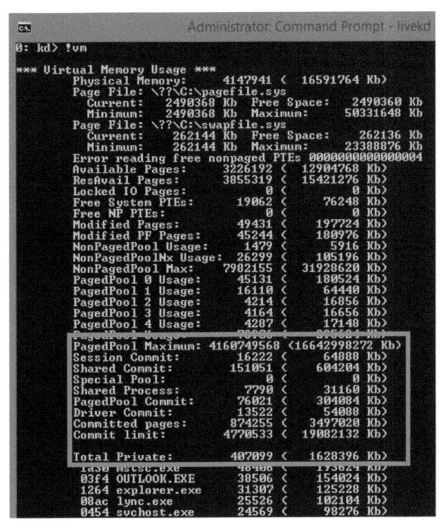

```
0: kd> !vm

*** Virtual Memory Usage ***
        Physical Memory:      4147941 (  16591764 Kb)
        Page File: \??\C:\pagefile.sys
          Current:   2490368 Kb  Free Space:     2490360 Kb
          Minimum:   2490368 Kb  Maximum:       50331648 Kb
        Page File: \??\C:\swapfile.sys
          Current:    262144 Kb  Free Space:      262136 Kb
          Minimum:    262144 Kb  Maximum:       23388876 Kb
        Error reading free nonpaged PTEs 0000000000000004
        Available Pages:      3226192 (  12904768 Kb)
        ResAvail Pages:       3855319 (  15421276 Kb)
        Locked IO Pages:            0 (         0 Kb)
        Free System PTEs:       19062 (     76248 Kb)
        Free NP PTEs:               0 (         0 Kb)
        Modified Pages:         49431 (    197724 Kb)
        Modified PF Pages:      45244 (    180976 Kb)
        NonPagedPool Usage:      1479 (      5916 Kb)
        NonPagedPoolNx Usage:   26299 (    105196 Kb)
        NonPagedPool Max:     7982155 (  31928620 Kb)
        PagedPool 0 Usage:      45131 (    180524 Kb)
        PagedPool 1 Usage:      16110 (     64440 Kb)
        PagedPool 2 Usage:       4214 (     16856 Kb)
        PagedPool 3 Usage:       4164 (     16656 Kb)
        PagedPool 4 Usage:       4287 (     17148 Kb)
        PagedPool Maximum: 4160749568 (16642998272 Kb)
        Session Commit:         16222 (     64888 Kb)
        Shared Commit:         151051 (    604204 Kb)
        Special Pool:               0 (         0 Kb)
        Shared Process:          7790 (     31160 Kb)
        PagedPool Commit:       76021 (    304084 Kb)
        Driver Commit:          13522 (     54088 Kb)
        Committed pages:       874255 (   3497020 Kb)
        Commit limit:         4770533 (  19082132 Kb)

        Total Private:         407099 (   1628396 Kb)
        1a30 mstsc.exe          48406 (    173624 Kb)
        03f4 OUTLOOK.EXE        38506 (    154024 Kb)
        1264 explorer.exe       31307 (    125228 Kb)
        08ac lync.exe           25526 (    102104 Kb)
        0454 svchost.exe        24569 (     98276 Kb)
```

FIGURE 6.13

Output of "!vm" in a kernel debugger.

of "!vm" using the kernel debugger Sysinternals LiveKD with the system committed memory-related fields highlighted including process private memory indicated by "Total Private."

PROCESS PRIVATE MEMORY

The most common consumer of system committed memory is processes. Processes need committed memory to operate and it is normal for the process of a busy application to consume a significant portion of system committed memory. Nonetheless, it is important to track which processes are consuming the most.

Process private memory can be tracked through many tools such as Task Manager, Resource Monitor, and Sysinternals Process Explorer. The performance counter for this is **\Process(*)\Private Bytes** and the closest WMI property is Win32_Process.PageFileUsage. Look for processes that are using a significant amount of private committed memory. The field for process private bytes has changed in Task Manager over the years. See Chapter 4 for more information about how to identify and troubleshoot memory leaks.

TIP

The terms "page file usage" and "page file backed" are often referring to system committed memory. Keep in mind that all versions of Windows and Windows Server that have implemented virtual memory can potentially run without a page file. In those cases, "page file backed" is actually backed by just physical memory.

It's important to note here that processes have private committed memory and shareable committed memory. Only the private committed memory of the process counts towards the system commit charge. An example of shareable committed memory is what is referred to as "image" files that are the portions of EXE and DLL files used to run the process. These files are "disk-backed" and therefore do not need to be backed by system committed memory.

TIP

Shareable process committed memory as seen in Sysinternals VMMap does not count toward the system commit charge.

AWE MEMORY USAGE

Processes have the option of using AWE to access memory even beyond its own virtual address space. For example, 32-bit versions of Microsoft SQL Server implemented AWE to access memory beyond its 2 GB virtual address space. This is similar to expanded or extended memory technique back in the MS-DOS days allowing it to "break out" of the memory confines. With that said, AWE is very specific in how it can be used and the application must be specifically written to use AWE memory.

To this day, the only application that I have seen that has implemented AWE is SQL Server, but it is certainly not limited to it.

The usage of AWE memory can be elusive since AWE memory usage has not been exposed as part of the process private committed memory until Windows 8 and Windows Server 2012. For example, on Windows Server 2008 R2, you might see a high system commit charge, but yet find no process consuming that much private committed memory. Thankfully, as of Windows 8 and Windows Server 2012 and later, the AWE memory usage of a process is included in the process private bytes seen in performance counters, Task Manager, Resource Monitor, and so on (Figure 6.14).

In the meantime, if you are on an earlier version of Windows or Windows Server, then the Sysinternals RAMMap tool can show AWE memory usage. If AWE memory usage is detected with RAMMap, then use Sysinternals VMMap to attach to a suspected process such as Microsoft SQL Server and the AWE memory should be exposed as "WS Shared" or "WS Shareable."

AWE memory is still often used in 64-bit versions of Microsoft SQL Server to do physical memory page locking. This makes it to where SQL Server manages the physical memory directly instead of the operating system. This is certainly a heated topic that should be tested before drawing a conclusion. In any case, as of Microsoft SQL Server 2008 R2, the configuration option, AWE enabled, is deprecated and users of 32-bit versions of SQL Server are encouraged to migrate to 64-bit versions

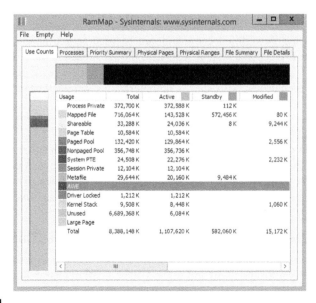

FIGURE 6.14

Sysinternals RAMMap with AWE memory highlighted.

of SQL Server. See the KB article, "The 'awe enabled' SQL Server feature is deprecated," at http://support.microsoft.com/kb/2644592 for more information on this topic.

KERNEL POOL MEMORY

The kernel has two memory pools that drivers use for normal operations. They are Pool Paged and Pool Nonpaged. As their namesake says, Pool Paged is for pagable memory and Pool Nonpaged is for nonpagable memory. In any case, both memory pools count toward the system commit charge and should be investigated if they are consuming a significant amount.

TIP

Window Sysinternals LiveKD can be used without enabling kernel debugging on a system. Go to http://technet.microsoft.com/sysinternals/bb897415.aspx for more information on LiveKD.

DRIVER LOCKED MEMORY

Drivers can lock memory outside of the kernel memory pools and that memory will be charged to the system commit charge. Driver locked memory can be shown using the Sysinternals tool, RAMMap (http://live.sysinternals.com/rammap.exe), or by using the kernel debugger command "!vm." Unfortunately, drive locked memory doesn't have an owner to track which driver created it, so look for the most likely "suspects" such as virtualization drivers, antivirus or anti-malware drivers, video card, and disk drivers.

The following PowerShell command can be used to get detailed information about all of the drivers on a system. This uses the WMI class Win32_SystemDriver. The "Select *" is needed to get all of the possible fields. Otherwise, it only returns a few fields for each driver. Also, the "-ComputerName" parameter can be used to get this data from a remote computer.

```
gwmi Win32_SystemDriver -ComputerName darksteel | Select *
```

A common consumer of driver locked memory is virtualization software. For example, in Figure 6.15, the Microsoft Hyper-V driver locked over 8 GB of physical memory on the host system to accommodate virtual machines. Also, VMware's memory "ballooning" within a virtual machine will show up as driver locked.

SYSTEM COMMITTED BACKED SHARED MEMORY SECTIONS

A process can create a shared memory section to share memory with another process and this memory allocation will add to the system commit charge immediately. As the process(es) uses the shared memory, it is mapped into their respective virtual address spaces that allow a system administrator to identify it through the virtual byte usage of a process. If the shared memory is allocated, but not used, then the only

FIGURE 6.15

Sysinternals RAMMap showing driver locked memory usage.

known technique to identify it is a kernel debug. This is because system committed backed shared memory sections have no owner to look up and this means that the Sysinternals tools VMMap, RAMMap, and Process Explorer cannot detect this kind of memory usage or show any further details to indicate its existence. With that said, shared committed memory can be detected using the command "!vm 1" in a kernel debugger as shown in Figure 6.16.

For more information about system committed backed shared memory sections, see Chapter 10, Memory Management of the Windows Internals, Sixth Edition, Part 2, http://technet.microsoft.com/sysinternals/bb963901.aspx.

DID YOU KNOW?

System cache resident memory uses physical memory and counted as "in use," but it doesn't count towards the system commit charge.

SYSTEM CACHE RESIDENT MEMORY

System cache consumes physical memory and yet is not counted towards the system commit charge. The reason that I am addressing it now is because for many years, I assumed that the physical memory side of system cache (**Memory\System Cache Resident Bytes** is the performance counter) also counted towards the system commit charge. I assumed wrong.

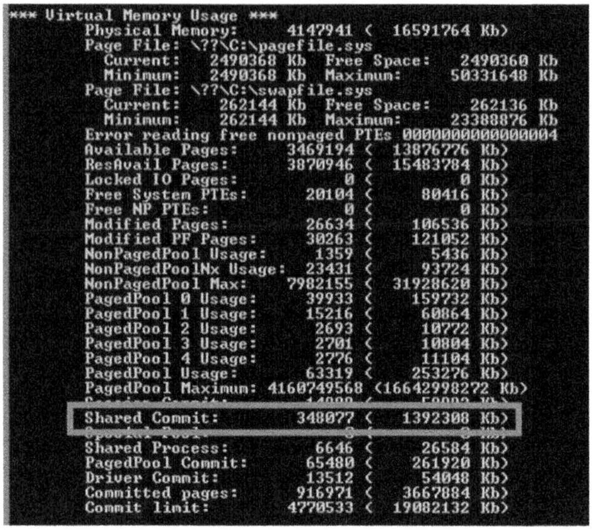

```
*** Virtual Memory Usage ***
    Physical Memory:      4147941 <  16591764 Kb>
    Page File: \??\C:\pagefile.sys
      Current:     2490368 Kb  Free Space:    2490360 Kb
      Minimum:     2490368 Kb  Maximum:      50331648 Kb
    Page File: \??\C:\swapfile.sys
      Current:      262144 Kb  Free Space:     262136 Kb
      Minimum:      262144 Kb  Maximum:      23388876 Kb
    Error reading free nonpaged PTEs 0000000000000004
    Available Pages:      3469194 <  13876776 Kb>
    ResAvail Pages:       3870946 <  15483784 Kb>
    Locked IO Pages:            0 <         0 Kb>
    Free System PTEs:       20104 <     80416 Kb>
    Free NP PTEs:               0 <         0 Kb>
    Modified Pages:         26634 <    106536 Kb>
    Modified PF Pages:      30263 <    121052 Kb>
    NonPagedPool Usage:      1359 <      5436 Kb>
    NonPagedPoolNx Usage:   23431 <     93724 Kb>
    NonPagedPool Max:     7982155 <  31928620 Kb>
    PagedPool 0 Usage:      39933 <    159732 Kb>
    PagedPool 1 Usage:      15216 <     60864 Kb>
    PagedPool 2 Usage:       2693 <     10772 Kb>
    PagedPool 3 Usage:       2701 <     10804 Kb>
    PagedPool 4 Usage:       2776 <     11104 Kb>
    PagedPool Usage:        63319 <    253276 Kb>
    PagedPool Maximum: 4160749568 <16642998272 Kb>
    Shared Commit:         348077 <   1392308 Kb>
    Shared Process:          6646 <     26584 Kb>
    PagedPool Commit:       65480 <    261920 Kb>
    Driver Commit:          13512 <     54048 Kb>
    Committed pages:       916971 <   3667884 Kb>
    Commit limit:         4770533 <  19082132 Kb>
```

FIGURE 6.16

Output of "!vm" in a kernel debugger highlighting shared committed memory.

If the system is low on available physical memory, then the system cache resident bytes is purged to disk as needed. It is effectively just using physical memory as "in use" memory while that physical memory is not actually being used by the system commit charge. This would be similar to system cache resident bytes living at a home that it doesn't own and then vacating the home when told to do so.

NOTE

Do not confuse system cache and standby cache. These are two very different kinds of cache memory. The difference is covered in "system cache" in Chapter 8 Physical Memory.

TREATING THE SYMPTOMS OF HIGH SYSTEM COMMITTED MEMORY

It is preferred to troubleshoot the highest consumers of system committed memory as discussed earlier in this chapter, but Windows performance analysis is like going through traffic. You can get where you want to go with enough time and effort. With that said, sometimes it might just be easier to treat the symptoms of high system committed memory usage.

Since the system commit limit is based on the size of physical memory and all paging files combined, increasing physical memory, increasing one or more paging files, or adding new paging files will increase the system commit limit allowing the system commit charge to grow larger. But, this just makes the limit larger. If the system has processes or drivers that leak memory, then the limit will eventually be reached unless the "leakers" are identified, stopped, and restarted before the limit is reached. Also, keep in mind that a system-managed paging file will automatically increase up to three times the size of physical memory or 4 GB whichever is larger so long as there is enough free disk space for it to expand.

If system committed memory regularly approaches the system commit limit and troubleshooting (discussed earlier in this chapter) has been followed as much as practically possible, then consider the following:

- *End or restart processes.* Processes that consume a significant part of the system committed memory can be identified in by the private memory usage of the process. Private committed memory of a process is the only part of the process memory that contributes toward the system commit charge. This can be identified in many ways such as Task Manager, Resource Monitor, Performance Monitor (the **\Process(*)\Private Bytes** counter), and Sysinternals Process Explorer. See the "monitoring system committed memory" sections discussed earlier in this chapter.

    Restarting processes that consume a significant amount of system committed memory is in many cases the easiest and most practical way of dealing with this condition. This is why Microsoft IIS has worker process recycling built into its infrastructure.

WARNING

Forcibly ending or restarting processes will force the process to lose the data resident in its virtual address space. Discuss this option with the developer or vendor of the application before considering this option.

- *Update or remove drivers.* If Pool Paged or Pool Nonpaged memory has significant memory usage, then consider updating or removing drivers. These can be measured using the performance counters **\Memory\Pool Paged Bytes** and **\Memory\Pool Nonpaged Bytes,** respectively, through Task Manager and various other tools.

    Keep in mind that viewing the usage of Pool Paged does not directly indicate system committed memory usage because counters and values mentioned above are measuring the reserved and committed memory usage. For the true amount of system committed memory that Pool Paged is using, use a kernel debugger with the "!vm" command and look at the PagedPoolCommitted field.

    In the case of Pool Nonpaged memory, it always uses physical memory and all of it counts towards the system commit charge.

    As a reminder, driver locked memory is separate from the kernel memory pools and can be identified using Sysinternals RAMMap. For example, a virtual machine might be running that is using up physical memory and system committed memory.

For more information about identifying and troubleshooting kernel memory pools, see Chapter 5.

- *Add more physical memory (RAM)*. Consider adding physical memory modules compatible with the system hardware. Note: Some virtualization hosting software such as Microsoft Hyper-V support "dynamic memory" that uses the "hot-add" RAM feature of Windows Server to add physical memory to a machine while it is still running. If the "hot-add" RAM feature is used, then it will immediately increase the system commit limit without a reboot. Otherwise, a reboot will be required.

- *Increase existing page file(s)*. Page files can be increased at any time immediately increasing the system commit limit, but page files cannot be decreased until after a reboot. Page files are covered in more detail later in this chapter.

- *Add new page files*. New page files can be added to Windows or Windows Server at any time, so long as there is enough free disk space to accommodate it. This will immediately increase the system commit limit without a reboot.

A CASE STUDY OF SYSTEM COMMITTED MEMORY

The following is an example of a system that ran out of system committed memory, how it was identified, and the recommendations provided to the customer. This is an analysis of a performance counter log file using Performance Monitor and the Performance Analysis of Logs tool (PAL). Performance Monitor is built into the operating system. The PAL tool is a free, open-source project that I created and maintain to make performance analysis easier.

This was a Microsoft Exchange Server 2007 running on 64-bit Microsoft Windows Server 2003. It has 16 GB of physical memory (RAM), eight logical processors, and experienced application and system-wide hangs due to the system commit charge reaching the system commit limit.

The **Memory\% Committed Bytes In Use** counter is the ratio of **Memory \Committed Bytes** to **Memory\Commit Limit**. Figure 6.17 (a chart created by the PAL tool) shows that this counter reached a value near 100, which means that the system commit charge (**Memory\Committed Bytes**) reached the system commit limit (**Memory\Commit Limit**). As mentioned earlier, this condition leads to frequent virtual memory allocation failures that lead to processes (applications and services) to hang, fail, or crash. So based on this counter alone, it is clear that the system is out of committed memory.

Using Performance Monitor with the counters **Memory\Committed Bytes** (green line) and **Memory\Commit Limit** (red line) (Figure 6.18), we can see that Committed Bytes reaches the Commit Limit and the Commit Limit doesn't change. When in this condition, the system commit limit should automatically increase if configured and able to do so. In this case, the physical memory on the system is 16 GB and the system commit limit (Commit Limit) is 32 GB, so we can assume that there is 16 GB worth of one or more page files.

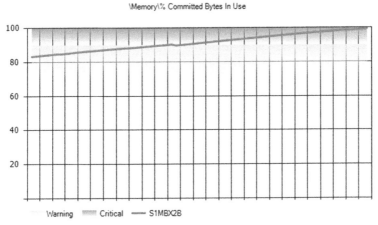

FIGURE 6.17

The % Committed Bytes In Use counter reaching near 100.

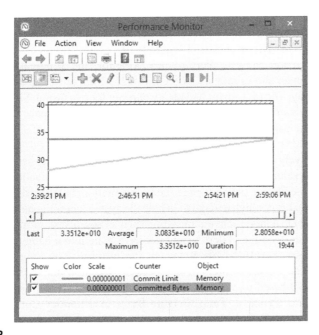

FIGURE 6.18

Performance Monitor showing Committed Bytes and Commit Limit.

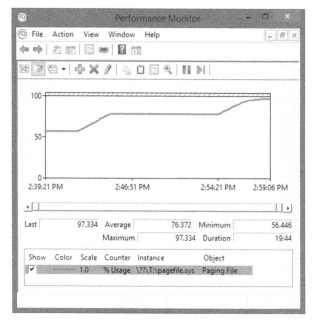

FIGURE 6.19

Performance Monitor showing Paging File % Usage.

As we expected, there is a page file, but in this case, it is on T: drive versus the default of C: drive. This is shown in Figure 6.19.

Using the report view of Performance Monitor, the **\LogicalDisk(T:)\Free Megabytes** counter shows roughly 17.8 GB (18,253 MB) of free space, which indicates that the page file on T: drive had plenty of room for expansion. Since the system commit limit was reached and there was plenty of free disk space on the logical disk hosting the page file, we can assume that the true maximum size of the page file was reached (Figure 6.20).

It is a relatively common practice for system administrators to set the minimum and maximum values of a page file to the same number. This preallocates the disk space to the page file and prevents page file fragmentation, but the risk here is a maximum setting that is not high enough to handle the system commit charge peak. If the page file was set to a larger maximum setting such as how a system-managed paging file grows larger, then the system would not have gone into a hang condition.

The **\Process(_Total)\Private Bytes** counter instance shows me the combined amount of private process memory of all processes. We know that the system commit limit is at 32 GB based on the value provided by **\Memory\Commit Limit**, so we want to compare **\Process(_Total)\Private Bytes** to **\Memory\Commit Limit** to see if there is a significant amount of usage (Figure 6.21).

In this case, I used a PowerShell session to convert the maximum value of **\Process(_Total)\Private Bytes** from a scientific notation value ($3.0743e+010$) to the amount in gigabytes, which in this case is 28.6 GB. This is a significant amount

LogicalDisk	**T:**
Free Megabytes	18,253.000

FIGURE 6.20

Performance Monitor in report view showing Free Megabytes of T: drive.

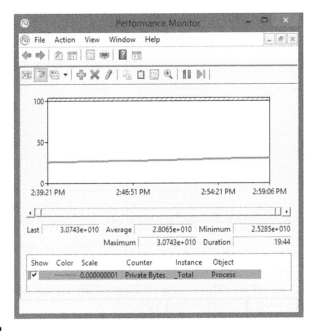

FIGURE 6.21

Performance Monitor showing the _Total instance of Process Private Bytes.

FIGURE 6.22

PowerShell makes converting scientific notation easy.

compared to the 32 GB system commit limit. At this point, I know that one or more processes are using a large amount of system committed memory (Figure 6.22).

I started a new instance of Performance Monitor with the same log file and added all of the **\Process(*)\Private Bytes** instances except for _Total. Next, I increased the chart size until I could visually see which processes are consuming the most private bytes. In this case, store.exe (the main Exchange Server process) is consuming

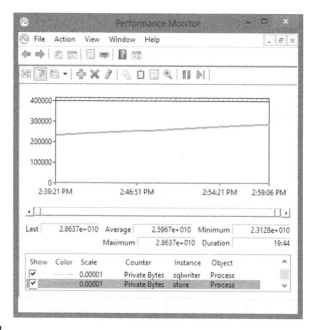

FIGURE 6.23

Performance Monitor showing the private bytes of store.exe.

the most. Again, using PowerShell to convert the scientific notation of the maximum value, it is using about 26.7 GB (Figure 6.23).

TIP

There are nine digits in a gigabyte, so scientific notation of $2.8637e + 10$ is a "ball park" figure of 28 GB, but remember that each digit grouping must be divided by 1024. In this case, the actual value is 26.7 GB. Powershell understands scientific notation and can make this easy.

```
PS C:\> 2.8637e+10 / 1GB
26.6702845692635
```

Finally, at this point, we know that Microsoft Exchange Server needs at least 26.6 GB of system committed memory. The next troubleshooting step is to identify why this process needs this much committed memory. This can be done in several ways such as using Exchange Server-related performance counters and tools or using the Sysinternals VMMap tool to attach to store.exe and refreshing VMMap periodically to see what is different about the memory usage. In any case, there are plenty of ways of analyzing committed memory usage of a process and these tools and techniques are covered in Chapter 4 "Process Memory". Though in regard to treating the symptoms of this condition, most Exchange Server experts simply said to add more physical memory (RAM).

CONCLUSION

This chapter covered the concepts of system committed memory, how to monitor system committed memory usage, and how to troubleshoot it.

Page files

7

INTRODUCTION

A page file (also known as a paging file) is an optional, hidden, system file on disk that can be used for backing system crash dumps and to extend the amount of system committed memory (also known as "virtual memory") that a system can back. It also allows the system to remove infrequently access modified pages from physical memory to allow the system to better use physical memory for more frequently accessed pages.

This section of the book covers what page files are actually used for and proper sizing considerations.

PAGE FILE SIZING

64-bit versions of Windows and Windows Server support significantly more physical memory (RAM) than 32-bit versions, but the reasoning for page file sizing has not changed. It has always been about accommodating a system crash dump, if needed, and/or extending the system commit limit, if needed. Unfortunately, many assumptions have been made such as multiples of physical memory (RAM) and such. When a large amount of physical memory is installed, a paging file may not be required to back the system commit charge during peak usage—physical memory alone might be large enough, but a paging file might still be needed to back a system crash dump.

Use the following considerations for page file sizing for all versions of Windows and Windows Server:

1. *Crash dump setting*: If a crash dump file is desired during a system crash, then a page file or a dedicated dump file must exist and be large enough to accommodate the system crash dump setting. Otherwise, a system memory dump file will not be created.
2. *The peak system commit charge*: is the sum of all of the virtual address space that has been committed. "Committed" means that the memory is "promised" to be backed by physical memory or a page file. The "peak" is the highest value that the system commit charge has reached since the last system start. The system commit charge cannot exceed the system commit limit, therefore the system commit limit must be made large enough to accommodate the needs of the system commit charge. The system commit limit is the sum of physical memory and all page files combined, therefore page file sizing depends on the expected system commit

Windows Performance Analysis Field Guide. http://dx.doi.org/10.1016/B978-0-12-416701-8.00007-7

charge peak in correlation with physical memory and page file sizes. Peak system committed memory usage can vary greatly between systems; therefore, physical memory and page file sizing will also vary.

3. *Reducing the number of infrequently access pages*: The purpose of a paging file is to back infrequently accessed modified pages, so that they can be removed from physical memory allowing more space for more frequently access pages. The performance counter **Memory\Modified Page List Bytes** measures, in part, the amount of infrequently accessed modified pages destined for disk. But, be aware that not all of the memory on the Modified Page List will be written out to disk. It is common to have a few hundred megabytes of memory resident on the modified list. Therefore, if more available physical memory (**Memory \Available MBytes**) is needed and the Modified Page List has a significant amount of memory on it and if the existing paging files are relatively full (**Paging Files(*)\% Usage**), then consider extending or adding a paging file.

NOTE

Some products or services might require a page file for reasons not mentioned above. Check your product documentation.

SYSTEMS WITH A LOW AMOUNT OF PHYSICAL MEMORY

This situation assumes the following:

- *Small amount of physical memory*: The system has a relatively small amount of physical memory that is insufficient for the workloads placed on it.
- *Regularly low on available physical memory*: Less than 10% of physical memory available (measured by **Memory\Available MBytes** in Performance Monitor).
- *Page files are frequently used*: The logical disks hosting page files are frequently used and the disks are overwhelmed. Disk overwhelmed means that the disk constantly has IO request packets in the disk queue and response times are greater than expected for the IO sizes. Keep in mind that tracking page file reads and writes can only be done by file IO tracing. See section "Tracking page file reads and writes" later in this chapter for more information.
- *A single page file is in use*: Page files are system-managed on the system partition by default.

In this situation, the system is regularly waiting on the disk hosting the page file. Since disks respond significantly slower than physical memory, the system will frequently feel sluggish or unresponsive.

ADD MORE PHYSICAL MEMORY

Adding more physical memory would considerably help in this situation, but we will assume that no more physical memory can be added to this system. Therefore, the system is relying heavily on page file performance, which is relying on disk performance.

REDUCE MEMORY USAGE

If physical memory cannot be added, then consider reducing unnecessary memory usage. Identify the highest consumers of system committed memory by following the guidance of section "Where did all of the system committed memory go?" in Chapter 6 "System Committed Memory." Process private memory usage is the most common consumer of system committed memory.

ADD OR MOVE PAGING FILES TO FAST DISKS

When multiple paging files are defined, the one that responds first is used; this means that a page file on a disk that is faster than the others will be used more frequently. Therefore, consider adding a page file on a solid state drive (SSD), a fast array of disks, or a disk with a relatively fast access time. Again, this guidance applies only to systems with insufficient physical memory.

SYSTEMS WITH A LARGE AMOUNT OF PHYSICAL MEMORY

A commonly asked question is, "How to size a page file for systems with a large amount of physical memory?" As mentioned earlier, the page file size requirements depend on the crash dump settings, accommodating the peak system commit charge and being large enough to back infrequently accessed modified pages in physical memory. Therefore, there really isn't a one-size-fits-all guideline.

This situation assumes the following:

- *Large amount of physical memory*: The system has a relatively large amount of physical memory that is well beyond the memory workload needs of the system.
- *Regularly plenty of available physical memory*: More than 10% of physical memory is available (measured by **Memory\Available MBytes** in Performance Monitor).
- *Page files are infrequently used*: The logical disks hosting paging files are infrequently used and relatively idle. Idle meaning that the disk rarely has IO requests queued up.
- *A single page file is in use*: Page files are system-managed on the system partition by default.
- *System crash dumps are not needed*: This assumes that a system crash dump is not needed in this case.

If a system has too much physical memory and/or too large of a paging file, there is no performance problem associated with this condition other than an inefficiency of power usage of the RAM modules and a waste of disk space for the page file.

OPTIONALLY REDUCE PHYSICAL MEMORY

Physical memory (RAM modules) consumes a significant amount of electricity, so reducing the amount of physical memory can be a way of saving on power costs and/ or using the RAM for other systems that need it more. The best way to determine if any of the physical memory is not serving any use is to see how much memory is "free"—not to be confused with "available" memory. Free memory is the sum of the free page list and the zero page list. Free page list is a list of physical memory pages that must be cleaned (all zeroes written to the page) and the zero page list a list of physical memory pages that are already clean. Simply put, the more free memory, the more that can be removed with no consequence to system performance.

Free memory and zero memory can be measured using the Memory tab in Resource Monitor, using the performance counter **Memory\Free & Zero Page List Bytes**, or by using the free and zeroed fields in the Memory tab of the System Information window in Sysinternals Process Explorer.

OPTIONALLY REDUCE THE PAGE FILE SIZE

If the peak system commit charge doesn't come anywhere close to reaching the system commit limit, then consider reducing the page file size only after taking into consideration system crash dumps and the size of the Modified Page List. For example, if you have 256 GB of physical memory and have a paging file of 256 GB—a 512 GB system commit limit, but yet the peak system committed memory usage is less than 200 GB—then it would be safe to reduce the page file size (or remove) only if system crash dumps and the Modified Page List have been considered. This is because physical memory alone is able to fully back the 200 GB of committed memory.

SYSTEM CRASH DUMPS

A system crash (also known as a "bug check" or "Blue Screen of Death (BSOD)") occurs when the system is unable to run properly. The dump file produced from this event is called a system crash dump and a page file or dedicated dump file is used to write the dump file to disk. Once written, the file is renamed to %windir%\memory.dmp and this is the crash dump file that can be analyzed with a debugger. According to the Chapter 14 of the Window Internals, Sixth edition, Part 2 book, *a common cause for a system crash is a reference to a memory address that causes an access violation, either a write operation to read-only memory or a read operation on an address that is not mapped.* This is in reference to poorly written device drivers and/or faulty hardware.

Paging files and dedicated dump files are used to collect or "back" system crash dumps. Therefore, these files must be large enough to accommodate the type of crash dump selected. Otherwise, the system will be unable to create a crash dump file (memory.dmp), which is used for postmortem analysis to discover the root cause of the crash dump (Figure 7.1).

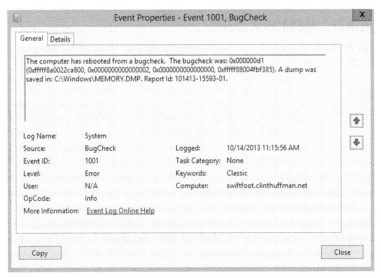

FIGURE 7.1

A bug check event on Windows Server 2012.

NOTE

During boot, system-managed paging files and system-managed dedicated dump files will automatically adjust their size according to the system crash dump settings. The size is usually slightly larger than the minimum page file or dedicated dump file size requirements listed below (Table 7.1).

The following Microsoft Knowledge Base article has more information on page file settings and considerations:

How to generate a kernel or a complete memory dump file in Windows Server 2008 and Windows Server 2008 R2 http://support.microsoft.com/kb/969028.

Table 7.1 The Minimum Page File Size Required for Each System Crash Dump Setting

System Crash Dump Setting	Minimum Page File or Dedicated Dump File Size Requirement
Small memory dump (256 KB)	1 MB
Kernel memory dump	Depends on kernel virtual address space usage
Complete memory dump	$1 \times$ RAM plus 257 MB[a]
Automatic memory dump	Automatically chooses small, kernel, or complete memory dump

[a] 1 MB of header data and device drivers may add up to 256 MB of secondary crash dump data.

AUTOMATIC MEMORY DUMP

Windows 8 and Windows Server 2012 introduced the "Automatic memory dump" feature, which is enabled by default. This is a new setting—not a new kind of crash dump. This setting will automatically choose the best system crash dump based on the frequency of system crashes.

The **Automatic memory dump** setting initially chooses a **Small memory dump** that requires a paging file or a dedicated dump file of at least 256 KB and the minimum size of the system-managed paging file will be large enough to accommodate it—roughly 200-400 MB on a system with 16 GB of physical memory, but this might vary greatly on systems with more physical memory. If the system crashes, then upon reboot, the automatic memory dump feature will choose a **Kernel memory dump** and will increase the minimum size of the system-managed paging file or the system-managed dedicated dump file to accommodate this kind of crash dump. Kernel memory crash dumps need enough paging file space or dedicated dump file space to accommodate the kernel mode side of virtual memory usage. If the system crashes again within 4 weeks of the previous crash, then upon reboot, **complete memory dump** is chosen, which requires a paging file or dedicated dump file of at least the size of physical memory (RAM), plus 1 MB for header information, plus up to 256 MB for potential secondary device driver dump date. Again, a system-managed paging file or the system-managed dedicated dump file will be increased to accommodate this kind of crash dump.

If the system is configured with a page file or a dedicated dump file of a specific size, then ensure that its size is large enough to accommodate the crash dumps setting mentioned above and the peak system commit charge.

> **The Microsoft Knowledge Base article has more on system crash dumps:**
> 969028 How to generate a kernel or a complete memory dump file in Windows Server 2008

SYSTEM COMMITTED MEMORY AND PAGING FILES

The system commit limit is the sum of physical memory and all paging files combined. It represents the maximum amount of system committed memory (known as the "system commit charge") that the system can back. The system commit charge is the total amount of committed or "promised" memory of all committed virtual address space in the system. If the system commit charge reaches the system commit limit, then the system and processes may fail to obtain committed memory resulting in, but not limited to, hangs, crashes, or other malfunctions. Therefore, it is important that the system commit limit is large enough to accommodate the system commit charge during peak usage.

The system commit charge and system commit limit can be measured in the Performance tab of Task Manager or by using **\Memory\Committed Bytes** and **\Memory\Commit Limit** performance counters, respectively. The counter **\Memory\% Committed Bytes In Use** is the ratio of **\Memory\Committed Bytes** to **\Memory\Commit Limit**.

NOTE

System-managed paging files will automatically grow up to three times physical memory or 4 GB whichever is larger when the system commit charge is near the system commit limit assuming there is enough free disk space available to accommodate the growth.

SYSTEM-MANAGED PAGING FILES

By default, paging files are system-managed. This means that the paging file(s) will grow and shrink based on many factors such as the amount of physical memory installed, accommodating the system commit charge and accommodating a system crash dump. For example, when the system commit charge is near the system commit limit, then the page file will be increased to accommodate it. This will continue to happen until the page file has reached three times the size of physical memory or 4 GB whichever is larger. This all assumes that the logical disk hosting the page file is large enough to accommodate the growth.

The following chart shows the minimum and maximum page file sizes of system-managed page files (Table 7.2):

Table 7.2 Minimum and Maximum System-Managed Page File Sizes

Operating System	Minimum Page File Size	Maximum Page File Size
Windows XP and Windows Server 2003 with less than 1 GB of RAM	1.5 × RAM	3 × RAM or 4 GB, whichever is larger
Windows XP and Windows Server 2003 with greater than 1 GB of RAM	1 × RAM	3 × RAM or 4 GB, whichever is larger
Windows Vista and Windows Server 2008	1 × RAM	3 × RAM or 4 GB, whichever is larger
Windows 7 and Windows Server 2008 R2	1 × RAM	3 × RAM or 4 GB, whichever is larger
Windows 8 and Windows Server 2012	Depends on crash dump setting[a]	3 × RAM or 4 GB, whichever is larger
Windows 8.1 and Windows Server 2012 R2	Depends on crash dump setting[a]	3 × RAM or 4 GB, whichever is larger

[a]See system crash dumps.

DEDICATED DUMP FILES

Computers running Microsoft Windows or Microsoft Windows Server normally must have a page file to back a system crash dump. As of Windows 7 Service Pack 1 with the hotfix 2716542 or Windows Server 2008 R2 Service Pack 1 with hotfix 2716542, system administrators have the option to create a dedicated dump file instead.

A dedicated dump file is a page file that is not used for paging. Instead, it is "dedicated" to back a system crash dump file (memory.dmp) in the event of a system crash. Dedicated dump files can be placed on any disk volume that can support a page file.

Similar to page files, dedicated dump files can be set to a specified size or be system-managed. When system-managed, the size of the file will be determined by the system crash dump setting. For example, if the system crash dump setting is set to complete memory dump, then the system-managed dedicated dump file will be at least the sum of physical memory.

Dedicated dump files can only be created by manually setting registry keys. Use the following procedure to create or modify dedicated dump file settings.

To create a system-managed dedicated dump file, create the following registry key and value:
Location: HKEY_LOCAL_MACHINE\System\CurrentControlSet\Control\CrashControl
Name: DedicatedDumpFile
Type: String
Value: C:\dedicateddumpfile.sys

The value must be the full path to the dedicated dump file such as C:\Dedicated-DumpFile.sys. It can be in a subdirectory and can be on a logical disk drive that is not the system partition. The initial size of the system-managed dedicated dump file will be determined by the system crash dump setting using the same automatic sizing as system-managed page files, unless a DumpFileSize setting is used. A reboot is required for this setting to take effect.

To set the dedicated dump file to a specific size (non-system-managed), create the following registry key and value:
Location: HKEY_LOCAL_MACHINE\System\CurrentControlSet\Control\CrashControl
Name: DumpFileSize
Type: DWORD (32-bit) value
Value: 16641

The value is the specified, non-system-managed, size in megabytes of the dedicated dump file. In this case, a value of 16641 is 16 GB plus 257 MB. The

Name	Type	Data
(Default)	REG_SZ	(value not set)
AutoReboot	REG_DWORD	0x00000001 (1)
CrashDumpEnabled	REG_DWORD	0x00000001 (1)
DedicatedDumpFile	REG_SZ	C:\dedicateddumpfile.sys
DisableEmoticon	REG_DWORD	0x00000001 (1)
DumpFile	REG_EXPAND_SZ	%SystemRoot%\MEMORY.DMP
DumpFileSize	REG_DWORD	0x00004101 (16641)
LastCrashTime	REG_QWORD	0x1cec9391f350668 (130262686414210664)
LogEvent	REG_DWORD	0x00000001 (1)
MinidumpDir	REG_EXPAND_SZ	%SystemRoot%\Minidump
MinidumpsCount	REG_DWORD	0x00000032 (50)
Overwrite	REG_DWORD	0x00000001 (1)

FIGURE 7.2

Registry Editor showing the CrashControl key after creating a dedicated dump file.

257 MB is 1 MB for the header data and the potential maximum of 256 MB of driver data. A reboot is required for this setting to take effect.

WARNING

If the dedicated dump file is too small to handle a system crash dump, then a crash dump file will fail to be created.

When done, the registry keys should look something like Figure 7.2. The following articles have more information on dedicated dump files:

- How to use the DedicatedDumpFile registry value to overcome space limitations on the system drive when capturing a system memory dump http://blogs.msdn.com/b/ntdebugging/archive/2010/04/02/how-to-use-the-dedicateddumpfile-registry-value-to-overcome-space-limitations-on-the-system-drive-when-capturing-a-system-memory-dump.aspx
- 969028 How to generate a kernel or a complete memory dump file in Windows Server 2008 http://support.microsoft.com/kb/969028
- 950858 Dedicated dump files are unexpectedly truncated to 4 GB on a computer that is running Windows Server 2008 or Windows Vista and that has more than 4 GB of physical memory http://support.microsoft.com/kb/950858

WHAT IS WRITTEN TO A PAGE FILE?

When data within a page is removed from physical memory, it is called a working set trim. If the memory is not part of a file on disk, then it must be backed up by the disk before the physical memory page can be reused. Since the data doesn't already exist on disk and has no association with a file on disk, then a page file is used to back the memory. This means that the only data that is actually written to a page file is data that is not already on disk.

For example, if I open Notepad, type "The quick brown fox jumps over the lazy dog." and don't save the document, then the only "modified" memory (data that does not exist on disk) is the sentence. This means that the sentence (the modified data) is data that potentially could be found on a page file. The portions of the DLLs and EXEs needed for Notepad to function are already on disk, so there is no reason to write this data to a page file when they already exist on disk.

OTHER CRASH DUMP-RELATED REGISTRY KEYS

Consider the following registry keys when working with page files and dedicated dump files:

IGNOREPAGEFILESIZE

If a page file or dedicated dump file has been set to a specific size, then consider adding the IgnorePageFileSize registry key that forces the system to attempt to write a dump out to a page file or a dedicated dump file even if the physical memory size is larger than the initial size of the page file or the dedicated dump file. This setting forces the system to attempt to write the dump file and is not a guarantee that a dump file will be written.

> **To set the IgnorePageFileSize setting, add the following registry key and value:**
> Location: HKEY_LOCAL_MACHINE\System\CurrentControlSet\Control \CrashControl
> Name: IgnorePagefileSize
> Type: DWORD (32-bit) value
> Value: 1

A value of 1 indicates enabled. A reboot is required for this setting to take effect.

DUMPFILE

By default, a system crash dump will default to %windir%\memory.dmp. If you wish to modify that location, then use the DumpFile registry key.

> **To specify the location of the crash dump file, modify the following registry value:**
> Location: HKEY_LOCAL_MACHINE\System\CurrentControlSet\Control\ CrashControl
> Name: DumpFile
> Type: expandable string value
> Value: D:\memory.dmp

The value is the file system location of where the system dump file will be created. A reboot is required for this setting to take effect.

The article "How to use the DedicatedDumpFile registry value to overcome space limitations on the system drive when capturing a system memory dump" at http://blogs.msdn.com/b/ntdebugging/archive/2010/04/02/how-to-use-the-dedicateddumpfile-registry-value-to-overcome-space-limitations-on-the-system-drive-when-capturing-a-system-memory-dump.aspx is a very good reference of creating on using dedicated dump files.

OTHER PAGE FILE-RELATED PERFORMANCE COUNTERS

There are several performance counters that are associated with paging files. This section describes the counters and what they measure.

\MEMORY\PAGES/SEC AND OTHER HARD PAGE FAULT COUNTERS

The performance counters **\Memory\Page/sec**, **\Memory\Page Reads/sec**, and **\Memory\Page Inputs/sec** measure hard page faults (faults that must be resolved by disk), which "may" or "may not" be related to a page file or a low physical memory condition. Hard page faults are a normal function of the operating system and happen when reading portions of files such as DLLs and EXEs as they are needed, when reading memory mapped files, or when reading from a page file. High values for these counters (excessive paging) indicate disk access (4 KB per page fault on x86 and x64 versions of Windows and Windows Server) that can increase the likelihood of system-wide delays assuming the related disks are overwhelmed. Therefore, it is recommended to monitor the disk performance of the logical disks hosting a page file in correlation with these counters.

NOTE

\Memory\Page Writes/sec and **\Memory\Page Output/sec** measure page file writes, but it is possible that future memory management changes might change this behavior.

TIP

There are no counters that directly measure page file reads. Hard page fault-related performance counters measure disk access that may or may not be related to page files.

Keep in mind that a system with a sustained 100 hard page faults per second is 400 KB per second disk transfers. Most 7200 RPM disk drives can handle about 5 MB per second with an IO size of 16 KB or 800 KB per second at an IO size of 4 KB. When possible, page file writes are done at 1 MB IO sizes, which means a

7200 RPM disk drive can sequentially write about 73 MB per second at 1 MB IO sizes, but not all disk drives can write at 1 MB IO sizes.

Unfortunately, there are no performance counters to directly tell us which disks are being used for page file reads and writes. This is where Event Tracing for Windows (ETW tracing)-related tools such as Microsoft Resource Monitor can provide file access details.

\PAGING FILE(*)\% USAGE

The performance counter **\Paging File(*)\% Usage** measures the percentage of usage of each paging file. 100% usage of a paging file does not indicate a performance problem so long as the system commit limit is not reached by the system commit charge and if there is not a significant amount of memory waiting to be written to a paging file—measured by the size of the Modified Page List (**Memory\Modified Page List Bytes**). If the Modified Page List (a list of physical memory pages that are the least frequently accessed) has a significant amount of memory on it and if the % Usage of all paging files is greater than 90, then increasing or adding a paging file can help make more physical memory available for more frequently access pages.

NOTE

Not all of the memory on the Modified Page List will be written out to disk. It is common to have a few hundred megabytes of memory resident on the modified list.

MULTIPLE PAGE FILES AND DISK CONSIDERATIONS

If a system is configured with more than one page file, then the page file that responds first will be used. This means that page files on faster disks will be used more often. In addition, placing a page file on a "fast" or "slow" disk only matters if the page file is frequently accessed and if the disk hosting the respective page file is overwhelmed. Keep in mind that actual page file usage depends greatly on the amount of modified memory that the system is managing—meaning files that already exist on disk such as an EXE or DLL will not be written to a page file.

RUNNING WITHOUT A PAGE FILE

Ever since Windows NT, Windows and Windows Server support the option of not running a page file. There are pros and cons of this configuration, so consider the facts below before considering running a system without a page file.

Also, keep in mind that hard page faults (errors that mean the data is not in physical memory and must be resolved from disk) will still occur because files must be read from disk before they can be used and reread from disk. Therefore, hard page fault-related counters will continue to show activity except for Page Writes/sec and Page Output/sec.

Facts when running a system without a page file:

- *Less available physical memory*: Infrequently accessed modified pages in physical memory cannot be backed and therefore must stay resident in physical memory.
- *Less disk access*: No disk IO related to page files.
- *No crash dump files*: Without a page file, the system cannot overwrite a page file in order to write a crash dump (memory.dmp file). If a crash dump file is needed, but a page file is not desired, then consider using a dedicated dump file, which is a page file that is dedicated only for crash dump and not for paging. See section "Dedicated dump files" earlier in this chapter for more information.
- *Immediate boot after a system crash*: Since a crash dump file cannot be written, if the system crashes (bug check), then the system can skip writing a dump file and immediately start a reboot. Unfortunately, there will be no dump file in order to determine the cause of the crash.
- *Smaller system commit limit*: Without a page file, the system commit limit will be smaller than the size of physical memory. This could make it more likely for the system commit charge to reach the system commit limit. See Chapter 6 "System committed memory" for more information.
- *More disk space*: A page file consumes space on disk. When no page files are configured, the disk space that would normally be consumed by a page file is free to use.

I used to have a 64-bit Windows 7 laptop with 16 GB of physical memory (RAM) and a 128 GB SSD. My system commit charge peak would never go above 8 GB and I didn't care about having a crash dump file because I can always configure one later if I wanted to. A 16 GB page file would have been a significant amount of disk space, so, I configured the system to run without a page file. This was a case where there was more than enough physical memory to accommodate my usage.

SHOULD THE PAGE FILE BE MOVED FROM C: DRIVE?

There is no general answer for all situations. This is why you should not find any official articles answering this question in any generalized form.

First, a page file must be able to accommodate the crash dump settings. Windows Server 2003 requires a page file to be on the system partition and be large enough to accommodate the crash dump setting. Windows Server 2008 and later versions allow a page file to be on other direct attached drives when accommodating a crash dump.

Second, it depends on the peak system commit charge and it will vary based on actual usage. With that said, the amount of system committed memory does "not" mean that a page file is actually being used. If the system commit charge is very large, but little of it is "touched," then having a page file on a slow disk drive is fine because the page file is not really being used—just there to accommodate the commit charge "if" it happens to become "touched" memory.

Third, assuming the system partition (typically C: drive) is a slow disk drive and that the system commit charge is greater than physical memory, and the committed memory is actually "touched," then the performance of the disk where the paging file is at is important. A page is 4 KB, so a sustained 1000 \Memory\Pages/sec (hard page faults) is 4 MB per second. Most 7200 RPM disk drives can generally handle more than 4 MB per second.

Finally, if multiple page files are configured, then the page file that is available first is used—meaning this is a load-balanced situation that can help in conditions where the page files are used frequently. Ultimately, if the page files are really being used that much, then consider adding more physical memory and/or placing the page files on faster disks.

In short, moving a page file off of the system partition really depends on how much the page file(s) are really being used (touched memory), the crash dump settings, version of the operating system, the system commit charge at peak, and disk drive performance.

PAGE FILE FRAGMENTATION

If the page files are constantly increasing and decreasing due to constant usage, then page file fragmentation can occur. To prevent fragmentation, the minimum setting and maximum setting of a page file can be set to the same value, but make sure that the setting is large enough to accommodate the desired system crash dump setting (if needed) and accommodate the peak system committed memory usage.

With that said, I have never seen evidence of page file fragmentation as a bottleneck. This is because most modern systems have a surplus of physical memory unlike older year 2000 systems. Furthermore, the system has to be constantly low on physical memory and it has to be using the page file(s) often enough to cause fragmentation.

If you suspect page file fragmentation, then consider placing the page files on faster disks. Also, consider the Sysinternals tool, PageDefrag available at http://technet.microsoft.com/en-us/sysinternals/bb897426.aspx. This tool will defragment the paging files on a regular basis, but be aware that this tool has been retired. It only works on x86 (32-bit) editions of Windows XP and Windows Server 2003.

TRACKING PAGE FILE READS AND WRITES

The only real way of knowing if a page file is actually being "read from" is to get a file IO trace. This can be collected and/or viewed with tools such as the Microsoft Performance Recorder/Analyzer, Microsoft Resource Monitor, and Sysinternals Process Monitor.

USING RESOURCE MONITOR

Resource Monitor is built into the operating system and can be launched from the Performance tab of Task Manager (Figure 7.3).

The Disk tab shows the processes and files involved in live disk activity. This data comes from ETW and shows much more data than what performance counters can provide. In this case, we can see the file C:\pagefile.sys being written to by the System process.

USING WINDOWS PERFORMANCE RECORDER/ANALYZER

Microsoft Windows Performance Recorder (WPR)/Analyzer (WPA) is part of the free Windows Performance Toolkit (WPT) and can capture activity related to hard page faults and the processes and files associated with them. In this case, I used WPR to record Disk IO and File IO activity while forcing the system to use the page file. In Figure 7.4, I am showing the Hard Faults chart within WPA and I aggregated the data to show the files most involved with hard page faults and in this case it was C:\pagefile.sys. This is proof that most of the hard page fault activity was related to the page file in this case.

USING SYSINTERNALS PROCESS MONITOR

Sysinternals Process Monitor (Procmon) can also show page file reads and writes. This can be done by enabling the Advanced Output option under Filter, Enable Advanced Output. Once enabled, set the filter to only show events where "Path is C:\pagefile.sys" or similar for other page files (Figure 7.5).

Disk Activity			■ 0 MB/sec Disk I/O		■ 0% Highest Active Time		⌃
Image	PID	File	Read ...	Write (B...	Total (B/sec)	I/O Priority	I ⌄
System	4	C:\pagefile.sys (Page File)	0	192,638	192,638	Normal	
System	4	C:\$Mft (NTFS Master File...	0	216	216	Normal	
System	4	C:\$Extend\$UsnJrnl:$J	0	683	683	Normal	
System	4	C:\$LogFile (NTFS Volum...	0	1,668	1,668	Normal	
System	4	C:\Windows\System32\7...	0	1,024	1,024	Normal	
System	4	C:\Windows\System32\7...	0	1,024	1,024	Normal	
svchost....	880	C:\Users\Clint\AppData\L...	16	0	16	Backgrou...	
svchost....	880	C:\Windows\assembly\N...	5,020	0	5,020	Backgrou...	⌄

FIGURE 7.3

The Disk Activity pane in Microsoft Resource showing reads and writes to pagefile.sys.

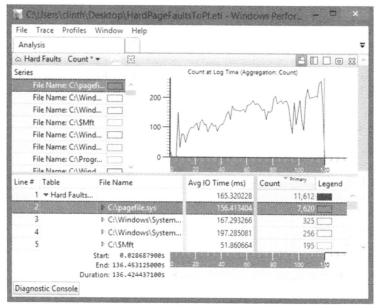

FIGURE 7.4

Windows Performance Analyzer (WPA) showing hard page fault activity.

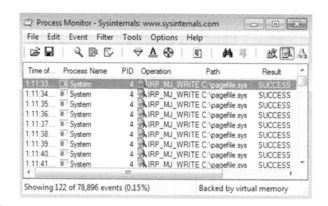

FIGURE 7.5

Sysinternals Process Monitor showing page file activity.

After capturing, click Tools, File Summary to get more details of the number of reads and writes to the page file.

HIGH SECURITY? CONSIDER CLEANING THE PAGE FILE

A page file contains modified memory of the system and has the potential to contain sensitive data such as unencrypted passwords and credit card information depending on how applications store the data.

TIP

Physical access to system hardware is just as important as network access.

Windows XP and Windows Server 2003 and later versions support the option to delete the page files upon shutdown of the system, but keep in mind that deleting the page files can be time-consuming and can significantly slow down the shutdown. Furthermore, if power is abruptly removed from the system (page file(s) not deleted) and if someone has physical access to the system, then they could still potentially get data from a page file. So, consider this if the shutdown delays are worth the security benefit and remember that physical security is still very important.

To delete all page files during shutdown, add the following registry key and value:
Location: HKEY_LOCAL_MACHINE\SYSTEM\CurrentControlSet\Control\ Session Manager\Memory Management
Name: ClearPageFileAtShutdown
Type: DWORD (32-bit) value
Value: 1

Refer to the following Microsoft Knowledge Base article for more information:
How to Clear the Windows Paging File at Shutdown http://support.microsoft. com/kb/314834

CONCLUSION

This chapter introduced page file concepts, how to monitor page files, and how to properly size them both for crash dumps and for accommodating the system commit charge.

Physical memory

INTRODUCTION

Physical memory (also known as random-access memory (RAM)) is a form of very fast, but volatile data storage. RAM modules are typically measured in nanoseconds (1000^{-3}), and physical disks are typically measured in milliseconds (1000^{-1}). This makes physical memory roughly 100,000 times faster than a common physical disk. Therefore, when possible, Windows and Windows Server keep the most frequently accessed pages of memory in physical memory and rely on a disk only if needed.

When a system is low on physical memory, it often leads to system-wide delays or, in extreme cases, a complete hang of the system. This chapter covers how physical memory is managed by the operating system, how to identify low-memory conditions, and how to alleviate those conditions.

FREE MEMORY IS DIFFERENT THAN AVAILABLE MEMORY

Before we jump right into low-physical memory conditions, it is important to define the difference between "Free" and "Available" memory. These terms are often mistakenly used interchangeably but, in fact, are significantly different in how they measure physical memory. Getting straight to the point, it is perfectly fine, if not desirable, to have no "Free" memory, but not okay to be low on "Available" memory.

Technically speaking, "Free" memory is the sum of the Free page list and the Zero page list. Memory on the Zero page list has all zeroes written to it. Memory on the Free page list is waiting to be overwritten with zeroes by the Zero page writer or waiting to be completely overwritten when allocated to a working set. In other words, "Free" memory is the memory that contains no useful data and is just waiting to be used. For example, if a system continuously has 16 GB of free memory even after peak load, then 16 GB of RAM modules can be removed without incurring any degradation in system performance, assuming that the workload remains the same. With that said, the longer a system is up and running, the more likely the memory will be put to use or used as disk cache making it available, but no longer free. This cycle is explained in more detail later in this chapter in "How physical memory is managed."

TIP

Save on electricity costs by removing RAM modules equivalent to the amount of free physical memory.

RAM modules consume a relatively large amount of electricity relative to the rest of the hardware, so if you need to save on power costs, then consider removing the amount of RAM equivalent to the amount of free memory. This is also a good tip when trying to assess the number of virtual machines a host can handle..

Depending on the version of Windows or Windows Server, Task Manager will show the amount of free memory, the amount of available memory, or both.

Available memory is much more important to monitor than Free memory simply because it represents all of the physical memory that can be used or reused without incurring a disk IO. The less memory a system has available, the more it relies on a disk, which is thousands of times slower than physical memory. This is the condition that system administrators fear most and the focus of most of this chapter.

A low-memory condition most often occurs when the system has less than 10% of its physical memory available. This is because when in this condition, most of the available memory is acting as disk cache. The more disk cache a system has, the less likely it needs to use the disk. The assumption being made is that the amount of physical memory installed dictates its workload—meaning that a system with a large amount of physical memory will do more work than a system with less physical memory.

Available memory is the sum of Free memory, which is the memory that has or will have all zeroes written to it, and Standby memory, which is the memory that contains data that is already on the disk. This is discussed in more detail later in this chapter.

IDENTIFYING A LOW-AVAILABLE-PHYSICAL MEMORY CONDITION USING PERFORMANCE MONITOR

If I had to choose a single, simple indicator of a low-physical memory condition, then it would be to monitor the performance counter **Memory****Available MBytes**. This is because when available memory is low (less than 10% of physical memory installed), then the system typically incurs additional disk IO than it normally does. Therefore, this is an "initial" indicator that warrants more investigation. This is helpful for automated monitoring solutions and other analysis tools. With that said, not all low-physical memory conditions are performance problems, hence why this is only an "initial" indicator (Table 8.1).

Table 8.1 A Simple, Initial Indicator of a Low Physical Memory Condition

Performance Counter	Healthy	Warning	Critical
\Memory \Available MBytes	More than 10% of physical memory installed	Less than 10% of physical memory installed	Less than 5% of physical memory installed or less than 100 MB, whichever is larger

TIP

Available memory of less than 10% of physical memory installed is an initial indicator of a low-memory condition.

To truly know if a system has system-wide delays due to a low-memory condition, hard page faults and the disk performance must also be considered. This is covered in more detail in "Tracking page file reads and writes" in Chapter 7 "Page Files".

LOW AVAILABLE MEMORY WITH NO PAGE FILE

If **\Memory\Available MBytes** is less than 10% of the physical memory installed and if no page file is configured, then the system is close to running out of system committed memory, which can lead to memory allocation failures, which is arguably worse than a slow system. See Chapter 6 "System Committed Memory" for more information on this subject. In addition, there are less disk cache (Standby list) and more hard page faults, which means increased disk IO. In any case, the system is at risk when low on available memory with no page file to support the system committed memory. For more information, see "Running without a page file" in Chapter 7 "Page Files".

LOW AVAILABLE MEMORY WITH A PAGE FILE

Assuming that the system has less than 10% physical memory available and the system has one or more available page files, then the disks hosting the page files need to be checked if they are overwhelmed and if they can handle the increased paging. Some of the telltale signs are low available memory (**\Memory\Available MBytes**), increased hard page faults (**\Memory\Pages/sec**), process working set reduction (**\Process(_Total)\Working Set**), and increased page file usage (**\Paging File(*)\ % Usage**). The "system-wide delays" occur when the disks hosting the page files cannot keep up with the increased load. For more information, see "Systems with a low amount of physical memory" in Chapter 7 "Page Files".

IDENTIFY THE LOGICAL DISKS HOSTING AN AVAILABLE PAGE FILE

First, identify which logical disks are hosting page files and are not full. This can be done by looking at the instances of **\Paging File(*)\% Usage** and looking for a value of less than 100.

ARE THE DISKS OVERWHELMED?

Next, determine if the logical disks hosting the page files have outstanding IO requests by checking the queue length. This can be done by monitoring the Current Disk Queue Length, Avg. Disk Queue Length, % Idle Time, or % Disk Time. The queue length can be quite erratic at times going from 0 to 1000 and back to 0 again in a quick succession, so the **Avg. Disk Queue Length** is a good choice because it calculates what the queue length might have been on average. We are checking the queue length not because of the number of spindles, but because it means that the disk constantly has work to do. Keep in mind that the queue length alone doesn't determine if a disk is overwhelmed, but it does tell us if the disk has constant work to do. If there was no IO requests queued, then the disk has no work to do (not busy) and the performance of the disk can be considered good until it has work to do again.

Finally, check the average IO sizes and response times of the outstanding requests. The larger the IO size, the longer the response times, but the more data can be transferred per second and vice versa. If the IO size is 64 KB or smaller, then use the hardware manufacturer's disk service times (use 15 ms if the disk service times are unknown). Disk service times are the manufacturer's guarantee of how long it should take at maximum to get an IO from the storage device. Now, as discussed in Chapter 3 "Storage," IO sizes have a significant impact on response times, so if the IO sizes are more than 64 KB, then add 10 ms to the service times of the storage device. The 10 ms increase in the threshold is based on my discussions with SAN vendors and the Microsoft Windows product team.

WORKING SET TRIMS AND PAGE FILE USAGE

Other symptoms that you might observe when in a low-memory condition is working set trims and increased page file usage both of which can be observed with performance counters.

The performance counter **\Processor(*)\Working Set** monitors the amount of physical memory in use by each process. When there is a sudden reduction—sometimes small, sometimes large—in all or most of the working set sizes, it is likely a condition commonly referred to as a "global working set trim." This happens when a system has to take physical memory from processes in order to make more memory available.

The performance counter **\Paging File(*)\% Usage** measures how much of a page file is in use and can be used in correlation with working set trimming as further evidence of a low-memory condition.

With all of that said, a large working set trim with a significant increase in page file usage only indicates that the activity is occurring. It is only a real problem if the disks hosting the page files become overwhelmed by the activity. Therefore, a low-physical memory condition that has system-wide delays is really all about avoiding disk IO and overwhelming those disks.

AN EXAMPLE

To see this analysis in action, let's take a look at a system that is clearly running poorly and incurring system-wide delays due to a lack of physical memory condition (Figure 8.1).

In this example, I induced a low-physical memory condition by causing a "touched" memory leak using the Sysinternals tool Testlimit. This tool can be freely downloaded from http://live.sysinternals.com/files/testlimit.zip.

The exact command that I used is the following:

Testlimit64 -d

WARNING

Be very careful when using this command. It will cause the system to quickly run out of physical memory. Use only for testing on nonproduction systems.

With that said, this condition can happen on any system when a number of processes or drivers consume a large amount of frequently accessed "touched" memory.

In this case, **\Memory\Available MBytes** goes down to less than 100 MB, which is less than 10% of the physical memory installed. There is a single page file on the C: drive and the response times (Avg. Disk sec/Transfer) of the C: drive goes over

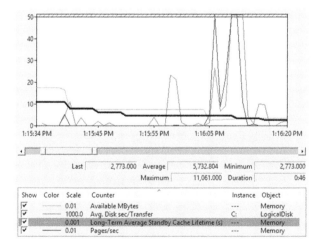

FIGURE 8.1

Performance monitor showing performance counter behavior during a low-physical memory condition.

0.025 (25 ms) in the second half of the PerfMon output at IO sizes of less than 64 KB (IO sizes are not shown) indicating that the disk is overwhelmed—this assumes that the disk queue length was at least 2 or more, which was very likely. Regarding the **\Memory\Pages/sec** counter, it shoots up to beyond 500, which indicates that there was at least 2 MB per second of disk activity due to hard page faults. Keep in mind that the page faults themselves have no real threshold other than knowing that it is IO that must be resolved by the disk.

IDENTIFYING A LOW AVAILABLE PHYSICAL MEMORY CONDITION USING TASK MANAGER

It is actually relatively easy to identify a system that is low on available memory but much more difficult (explained in "Identifying a low-available-physical memory condition using Performance Monitor" earlier in this chapter) to determine if the low-memory condition is causing a system-wide delay. Task Manager (part of the operating system) provides some initial indicators of this condition.

The Performance tab of Task Manager in Windows 7 and Windows Server 2008 R2 and earlier provides the "available" field, which is the equivalent of the **\Memory \Available MBytes** performance counter. It doesn't provide any indication of when memory is low, so you have to look for the total physical memory usable by the system using the "Total" field, do a 10% calculation on it, and determine if the current value of available memory is less than it (Figure 8.2).

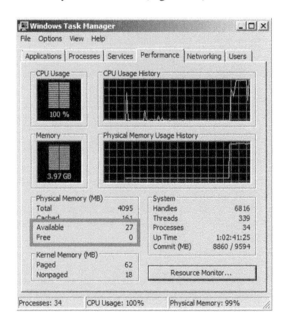

FIGURE 8.2

Task Manager on Windows Server 2008 R2 showing a low-available memory condition.

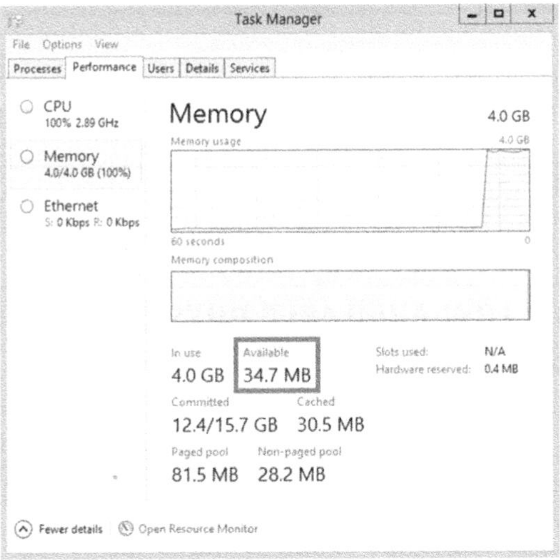

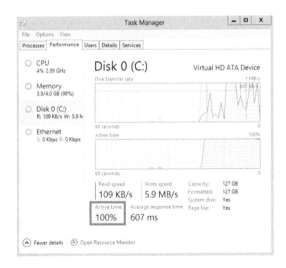

FIGURE 8.3

Task Manager on Windows Server 2012 showing a low-available memory condition.

Task Manager in Windows 8 and Windows Server 2012 and later has changed significantly and provides a bit more detail. The performance tab now has tabs for each resource, so we can see the Available memory on the Memory tab and the disk usage on the "Disk" tab (Figures 8.3 and 8.4).

FIGURE 8.4

Task Manager on Windows Server 2012 showing 100% active time on C: drive.

NOTE

By default, the "Disk" tab does not appear in Task Manager on Windows Server 2012 and later. To enable it, run "diskperf -y" at an admin command prompt. This is not recommended for systems with a large number of disks.

IDENTIFYING A LOW-AVAILABLE PHYSICAL MEMORY CONDITION USING RESOURCE MONITOR

Resource Monitor has been part of the operating system since Windows Vista and Windows Server 2008 with significant features (such as the "tabbed" details of each resource) added in the version that ships with Windows 7 and Windows Server 2008 R2 (Figure 8.5).

The Memory tab shows the overall physical memory usage (bottom pane in Figure 8.5) and the memory usage of each process (top pane in Figure 8.5). In this case, the sum of Standby (18 MB) memory and Free (0 MB) memory makes up the Available field with 18 MB, which is very low since it is less than 10% of the amount of total physical memory. As a reminder, available memory is the amount of physical memory that can be reused without incurring a disk IO to make more memory available. It is arguably the simplest way of determining if the system is low on physical memory.

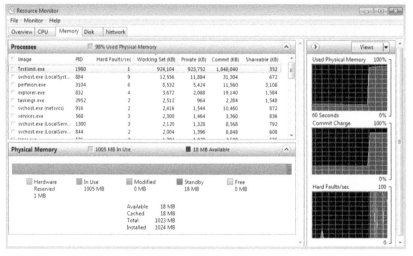

FIGURE 8.5

Resource Monitor showing a low-physical memory condition.

While we are here, I'll explain the fields shown in this pane:

Hardware Reserved: This is memory that is reserved for the BIOS and some drivers for other peripherals. This is also used to truncate the memory that the system cannot use. For example, my wife's Windows 7 computer has 8 GB of physical memory installed, but it is the 32-bit version of the operating system, which is limited to 4 GB. Therefore, at least 4 GB (4096 MB) of it is marked as hardware reserved preventing the operating system from using it. This is due to 32-bit drivers stability. The 64-bit version of Windows 7 can address all 8 GB of physical memory. This is due to 32-bit drivers stability. The 64-bit version of Windows 7 can address all 8 GB of physical memory. You can see this in Figure 8.6.

Nearly all 32-bit versions of Windows XP and Windows Server 2003 and later have Physical Address Extensions enabled with hardware support, which allows the operating system to access up to 64 GB of physical memory. With that said, many of the device drivers on consumer versions of the operating system are less reliable when the system has more than 4 GB of physical memory, so it was decided to limit the 32-bit versions of Windows to 4 GB. Enterprise versions of 32-bit Windows Server 2003 and later can address up to 64 GB of physical memory.

In Use: This is the amount of physical memory in use by processes, drivers, and the operating system. It is largely made up of, but not limited to, a combination of process working sets, nonpageable kernel memory, the portion of pageable kernel memory currently in physical memory. Address Windowing Extensions (AWE) memory usage, and/or driver-locked memory. This is only the "physical memory" (RAM) usage and not related to the system commit charge.

Modified: This is "dirty" memory that was once in the working set of a process but has been trimmed by the memory manager—meaning that it was removed from the process and placed on the Modified list. It is not "in use" memory, but the physical pages that contain the data cannot be removed or reused yet. Page lists are explained later in this chapter. "Dirty" means that it must be written to a disk (backed up) before the physical page in which the data is contained can be reused. This memory contains data waiting to be written to a disk such as but not limited to a page file or a memory-mapped file.

Standby: This is unmodified memory that was once in the working set of a process but has been trimmed by the memory manger—meaning that it was removed

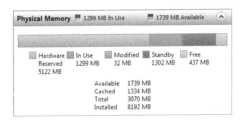

FIGURE 8.6

The Physical Memory pane from Resource Monitor on Windows 7.

from the process and placed on the Standby list. It is not "in use" memory. Page lists are explained later in this chapter. The memory already exists on disk, so it is "backed up". Therefore, the data can be retrieved from physical memory instead of going to a disk making this memory serve as disk cache increasing the performance of the system. In addition, since these physical pages of memory are not in use, they can be wiped (either all zeroes written to it or overwritten) and given to the working set of a process needing more physical memory. Standby memory is considered disk cache and is often, but not always, associated with the "Cached" field in Task Manager and Resource Monitor.

Since the physical pages in which the data is contained can be reused at any time, this memory is considered "available" for reuse and counts toward the Available field in Task Manager and Resource Monitor.

Free: This is the memory where the physical pages containing the data, if any, are free to be reused by another process. The data within it was once private data within the working set of a process or had all zeroes written to it. Private data cannot be given to another process, so it must be "cleaned" or overwritten before the physical page can be reused.

TIP

The best way to know if a system has too much physical memory is by measuring its Free memory. This memory serves no purpose other than waiting to be used.

Available: This is the sum of Free memory and Standby memory and consists of physical memory pages that can be immediately reused without incurring a disk IO. Low available memory is arguably the simplest indicator of potential system-wide delays due to increased disk paging. For more information, see "Free memory is different than available memory" earlier in this chapter.

Cached: The Cached field is calculated differently depending on the version of Windows or Windows Server. Without elaborating too much, there are many kinds of "cache" in the operating system depending on the perspective. In the case of Resource Monitor, this value is the sum of Standby memory and Modified memory. Standby memory is disk cache based on the description above, but Modified memory is difference since it is not backed by the disk yet. When pages with a working set are infrequently accessed, they are removed from the working set and placed on the Modified list (pending to be written to a page file), and if the process accesses the virtual memory pages associated with the data, then the data is returned to the working set. In this way, it is cache.

Total: This is the total amount of physical memory (RAM) that the system has access to.

Installed: This is the total amount of physical memory (RAM) installed in the system. This sounds similar to Total, but remember that a 32-bit Windows 7 system can only use up to 4 GB (Total) of physical memory even if 8 GB (Installed) is installed.

MONITORING FOR LOW-MEMORY CONDITIONS USING SCRIPTING

When working with hundreds of computer systems, it may be more convenient to run a script to gather the physical memory data than to log in to the desktop of each machine. Therefore, I'll try to provide some scripting tips on how to gather the physical memory data from remote computers.

The following Powershell command returns the amount of available physical memory (in MB) from localhost:

Get-WmiObject Win32_PerfFormattedData_PerfOS_Memory -ComputerName localhost | Select AvailableMBytes

The following Powershell command returns the amount of physical memory (in bytes) installed:

Get-WmiObject Win32_ComputerSystem -ComputerName localhost | Select TotalPhysicalMemory

WHERE DID ALL OF THE PHYSICAL MEMORY GO?

You have arrived here because the system is low on available physical memory (**\Memory\Available MBytes** is less than 10% of addressable physical memory), running very slow, and you're not sure why. A system can run out of available physical memory for many reasons. The most common consumer of physical memory is processes that are frequently accessing memory.

PHYSICAL MEMORY IS CONSUMED BY, BUT NOT LIMITED TO, THE FOLLOWING

1. *Process working set memory (\Process(*)\Working Set)*: A working set is the physical memory usage of a process. Under normal circumstances, the more frequently the pages of a process are accessed, the closer the working set is to the committed memory usage of the process. With that in mind, one might think that if you add up all of the working sets of all of the processes, then you should be close to the amount of physical memory usage on the system. Well, that is "mostly" true. You have to keep in mind that more than one process can reference the same pages of physical memory and counting those pages in its working set. When more than one process counts the same physical memory pages as its own, then it is possible to add up all of the working sets of all of the processes and end up with a value larger than the physical memory of the system.

   Start off with the _Total instance of the process working set performance counter (**\Process(_Total)\Working Set**) to see if all of the process working sets combined is consuming a large amount of memory. For more information, see "Process working sets" later in this chapter. Next, look at each process working set individually.

2. *Driver locked*: This is physical memory that has been locked by a driver and commonly used by a virtualization software such as Microsoft Hyper-V to lock physical memory for a virtual machine. For more information, see "Driver-Locked memory" later in this chapter. There is no performance counter to directly measure driver-locked memory. This is also commonly used by VMWare to "balloon" physical memory within a virtual machine.

3. *Address Windowing Extensions (AWE)*: AWE is an object model that allows an application to directly address physical memory by-passing the operating system's normal memory management. As of Windows 8 and Windows Server 2012 and later, AWE memory is included in the process private bytes (**Process (*)\Private Bytes**). Otherwise, tools like Sysinternals RAMMap can be used to identify AWE memory usage.

NOTE

Microsoft SQL Server uses AWE memory to lock physical memory. For more information, see "Address Windowing Extensions (AWE)" later in this chapter.

---

4. Kernel pool memory: Pool Nonpage memory *(\Memory\Pool Nonpaged Bytes)* must be resident in physical memory. It counts as "In use" memory. Furthermore, a portion of Pool Paged memory (**Memory\Pool Paged Bytes**) will use physical memory.

5. *System Cache (\Memory\System Cache Resident Bytes)*: System cache uses physical memory and the memory usage is considered "in use." With that said, when the system needs the physical memory, the system cache will give up its memory. This is why the system cache is not counted toward the system commit charge (**Memory\Committed Bytes**) discussed in the Chapter 6 "System Committed Memory". The system cache is similar to a squatter staying in a house that he or she doesn't own and when the owner reclaims the residence, then the squatter must leave. And just like in the real world, sometimes, the squatter doesn't leave.

ADDING IT UP WITH PERFORMANCE COUNTERS

The fact is that there is not enough performance counters to truly account for all of the physical memory usage. This is primarily due to the "not so obvious" ways that physical memory is actually used and referenced. With that said, some of the performance counters can provide some clues such as **Memory\Available MBytes**, **Memory\Pool Nonpaged Bytes**, **Memory\System Cache Resident Bytes**, and **Process(*)\Working Set**, which directly measure physical memory usage. Other counters such as **Memory\Pool Paged Bytes** and **Process(*)\Private Bytes** do not directly measure physical memory usage, but a portion of these resources will be in the physical memory (Figure 8.7).

Memory

Available MBytes	9,145.000
Free & Zero Page List Bytes	7,068,168,192
Long-Term Average Standby Cache Lifetime (s)	14,400.000
Modified Page List Bytes	139,034,624.000
Pool Nonpaged Bytes	227,942,400.000
System Cache Resident Bytes	192,585,728.000

Process	_Total
Working Set	5,053,906,944

FIGURE 8.7

Performance counters directly related to physical memory usage.

For example, I have a Windows 8.1 laptop with 16 GB of physical memory. According to **\Memory\Available MBytes**, the system has 8.9 GB (9145 MB) available, so this means that there is roughly 7 GB of physical memory usage. Alternatively, Task Manager shows the amount of physical memory usage on the Performance tab.

NOTE

There is no performance counter for total physical memory, so the amount of physical memory in gigabytes is shown in Task Manager, Resource Monitor, or the following Powershell command:

gwmi Win32_ComputerSystem | % {$_.TotalPhysicalMemory /1GB}

Take the returned value minus the amount of available memory to get the physical memory usage.

So, where did the 7 GB of physical memory usage go? Well, the most likely suspect is process working sets. In this case, **\Process(_Total)\Working Set** is 4.7 GB (5,053,906,944 bytes); this leaves roughly 2.3 GB unaccounted for. Next, we know that nonpageable kernel memory and system cache both use physical memory and are not part of process working set. Added together (227,942,400 + 192,585,728) is 400 MB, so we still have roughly 1.9 GB unaccounted for.

This is as far as we can go with performance counters, and it is time to bring out Sysinternals RAMMap (Figure 8.8).

In this case, just over 1 GB (1,128,480 KB) of physical memory is driver-locked. I happen to be running a virtual machine with 1 GB of RAM allocated to it, so this explains where 1 GB of the physical memory went leaving roughly 900 MB. The rest of the 900 MB is in use by the physical memory portions of Paged Pool, shareable memory, and various other resources. Paged Pool happens to be using 843 MB of committed memory on my system, but there is no performance counter to tell us how much of that is resident in physical memory, so again, RAMMap is able to provide this to us showing the "active" portion of it that is in physical memory, which in this case is 546 MB (558,952 KB) leaving roughly 354 MB taken up by various resources.

Remember that just because committed memory is "promised" by the system to be backed by the physical memory or the disk, it doesn't lock that memory or make that much memory "in use." We can only assume that some portion of that memory is in physical memory, and for that, we have to use tools other than Performance Monitor.

FIGURE 8.8

RAMMap provides details of physical memory usage.

In summary, performance counters can give us an idea of the physical memory usage, but it takes a memory analysis tool like RAMMap to see the actual physical memory usage.

PROCESS WORKING SETS

The most common cause of running out of physical memory is simply one or more processes frequently accessing their respective memory in which in turn the operating system will keep those pages of memory in physical memory as much as possible. Keep in mind that processes do not directly access physical memory except under rare conditions described later.

NOTE

Processes can reference the same pages of physical memory, and all of them are counting that memory in their respective working sets. This means that in theory, it is possible to add up all of the process working sets and end up with a value larger than the physical memory total of the system. This is why process working sets are a starting point.

The operating system controls the working set sizes of processes, and it will reduce or "trim" these working sets as needed without consent from the application. With that said, when one or more processes are frequently accessing their respective memory, then the memory manager tries to accommodate it.

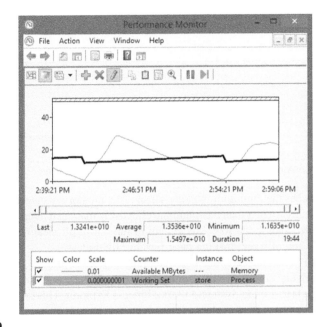

FIGURE 8.9

Performance monitor showing store.exe consuming the most physical memory.

The physical memory usage of a process is measured by its working set. The performance counter **\Process(*)\Working Set** is the physical memory usage of a process. In the case of Figure 8.9, the working set of store.exe (Microsoft Exchange Server 2007) is consuming up to $1.5497e+010$ (14.4 GB) of the 16 GB of physical memory and running Available MBytes down to critical levels forcing the system to trim the working set. The system partially succeeds with trimming, but the process continues to demand more memory.

When a process is busy doing work, it will naturally need memory to do the work. In this particular case, store.exe was very busy and legitimately needed the memory to do the work; therefore, simply adding more physical memory to the system was the best course of action.

When a process consumes memory and retains it unnecessarily, then it is considered a memory leak. Memory leaks are difficult to troubleshoot because it is difficult to determine which memory usage is needed versus which memory usage is not needed. With that said, tools such as Sysinternals VMMap, DebugDiag, and Windows Performance Analyzer are helpful in identifying areas of the most memory consumption within a process. This topic is covered in more detail in Chapter 4 "Process Memory" (Figure 8.10).

MINIMUM WORKING SETS

If given the user right, "Increase a process working set" (SeIncreaseWorkingSetPrivilege), an application can set its process minimum working set size. This means that after

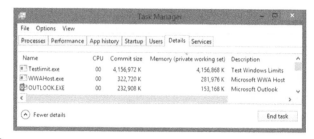

FIGURE 8.10

Task Manager on Windows Server 2012 showing processes with the largest working sets.

the process reaches the minimum working set size, the memory manager will not trim the working set any smaller than the minimum effectively making it nonpageable. If this setting is abused, then it can force the system to run out of physical memory and be unable to page any of it out, making page files mostly useless.

There is no performance counter to determine a process' minimum working set size, so a relatively quick way of identifying use and abuse of minimum working set size settings is to use the Sysinternals tool Process Explorer. This tool is a free tool from Microsoft and can be downloaded from http://live.sysinternals.com/procexp.exe and does not require installation (Figure 8.11).

The minimum working set size is not shown by default in Process Explorer, but it can be added by right-clicking the column headers, selecting "Select columns," navigating to the Process Memory tab, and enabling **Minimum Working Set** (Figure 8.12).

In this case, WWAHost.exe (the Windows Store App host process) has set a minimum working set size of 280,172 KB, but its working set has not yet reached it. This means that the memory manager will not reduce this working set until it reaches a size of 280,172 KB and then will not reduce it below that amount.

If one or more processes are setting a large minimum working set size, then discuss the application's memory requirements with the developer of the application. If the size cannot be reduced, then moving nonessential applications to other servers or adding more physical memory may be necessary.

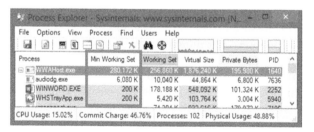

FIGURE 8.11

Process Explorer showing the minimum working set sizes of processes.

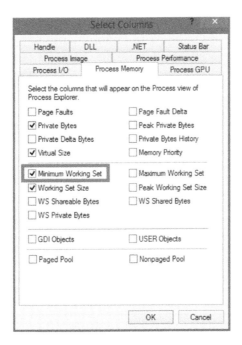

FIGURE 8.12

The Process Memory tab of Process Explorer.

DRIVER-LOCKED MEMORY

Drivers have the ability to lock physical memory making it nonpageable memory. A common reason for this is to lock physical memory for one or more virtual machines. The Sysinternals tool RAMMap is helpful in initially identifying a driver-locked memory condition (Figure 8.13).

In this case, the Microsoft Hyper-V driver has locked 4 GB of physical memory in order to host a virtual machine with 4 GB of physical memory, but this is as far as RAMMap can go. It is unable to identify which driver or drivers are responsible for locking this memory. Therefore, determine if there are any virtual computers running within the system and/or search for unnecessary drivers. Sysinternals Autoruns is a great way of validating system drivers. For more information on validating system drivers, see my blog post "Using Autoruns to validate system drivers," at http://blogs.technet.com/b/clinth/archive/2013/11/21/using-autoruns-to-validate-system-drivers.aspx.

For clarification, driver-locked memory is not the same as a driver using Nonpaged Pool memory. This means that driver-locked memory does not show up in Nonpaged Pool.

FIGURE 8.13

Sysinternals RAMMap showing 4 GB of driver-locked memory.

ADDRESS WINDOWING EXTENSIONS (AWE)

According to the book "Windows Internals" 5th edition, AWE *allows a 32-bit application to allocate up to 64 GB of physical memory and then map views, or windows, into its 2-GB virtual address space*. This is one of the few ways that a 32-bit application can access more than 2 GB of virtual address space, but it comes at a price.

CONSIDERATIONS OF AWE MEMORY USAGE

- *Exceed virtual address space*: Allows 32-bit apps to access virtual address space beyond 2 GB.
- *Written specifically for AWE:* The developer of the application has to write the code specifically for this feature.
- *It is not "all-purpose" memory*: It can only be used for heap memory.
- *Nonpageable*: All of the memory allocated through AWE is nonpageable— meaning that the operating system is not able to reduce it or manage it. AWE effectively takes the memory away from the operating system.
- *Difficult to monitor*: In Windows 7 and Windows Server 2008 R2 and earlier operating systems, AWE memory usage is not tracked by performance counters— meaning that AWE memory usage will not show up in a process' virtual bytes, private bytes, or working set. With that said, the AWE memory usage is charged against the system commit charge (\Memory\Committed Bytes) and available

memory (\Memory\Available MBytes). Therefore, if a system is low on available memory and none of the "usual suspects" listed in "Where did all of the physical memory go?" are consuming physical memory and if the system is running Microsoft SQL Server, then likely, it is locking memory with AWE.

As of Windows 8 and Windows Server 2012 and later operating systems, AWE memory usage is charged against the process' virtual bytes, private bytes, and working set.

As of this writing, Microsoft SQL Server is the only application that I know of that takes advantage of AWE, but in my own experience with enterprise customers, SQL Server implementations are common, so this topic comes up often.

LOCKING MEMORY WITH MICROSOFT SQL SERVER

Whether it is 32-bit SQL Server or 64-bit SQL Server, they both use the AWE object model to lock physical memory for exclusive use of SQL Server. 32-bit SQL is limited to 2 GB of virtual address space, so it used AWE to access additional memory. 64-bit SQL Server has 8 TB or 128 TB of virtual address space, but that memory is not guaranteed to be in physical memory. For this reason, AWE is still used in 64-bit SQL Server. This debate really comes down to allowing the operating system to manage the physical memory or allowing SQL Server to directly manage it. If you decide to allow SQL Server to lock the memory, keep in mind that the memory is exclusive to SQL Server's processes. This means that if another process such as SQL Server reporting services needs memory, then it might not have enough to operate efficiently. This ends up being a balance of SQL Server memory usage and just enough for everything else.

With that in mind, I've had plenty of customers who ask me what is the proper amount of memory to allow the operating system to function properly. My response has been the minimum hardware requirements of the operating system, but often, that is not enough. The problem is that I can't predict how much memory that all of the other non-SQL Server processes will need—see "Process working sets" earlier in this chapter. This is something that just has to be measured and adjusted because each server and its respective workload are unique.

In the example in Figure 8.14, SQL Server (shown as sqlservr), the system has 16 GB of physical memory installed and has 1728 MB of it available

Memory		
Available MBytes	1,728.575	
Commit Limit	38,773,915,648.0000	
Committed Bytes	19,007,856,640.0000	
Pool Nonpaged Bytes	98,078,003.200	
Process	_Total	sqlservr
Private Bytes	5,021,886,874	350,670,438.400
Virtual Bytes	...	21,959,412,940.8000
Working Set	4,184,129,638	101,197,824.000
SQLServer:Memory Manager		
Total Server Memory (KB)	12,582,912.000	

FIGURE 8.14

Performance Monitor showing physical memory-related performance counters.

(\Memory\Available MBytes). If we look at all of the process working sets added up (**Process(_Total)\Working Set**), it unfortunately only shows only 3.9 GB (4,184,129,638 bytes). Where did all of the physical memory go? Pool Nonpaged bytes is not responsible because it is only using about 93 MB (98,078,003 bytes). Normally, I would start using Sysinternals RAMMap to identify physical memory usage, but since this is an active Microsoft SQL Server, I took a quick look at **\SQLServer:Memory Manager\Total Server Memory (KB)**, and it shows 12 GB of memory usage even though the private bytes and working set of sqlservr show only a very small portion of it.

This is a Windows Server 2008 R2 system, so the physical memory locked by SQL Server's AWE feature is not counted toward its private bytes and working set. In this case, 1.7 GB of available memory is likely sufficient for the system to operate, so there is little to no danger here. With that said, this shows that AWE memory usage can be very difficult to track. Luckily, the Total Server Memory (KB) counter counts AWE memory usage. In addition, Windows 8 and Windows Server 2012 include AWE memory usage in process private bytes.

OUT OF PHYSICAL MEMORY, BUT NOT OUT OF COMMITTED MEMORY

A system can run out of physical memory due to a large amount of nonpageable memory usage such as, but not limited to, Pool Nonpaged kernel memory usage, page locked memory, or driver-locked memory. This condition prevents the system from trimming the working sets and prevents it from using a page file to back this memory.

As an experiment, I induced a driver leak in Pool Nonpaged, which consumed all of the physical memory in the system. Since it is nonpageable memory, the system is not able to use the disk to back the memory. This resulted in a complete hang of the system—meaning that the system is unable to "paint" screen updates and is unresponsive to input devices such as mouse clicks and keyboard strokes.

Figure 8.15 shows nearly all of physical memory in use, 26.3 MB available, but plenty of system committed memory since the system commit limit could expand from 4.7 GB to up to 16 GB. This is a rare condition where the system is out of physical memory and is unable to page out any of it.

A system that is out of physical memory will likely have the following symptoms:

- "Laggy" or failure to properly "paint" the user interface
- Sluggish or unresponsive mouse clicks and keyboard strokes
- Unresponsive or very slow applications and services
- High "in use" memory and very low available physical memory

If a lack of physical memory is suspected, then use the troubleshooting steps first mentioned in "Where did all of the physical memory go?" earlier in this chapter.

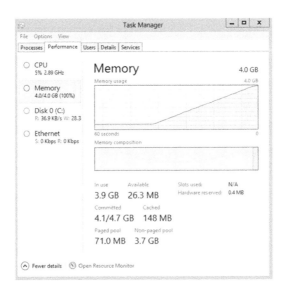

FIGURE 8.15

Task Manager of Windows Server 2012 showing an out of physical memory condition.

HOW PHYSICAL MEMORY IS MANAGED

The operating system has a database called the Page Frame Number database where it keeps track of all of the pages of physical memory on the system. In the context of this explanation, when a page (a 4 KB unit of memory for ×86 and ×64 systems) is moved from once place to another, nothing is physically moving. The address of the page is moved from one list to another.

When a computer running Microsoft Windows or Windows Server is booted up, all pages of physical memory are zeroed—meaning that all of the pages are filled with zeroes. Once zeroed, the pages are placed on the Zero page list ready to be used (Figure 8.16).

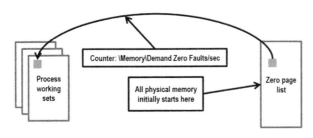

FIGURE 8.16

Physical memory starts off in the Zero page list.

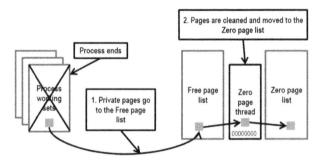

FIGURE 8.17

Deallocated private pages moved to the Free page list, zeroed, and then moved to the Zero page list.

When a process exits or deallocates memory, the private portion of the memory is moved to the Free page list. The data in these pages cannot be given to another process—it would be a security violation; therefore, the data in these pages must be wiped before the pages can be reused. A system process thread called the zero page writer runs at the lowest priority in the system, and its job is to watch the Free page list for pages that arrive there and then wipe them clean. Once wiped, the page is moved to the Zero page list (Figure 8.17).

When a page of memory is needed to go into the working set of a process, then it comes from either the Free page list or the Zero page list first depending on if the page will be completely overwritten or not. In any case, since memory on the Free page list and the Zero page list is readily available for reuse, it is the primary location for the system to get physical memory. Most tools combine both the Free page list and the Zero page list and just call it "Free" memory (Figure 8.18).

When a page of memory is trimmed from a working set (there are many reasons for this, but the most common is that the page is the least recently accessed page), the page is moved to either the Standby list or the Modified list. It is not moved to the Free page list because the process has not deallocated or freed the memory. As far as the process is concerned, it still has a virtual memory reference to the page.

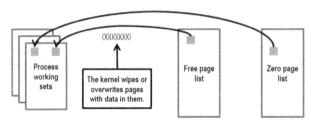

FIGURE 8.18

"Free" memory comes from the Free page list and the Zero page list.

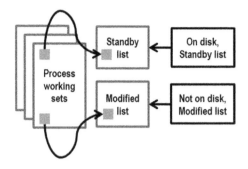

FIGURE 8.19

Pages trimmed from a working set are moved to the Standby list or the Modified list.

If the data in the page already exists on disk, then the page and its data are moved to the Standby list and used as disk cache. If the physical page's respective virtual address space page is accessed, then the page is moved from the Standby list and back into the working set of the process without the process knowing about this exchange—this is called a soft page fault. Otherwise, the page remains on the Standby list until needed to be reused (Figure 8.19).

If the data in the page does not already exist on disk, then the page and its data are moved to the Modified list. Pages on the Modified list are destined to be written to disk but might remain in memory depending on what it is. For example, if the system is configured with no page file, then the data will remain on the Modified list until a page file is created with enough space to handle it or if the virtual address space page associated to the physical page is accessed in which the page is referenced back into the respective working set (Figure 8.20).

When the system needs a physical memory page to give to a working set, it will attempt to get the page from the Free page list or the Zero page list depending on if the page will be completely overwritten by the process receiving it or not. It would be a security violation if the receiving process was able to get access to the existing data on the page. As a reminder, the sum of the Free page list and the Zero page list is often referred to as free memory since it is readily available for use.

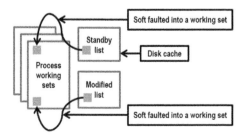

FIGURE 8.20

Pages accessed by the respective working set are faulted back into that working set.

```
Paging Lists (K)
Zeroed                  88,276
Free                         8
Modified                27,036
ModifiedNoWrite              4
Standby              9,829,120
    Priority 0               0
    Priority 1              16
    Priority 2       1,947,632
    Priority 3          42,808
    Priority 4         861,004
    Priority 5       6,907,456
    Priority 6              48
    Priority 7          70,156
PageFileModified         26,740
```

FIGURE 8.21

The physical memory paging lists as shown by Sysinternals Process Explorer.

If the Free page list and the Zero page list are depleted, then the system goes to the Standby list and will reuse the pages (not the data) in order of priority (Figure 8.21).

The Standby list contains pages of physical memory that has data that already exists on disk; therefore, it is used as disk cache. Some data is more important or more frequently accessed than others. So, when the system needs physical memory from the Standby list, it uses the pages in order of priority. Pages in priority 0 contain data with the lowest priority such as network file transfers, so these are used first followed by priority 1 data and so on. Priority 7 data is the highest priority data and is used last.

To demonstrate this behavior, I induced a leak of 8 GB of "touched" (committed and then accessed) memory; we can see that the pages in priority 0 through priority 4 were used first followed by a portion of priority 5. The data in priority 6 and priority 7 were not used (Figure 8.22).

As a reminder, the memory on the Standby list is already on disk and it is not in use. However, once the Zero, Free, and Standby page lists are depleted (this is a low-available memory condition), then the next page list to get memory from is the Modified list. The Modified list contains data that does not exist on disk yet, so in order to use that memory, it must be backed up to the disk first. This results in an increase in hard page faults, which can potentially overwhelm a disk if severe enough. Page faults are covered in more detail later in this chapter (Figure 8.23).

Finally, once the Zero, Free, Standby, and Modified page lists are depleted, then the last place that the system can go to get more physical memory is process working sets. When in this condition, the system will do what is known as a "globally working set trim." This means that all processes will undergo a working set trim so long as

Paging Lists (K)	
Zeroed	240
Free	20
Modified	90,836
ModifiedNoWrite	4
Standby	2,248,296
Priority 0	0
Priority 1	0
Priority 2	0
Priority 3	0
Priority 4	0
Priority 5	2,177,812
Priority 6	44
Priority 7	70,440
PageFileModified	90,804

FIGURE 8.22

The physical memory paging lists after an aggressive memory leak.

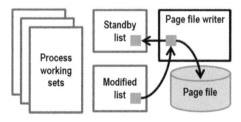

FIGURE 8.23

Pages on the Modified list must be written to disk before being moved to the Standby list.

there are no special circumstances such as a minimum working set or page locking that would make the memory nonpageable (Figure 8.24).

When a working set is trimmed, the page and the memory within it are moved out of the process' working set and into the Standby list (backed by disk) or the Modified list (not backed by disk) depending on if the data already exist on disk or not, and then, the page is wiped and reused in the procedure mentioned above. It is repeated until the system has more available memory.

DETECTING BAD PHYSICAL MEMORY

"Bad" physical memory is RAM modules that are not functioning properly. Modern versions of Windows and Windows Server have an internal consistency check that places pages that fail on the Bad page list. The Bad page list can be viewed using the Sysinternals tool, RAMMap. Again, RAMMap does not require installation. Just download and run it (Figure 8.25).

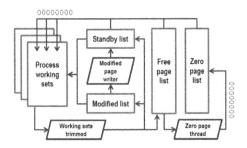

FIGURE 8.24

The life cycle of physical memory pages.

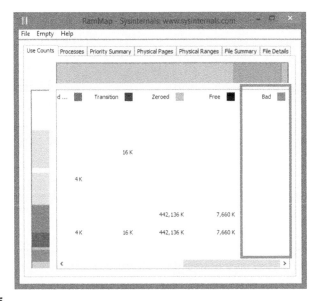

FIGURE 8.25

The Sysinternals RAMMap tool shows how much memory is on the Bad page list.

The internal consistency check isn't a guaranteed check of the reliability of physical memory pages. When a more thorough check is needed, Windows 7 and Windows Server 2008 R2 and later have a built-in physical memory diagnostics tool. Go to Control Panel, search for "memory," and then, select "Diagnose you computer's memory problems." This should start the Windows Memory Diagnostics Tool (Figure 8.26).

Once the system is rebooted, it will automatically start the Windows Memory Diagnostics Tool (in a DOS-like mode), and then, Windows will automatically restart the computer again and display the results when you log on (Figure 8.27).

The results might look something like what is in Figure 8.28.

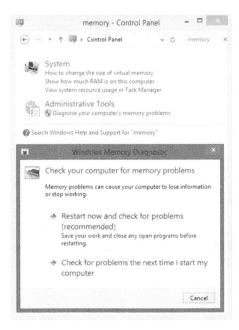

FIGURE 8.26

The Windows Memory Diagnostics Tool is built into the operating system.

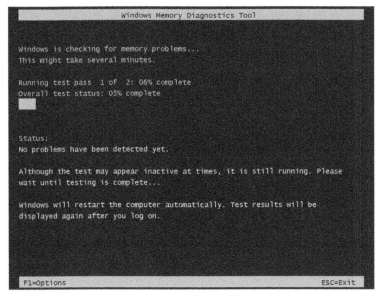

FIGURE 8.27

The Windows Memory Diagnostics Tool running.

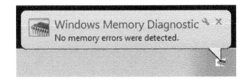

FIGURE 8.28

The results of running the Windows Memory Diagnostics Tool.

For systems running Windows or Windows Server earlier than Windows 7 or Windows Server 2008 R2, there is an ISO image that can be burned to a CD-ROM or floppy disk. The tool is relatively old, and I was only able to find a download for it at CNet. com at http://download.cnet.com/Memory-Diagnostic/3000-2094_4-10629429.html. Since it is relatively hard to find, I have placed it on my personal Microsoft OneDrive at http://aka.ms/clinth, and then, go to Tools. Download and burn windiag.iso to a CD-ROM, and then, restart the computer with the system set to book from that media.

PAGE FAULTS

A page fault is an error condition that simply means "not in working set" (not in RAM). When a virtual address space page is accessed and there is no physical memory page associated with it, then a page fault occurs. If a physical page is associated with the virtual address space page when accessed, then no page fault occurs because there is a page in the working set (Figure 8.29).

TIP

Page faults are often associated with reading and writing to a page file on disk, but this is only one of many operations that are used to resolve a page fault.

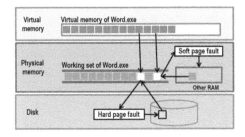

FIGURE 8.29

Soft page faults are resolved from physical memory, while hard page faults are resolved from disk.

If a page fault is resolved from elsewhere in physical memory such as the Standby list or Modified list, then it is called a "soft" page fault. These kinds of faults are relatively "cheap" and of no significant consequence since the time to retrieve the data was in nanoseconds.

If a page fault is resolved from disk, then it will take much longer to retrieve depending on the performance of the storage device. A high number of hard page faults even if consisting happening is not necessarily a problem. Hard page faults are a normal function of the operating system. All it means is that the data is coming from disk.

TIP

Hard page faults mean disk access that may or may not involve a page file.

The following could be the cause of consistent hard page faults:

APPLICATIONS READING IMAGE FILES

When an application starts, no amount of physical memory will help. It has to read the portions of the DLLs and Exes (DLLs and Exes are known as image files) needed to get the application up and running. The DLLs and Exes are fully loaded in virtual address space, but only the portions of those files that are actually needed are loaded into physical memory on an ongoing basis (Figure 8.30).

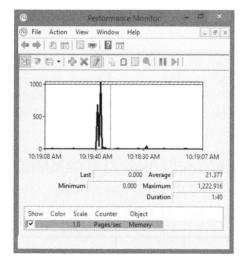

FIGURE 8.30

Over 1000 hard page faults when opening an application.

For example, when I open Microsoft Word for the first time since booting my laptop, the system has 1222 hard page faults (\Memory\Pages/sec measures the number of hard page faults per second) just to read the portions of the DLLs and Exes needed to get it up and running. As I use Microsoft Word, more of the DLLs and Exes are hard page faulted into the working set of word.exe. Again, there is no page file involved in this. As a matter of fact, this particular system is not running a page file.

MEMORY-MAPPED FILES

Many applications like Microsoft Word open files as a memory-mapped file. This means that the document is loaded into the virtual address space of the process and accessed as if it was memory. As the document is being read [document] page by [document] page, the respective virtual address space pages (4 KB memory unit) are being accessed, and since those portions of the file are not in the working set (physical memory) of word.exe yet, a hard page fault is used to read the data from disk and place it in the working set.

TIP
It is relatively common to see constant hard page faults per second due to backup software and/or antivirus software reading files as memory-mapped files.

PAGE FILE READS AND WRITES

A read or write operation to a page file is a hard page fault since it is accessing the disk, and the only "real" way of knowing if a page file is actually being "read from" is to get a file IO trace. This can be collected and/or viewed with tools such as the Microsoft Performance Recorder/Analyzer, Microsoft Resource Monitor, or Sysinternals Process Monitor. Keep in mind that the performance counter \Memory\Page Writes/sec measures only page file writes, but \Memory\Page Reads/sec includes both page file reads and other hard page faults such as memory-mapped files.

Chapter 7 "Page Files" has more information about how to accurately measure page file reads and writes in the "Tracking page file reads and writes" section.

HARD PAGE FAULTS AND DISK PERFORMANCE

In the counter description of \Memory\Pages/sec, it says, "This counter is a primary indicator of the kinds of faults that cause system-wide delays." This statement is accurate, but only when the hard page faults are frequently waiting on overwhelmed disks ... which the counter description fails to mention.

I often see documents referring to a threshold of 100 or more on \Memory\Pages/sec. I used to laugh at this because I know most disk drives can do far more than 400 KB of data transfers per second, but in retrospect 100 IOs per second could be considered significant load. Again, it depends on if the disk is overwhelmed or not.

If a system is constantly at 100 hard page faults per second, then it translates to 400 KB per second since standard page sizes are 4 KB on both ×86 (32-bit) and ×64 (64-bit) versions of Windows and Windows Server. Assuming all of the hard page faults target the same disk, then generally speaking, at 4 KB IO sizes, most modern disk drives can do more than 100 random write operations per second with more than 1 MB per second of data written.

Figure 8.31 shows that a 7200 RPM disk drive can do 72 MB/s at 1 MB IO sizes, but it doesn't show the performance of 4 KB IO sizes.

In Figure 8.32, I demonstrate a constant load of random write IO requests at 4 KB IO sizes to simulate hard page faults on a 7200 RPM disk drive. It shows that it can do

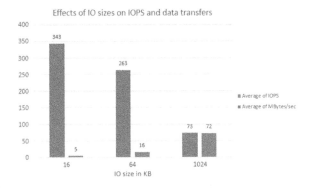

FIGURE 8.31

The effects of IO sizes on IOPS and data transfers.

LogicalDisk	D:
% Disk Read Time	0.000
% Disk Time	194.448
% Disk Write Time	194.448
% Free Space	49.060
% Idle Time	0.000
Avg. Disk Bytes/Read	0.000
Avg. Disk Bytes/Transfer	4,096.000
Avg. Disk Bytes/Write	4,096.000
Avg. Disk Queue Length	1.944
Avg. Disk Read Queue Length	0.000
Avg. Disk sec/Read	0.000
Avg. Disk sec/Transfer	0.006
Avg. Disk sec/Write	0.006
Avg. Disk Write Queue Length	1.944
Current Disk Queue Length	2.000
Disk Bytes/sec	1,373,026.623
Disk Read Bytes/sec	0.000
Disk Reads/sec	0.000
Disk Transfers/sec	335.212
Disk Write Bytes/sec	1,373,026.623
Disk Writes/sec	335.212
Free Megabytes	149,753.000
Split IO/Sec	0.000

FIGURE 8.32

Logical disk counters of a 7200 RPM disk under 4 KB sized IO.

about 335 write operations at 4 KB IO sizes (random IO) at roughly 1.3 MB/sec. This is a surprising result. This means that a threshold of 100 pages/sec (1/3rd of the writes/sec we are seeing) has some merit, "but" it is assuming that all of the hard page faults are being resolved from the same disk, that the disk is a single 7200 RPM drive, and that there is no other IO occurring on that disk. That is just too much to assume. Therefore, when dealing with hard page fault performance, go back to the basics of disk performance looking to see if the disk queue has outstanding IO (not how long the queue is, but "if" it has constant work to do) and if the IO response times are acceptable (generally under 15 ms on average) with the IO size considered—larger IO sizes produce much higher data transfer rates but increases response times.

Therefore, getting back to the question on hand, is 400 KB per second a problem? Are we only taking hard page faults into consideration? What if the disk is already overwhelmed by other IO requests? What if the logical disk actually has eight solid-state drives behind it? What about IO request sizes greater than 4 KB?

This is why you must "know thy disk" and how it performs under these conditions. This problem is difficult enough when just dealing with a single disk array. Imagine trying to deal with this if it was on a SAN where the performance is not consistent. This is why when dealing with constant hard page faults, you have to go back to the basics of disk performance analysis discussed in Chapter 3 "Storage" to see if the disks are overwhelmed.

In summary, we still can't put a static threshold on hard page faults due to the greatly varying disk hardware, disk sharing, and other IO occurring on the disk(s), but it should be considered when identifying the cause of the IO demand. With that said, we can safely say that if there are less than 100 hard page faults per second, then it is not significant and does not warrant more investigation. Thank you to Ben Christenbury for reminding me of this fact.

SIZING PHYSICAL MEMORY

Okay, so now, we are at the money question—how much physical memory does a system need? If you have read everything in the book up to this point, then you should know by now that this requires constant monitoring of available memory and adjustment after the system is in production use. See the "identifying low available physical memory" sections earlier in this chapter for more information. In addition, proper physical memory sizing is subjective since the goal might be to maximize the physical memory efficiency or to get the best performance out of the system by reducing paging. In the context of this section, I will try to strike a balance of efficiency and performance.

What if we need to provision 100 new servers that will be running a new software package? We have no existing data to size the physical memory. In these cases, it's just a shot in the dark. Start off with more physical memory than what the system is expected to need, and then, adjust it from there based on the amount of minimum available memory after the system has been under heavy load. Specifically, monitor

\Memory\Available MBytes for values of less than 10% of physical memory usable by the system. Keep in mind that the larger the Standby list (part of available memory), the less often that the system will need to go to disk.

Using Free memory (sum of the Free page list and the Zero page list) minus the physical memory usable by the system might sound like a good starting point, but once the system has accessed the disk enough, the system should have little to no free memory regardless of the amount of physical memory installed. For example, if a system has 16 GB or 256 GB of physical memory installed, it could still be at 4 GB of free memory given identical working conditions. The difference would simply be the size of the Standby list, which is acting as disk cache. Certainly with 256 GB of physical memory installed, it will be accessing the disk less often than with 16 GB of physical memory installed, but the disks might be able to handle it. With that said, if the system has been up and running for weeks and been through heavy load and "still" has free memory (this is very unlikely by the way), then that is the amount of physical memory that can be safely removed without effecting the performance of the system.

What about transforming existing physical servers to be virtual machines? In this situation, it is easier to size the physical memory because we have some data to work with. After the system has been in heavy use and has been up and running long enough to be a proper profile of the regular usage of the system (that is the assumption with a VM that has been running for awhile), then identify the minimum amount of available physical memory observed. If the amount of available memory is less than 10% of the installed memory, then increase the physical memory size until it is at or greater than 10% of the installed memory. Likewise, if the available memory is greater than 10% of the installed memory, then decrease it until it is less than 20%.

A quick and simple "future-proofing" technique that I like to use is to take the peak system committed memory usage (\Memory\Committed Bytes) and use this as the new physical memory size as an adjustment to an existing system or as the proposed amount for the next version of hardware that the system will be running on. Keep in mind that the peak system committed memory usage is "not" measuring physical memory usage (it measures all of the "in use" and promised physical memory and page file), but it represents the potential usage. This means that it will have some extra padding for increased system usage. This assumes that the page file sizing techniques discussed in Chapter 7 "Page Files" are also being followed.

READYBOOST

The more physical memory installed on a system, the more potential disk cache it has. This is why the more physical memory installed, the better the performance. For systems that are regularly low on available memory and have a relatively slow disk and where it is impractical to increase the physical memory installed, then ReadyBoost can help.

ReadyBoost is a feature of Windows Vista, Windows Server 2008, and later that uses removable flash drives as disk cache to improve read performance. In other words, it is more or less an extension of the Standby list disk cache discussed earlier in this chapter. This means that the data is already backed by disk.

According to the article "Understand ReadyBoost and whether it will Speed Up your System" at http://technet.microsoft.com/en-us/magazine/ff356869.aspx, there are three criteria that the external media must support:

- Capacity of at least 256 MB, with at least 64 KB of free space
- At least a 2.5 MB/sec throughput for 4 KB random reads
- At least 1.75 MB/sec throughput for 1 MB random writes

ReadyBoost is often not used on systems with a solid-state hard drive (SSD), since it is faster than the removable media.

In addition, according to the article, ReadyBoost provides the most significant performance improvement under the following conditions:

- The computer has a slow hard disk drive. Computers with a primary hard disk Windows Experience Index subscore lower than 4.0 will see the most significant improvements.
- The flash storage provides fast, random, nonsequential reads. Sequential read speed is less important.
- The flash storage is connected by a fast bus. Typically, USB memory card readers are not sufficiently fast. However, connecting flash memory to an internal memory card reader might provide sufficient performance.

If you are considering this option, then I recommend using removable media that does not protrude from the system case such as most SD or MicroSD cards. If the media protrudes, there is a higher risk of it being broken off and damaged.

To use ReadyBoost, simply plug in the removable flash media and wait for the Autoplay options. If the media meets the criteria above, then it will offer "Dedicate this device to ReadyBoost."

Go to the article "Turn ReadyBoost on or off for a storage device" at http://windows.microsoft.com/en-us/windows/turn-readyboost-on-off-storage-device#1TC=windows-7 for more information on enabling and disabling ReadyBoost.

PREFETCH

As shown earlier in this chapter, the startup sequence of an application (processes) can be disk-intensive. This is because the process needs to read the portions of DLLs, EXEs (or other code files), and data from disk to be functional. To improve the startup time of the process for the next time, the logical prefetcher built into Windows XP and Windows Server 2003 and later profiles the first 10 seconds of the startup sequence and stores the data in a single, defragmented file under %windir%\Prefetch.

According to the "Windows Internals," 5th edition book, the file's name is the name of the application to which the trace applies followed by a dash and the hexadecimal representation of a hash of the file's path and ending with a PF file extension. An example of a file might be the following:

CALC.EXE-0FE8F3A9.pf

SUPERFETCH

Superfetch is a Windows service (the short name is SysMain) that preloads data from disk to the Standby list (disk cache) in physical memory. The idea is that if you start Microsoft Outlook every weekday at 9 AM, then Superfetch will preload the data needed to launch Outlook so that when you actually start Outlook, it will load much faster than it would had if it had to read it from disk.

With that said, Superfetch is often one of the reasons why the disk is grinding away when there is little activity on the system. It is simply taking advantage of the idle time. Therefore, if you are trying to avoid disk IO, then consider disabling this service.

SYSTEM CACHE

The system cache and the Standby list are often thought of as the same thing since they are both referred to as "cache" and they are closely interrelated. With that said, one has "in use" memory and the other does not. In short, it is perfectly fine and desirable for most of physical memory to be on the Standby list, but not good if the system cache working set is consuming most of physical memory.

As explained earlier in this chapter, the Standby list contains memory that used to be part of a process' working set or preloaded by the logical prefetcher. Memory on the Standby list is available meaning that the page containing the data can be wiped and reused without incurring a disk IO since the data is already backed by disk. It's actually best to have no "free" memory so long as there is plenty of memory on the Standby list because these data can potentially be reused avoiding a disk IO. The Standby list size can be measured by the performance counter **Memory\Standby Cache Normal Priority Bytes**.

The purpose of the system cache (**Memory\System Cache Resident Bytes**) is to buffer updates to the file system allowing more than one process to read and write to the same portion of a file at the same time. The system cache contains the most up-to-date version of the data. The data is considered "dirty" since it is not yet backed by the disk. The point of keeping this data in physical memory is because if the same data is updated frequently, then only the latest bits of data needs to be written to disk versus every update in sequence resulting in less disk IO. Since the data is not yet backed by disk, memory in the system cache is in its own working set and is considered "in use"—meaning that it takes away from the available memory of the system. With that said, it does not count toward the system commit charge—meaning that the system can promise away the memory that the system cache's working set is currently occupying similar to someone "squatting" on a house that they don't own. When the system is low on available memory, then it will be actively purged to disk to make more memory available.

The working set of the system cache is limited to 900 MB on 32-bit versions of Windows and Windows Server and 1 TB on 64-bit versions of Windows and Windows Server. This means that it can become quite large on 64-bit systems and therefore needs to be monitored closely if the system becomes low on available memory.

The working set of the system cache should not cause any real problems on Windows 8, Windows Server 2012 or later there were some system cache "runaway" issues on 64-bit versions of Windows Server 2008. With that said, if the system cache's working set (\Memory\System Cache Resident Bytes) consumes a significant amount of physical memory when the system is low on available memory, then the size of the system cache working set can be reduced using the Microsoft Windows Dynamic Cache Service, which is a free download at http://www.microsoft.com/en-us/download/details.aspx?id=9258.

Inconsequently, you can temporarily empty the system cache working set using Sysinternals RAMMap or Sysinternals CacheSet tools, but these effects are only temporary.

TOO MUCH PHYSICAL MEMORY AND POWER CONSIDERATIONS

Ever wonder if a system has too much physical memory? This is actually a lot easier to answer than the question of not enough physical memory. Just monitor the amount of free memory on the system. As mentioned earlier in this chapter, "free" memory pages contain no useful data and are just waiting to be used. This is the amount of physical memory that can be removed and incur no performance degradation.

Free memory can be monitored using Task Manager, Resource Monitor, the performance counter **\Memory\Free & Zero Page List Bytes**, and many other memory-related tools.

Before you start yanking gigabytes of memory from your systems, there is a catch. Keep in mind that the more that the disk is used, the more data that will be in use or on the Standby list. Having a large Standby list means a large disk cache, which allows the system to avoid going to disk since it is already in physical memory. This means wait awhile before yanking the memory to see if the system eventually uses the free memory and increases the size of the Standby list as it goes. In theory, the contents of the entire file system could eventually be in physical memory.

CONCLUSION

This chapter covered the concepts of physical memory (RAM), how to monitor physical memory, and how to troubleshoot it.

Network

9

INTRODUCTION

This chapter covers how to identify poor network performance conditions using various tools and techniques. It is not intended to be a comprehensive guide to network performance analysis.

Bandwidth is the amount of potential data that a network adapter can send or receive per second and it is often the single consideration when judging the performance of a network, but other factors such as latency, packet loss, collisions, retransmissions, and hardware should all be considered. One of my customers had a poorly performing wireless network with frequent connection losses. I ran a wireless network application that showed that there was another, very close, wireless access point on the same 2.4 GHz channel—a visiting sales team had brought it in. Once identified, we asked the sales team to use a different channel and order was restored.

I often find that the 5 GHz wireless band is wide open, so I generally recommend using it instead of the often excessively overlapping 2.4 GHz band. My neighborhood is teaming with 2.4 GHz networks where there is no channel that is clear. Once I moved all of my network devices to 5 GHz, all is good now . . . especially my wife's TV watching experience.

INITIAL INDICATORS

There are quite a few performance counters related to networking, but few offer an indication of a network performance condition. On Windows XP, Windows Server 2003, and earlier, a threshold value of 2 or more for **\Network Interface(*)\Output Queue Length** served for years as the initial indicator of a potential problem. This counter measures the number of network packets waiting to be placed on the network. There are many reasons why packets can queue up on the network adapter such as jitter, packet loss, or latency, so this serves only as an initial indicator that more investigation is needed.

Unfortunately, the **\Network Interface(*)\Output Queue Length** performance counter is nonfunctional on Windows Vista, Windows Server 2008, and later. This is due to the network driver architecture changes. The counter always returns 0 in all conditions, so avoid using it on those systems as it will give a false sense of security.

Windows Performance Analysis Field Guide. http://dx.doi.org/10.1016/B978-0-12-416701-8.00009-0

Fortunately, Windows 7, Windows Server 2008 R2, and later ship with a version of Resource Monitor that provides network latency, packet loss, and other details of each TCP/IP session—far more detail than has ever been possible. Really cool stuff indeed! Unfortunately, this data is not available in the form of performance counters. In addition, the Windows Performance Analyzer (WPA) tool does not have a parser for network-related ETW data. In summary, there are no performance counters that can be used as an initial indicator of a network performance problem on Windows Vista, Windows Server 2008, and later. Use network performance related tools for now.

MEASURING THE SLOWEST NODE AND BLACK HOLE ROUTERS

There are no performance counters for measuring network performance outside of the local system, so tools are needed to identify a slow TCP/IP node such as a network switch or router.

When a TCP/IP session is established, the maximum packet size is established, but when the packet is routed through a different path than intended and if the packet is too large for the router, then it is discarded. The router that discarded the packet is called a "black hole router" since the packet will never make it to its destination. This condition can be detected by running Ping.exe with increasingly larger packet sizes to see the largest size that makes it through. If the maximum packet size is smaller than what is needed for network services to function, then investigation is needed.

Ping.exe is a command-line tool that is part of the operating system and provides data on the network round-trip latency of a single ping packet. It is most commonly used to determine if another system is on the network (Figure 9.1).

Packet loss and latency between two systems are important when it comes to network performance since either of these conditions can result in poor application performance. The command-line tool, PathPing.exe, is part of the operating system and was first introduced in Windows 2000 Workstation and Windows Server 2000. This

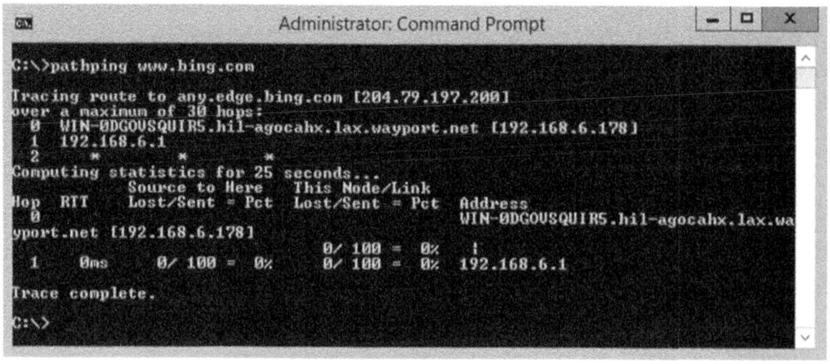

FIGURE 9.1

A PathPing.exe trace to www.bing.com.

tool traces the route (all of the network nodes along the way) and sends a burst of 100 ping requests to each node along the way. It calculates the packet loss and average latency for each node. This is very helpful when trying to determine if there is a bad node along the path. In addition, this helps with determining where there are slow (high-latency) connections that can have a significant impact on network applications such as international web applications.

MONITORING NETWORK UTILIZATION USING PERFORMANCE MONITOR

It's important to ensure that network adapters are operating at the bandwidth (connection speed) they were intended. If not, performance may be degraded. The performance counter **\Network Interface(*)\Connection Bandwidth** is the current connection speed that the network adapter negotiated with a wired network switch or wireless access point. In a case I had a few years ago, a 1 Gbps network adapter negotiated a 10 Mbps half-duplex connection with a wired network switch. This caused the entire banking application to perform much slower than expected. Once we forced it to be 1 Gbps full duplex on both the NIC and the switch port, the solution's performance was dramatically faster. This doesn't mean that this works in all situations, so be sure to refer to your network interface card (NIC) and network device documentation and support services for the best configuration (Figure 9.2).

The following performance counters are related to bandwidth and utilization:

- **\Network Interface(*)\Current Bandwidth** is an estimate of the current bandwidth of the network interface in bits per second (bps). The value should be what is expected—meaning a 1 Gbps connection should be at 1,000,000,000. Keep in mind that network teaming might make this value double the expected value.
- **\Network Interface(*)\Bytes Sent/sec** is the rate at which bytes are sent over each network adapter, including framing characters. If the NIC is full duplex, then this value can go up to the current bandwidth, but keep in mind that current bandwidth is in bit and Bytes Sent/sec is in bytes.
- **\Network Interface(*)\Bytes Received/sec** is the rate at which bytes are received over each network adapter, including framing characters. If the NIC is

Network Interface	Intel[R] 82579LM Gigabit Network Connection
Bytes Received/sec	128,120.117
Bytes Sent/sec	16,583.353
Bytes Total/sec	144,703.471
Current Bandwidth	100,000,000.000
Output Queue Length	0.000

FIGURE 9.2

Common performance counters used in network troubleshooting.

full duplex, then this value can go up to the current bandwidth, but keep in mind that current bandwidth is in bit and Bytes Sent/sec is in bytes.

- **\Network Interface(*)\Bytes Total/sec** is the rate at which bytes are sent and received over each network adapter, including framing characters. Bytes Total/sec is a sum of Bytes Received/sec and Bytes Sent/sec. If the NIC is simplex, then this value can go up to the current bandwidth, but keep in mind that current bandwidth is in bit and Bytes Sent/sec is in bytes.

The percentage of network utilization (the ratio of usage to maximum) is helpful in determining if the network adapter is overwhelmed, but keep in mind that this is only measurable between the NIC and the network device (switch, router, WAP) that it is connected to.

Although Task Manager and Resource Monitor both provide a % Network Utilization chart, there is no % network utilization performance counter. Therefore, we have to calculate it manually using **\Network Interface(*)\Bytes Received/sec**, **\Network Interface(*)\Bytes Sent/sec**, and **\Network Interface(*)\Current Bandwidth** for full duplex NICs. For half-duplex NICs, use **\Network Interface(*)\Bytes Total/sec** and **\Network Interface(*)\Current Bandwidth**.

Use the following formulas to calculate the percent network utilization using performance counters:

% Network utilization for full duplex Bytes Sent = ((Bytes Sent/sec * 8)/Current Bandwidth) * 100

% Network utilization for full duplex Bytes Received = ((Bytes Received/sec * 8) /Current Bandwidth) * 100

% Network utilization for simplex Bytes Total = ((Bytes Total/sec * 8)/Current Bandwidth) * 100

NOTE

The PAL tool at http://pal.codeplex.com automatically applies this formula and generates a fake counter called **\Network Interface(*)\% Network Utilization**, charts it, and creates alerts if greater than 30%.

It is difficult to place a threshold on % network utilization simply because it is localized to the NIC. For example, a sustained value of over 30% could be nothing if doing a transfer over the local area network or significant if doing a network transfer over a wide area network connection.

MONITORING NETWORK UTILIZATION USING TASK MANAGER

Task Manager is often the first tool to bring up when a system is running slow since it is already part of the operating system. Windows 8 and Windows Server 2012 introduced a redesigned Task Manager that features resource usage of all of the major resources. The Performance tab has a minichart on the left for each of the network

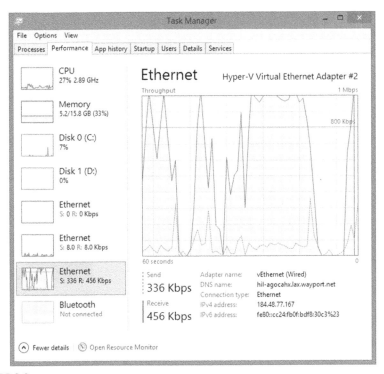

FIGURE 9.3

Task Manager showing Ethernet details.

adapters and provides more details of its usage when selected. This really isn't anything new though. The Task Manager in Windows Server 2008 R2 has a Networking tab that shows similar information (Figure 9.3).

Keep in mind that Task Manager only shows the amount of data being sent or received per second and does not show network bottlenecks outside of the system such as a slow web site or packet loss. In my experience, chattiness (the number of network round trips) and latency (the amount of time it takes a packet to make a round trip), not utilization, are the most common network bottlenecks. Thankfully, the version of Resource Monitor that ships with Windows 7, Windows Server 2008 R2, and later provides packet loss and latency of active TCP/IP connections.

MONITORING NETWORK UTILIZATION USING RESOURCE MONITOR

Microsoft Resource Monitor was first introduced in Windows Vista and Windows Server 2008, but features such as TCP Connections was first introduced in Windows 7 and Windows Server 2008 R2. It provides live data on the processes,

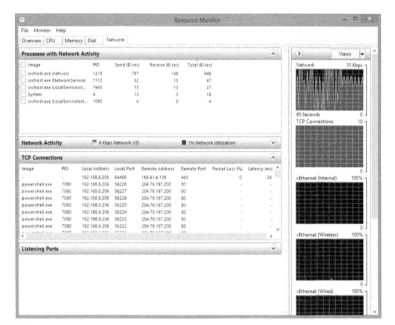

FIGURE 9.4

The Network tab of Resource Monitor.

IP addresses, ports, packet loss, and latency of current TCP connections. This data is coming from ETW data—not from performance counters (Figure 9.4).

Similar to Task Manager, each network adapter has a corresponding chart on the right side showing the overall utilization. As mentioned earlier, network problems can manifest in the form of packet loss and/or latency, so it is important to look at all aspects.

To filter on one or more specific processes, use the checkboxes next to the process list.

DETECTING NIC DUPLEX SETTINGS

Most network adapters are set to an autodetect speed and duplex setting by default. If the NIC negotiates a poor speed and duplex setting, then the performance can be greatly hindered. Unfortunately, the duplex setting of a NIC is unusually difficult to get programmatically—it is not a part of the Win32_NetworkAdapterConfiguration class in WMI. This is because this setting is unique to the driver manufacturer such as **HKEY_LOCAL_MACHINE\SYSTEM\CurrentControlSet\Control\Class\{4d36e972-e325-11ce-bfc1-08002be10318}\0002*SpeedDuplex** in the case of my Intel(R) 82579LM gigabit network adapter. If you know the registry location of the network driver, then this data could be retrieved remotely using the WMI registry provider (RegProv) in the root\default namespace.

Here is an example:

```
$wmiRegProv = [wmiclass]'\\.\root\default:StdRegprov'
$HKLM = 2147483650
$sKey  =  'SYSTEM\CurrentControlSet\Control\Class\{4d36e972-e325-11ce-
bfc1-08002be10318}\0002'
$wmiRegProv.GetStringValue($HKLM, $sKey, '*SpeedDuplex') | Select sValue
```

The period (.) in the first line can be replaced with the computer name, DNS name, or IP address of a remote computer in which your logged-in account has administrator rights and DCOM connectivity (Figure 9.5).

The result is the speed/duplex setting. In this case, a value of 0 is "autonegotiation" based on the enumeration documentation at http://msdn.microsoft.com/library/ff548866.

CHATTINESS AND LATENCY

One of my pet peeves is a web application that does frequent and unnecessary round trips to the web server. The round trips have a latency (delay) for the request to reach the server and for the web application (client) to receive it. Even if no data is being transferred, the act of just making a request significantly slows down the application waiting on it. This is why testing network applications over a slow network is important.

I once dealt with a web application where every click on the form resulted in a round trip to the web server. It made the application very tedious and time-consuming to use. In many cases, a simple HTTP trace with Internet Explorer's F12 Developer Tools can show this behavior and help the developer understand where to make optimizations.

My point is to be aware of the number of round trips that any network application is doing and try to reduce them as much as reasonably possible. Your low-bandwidth, high-latency users will thank you.

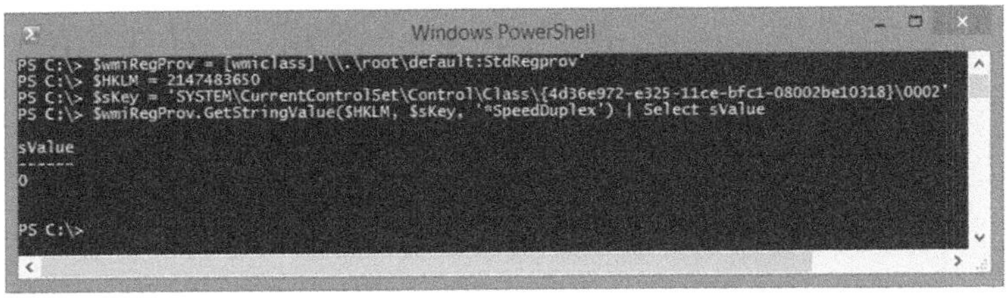

FIGURE 9.5

An example of using Powershell and WMI to access a registry key.

CONCLUSION

If a deeper investigation is needed into network analysis, then consider using network tools such as Microsoft Network Monitor. Microsoft Network Monitor 3.4 can be downloaded from http://www.microsoft.com/download/details.aspx?id=4865. In this chapter, I showed various ways of monitoring network performance. This chapter was not intended to be a comprehensive network performance analysis guide, but it should help with initially identifying when deeper network analysis is needed.

Processor

10

INTRODUCTION

A system's performance is often related to the number of processors and their clock speed, but more often than not, other resources such as disk are more often the most overwhelmed resource. This is the reason why the processor chapter is after the storage, memory, and network chapters.

When the processors are overwhelmed, it is most often due to one or more threads that are executing code. This means that any changes to make it more efficient will require changes to code. Looking at call stacks can be difficult and often leads to debugging deeper than this book will cover. Deep debugging is covered in the "Advanced Windows Debugging" book by Mario Hewardt. With that said, this chapter will introduce how to identify the processes and thread stacks consuming the most processor time.

Throughout this chapter and book, the words "processor" and "CPU" will be used synonymously.

IDENTIFYING HIGH PROCESSOR USAGE USING TASK MANAGER

Arguably, the easiest way to identify a high processor condition is to open Task Manager (Ctrl-Shift-Esc) and navigate to the Performance tab. If any processor is at 75% or more of sustained usage, then it's worth investigating the threads and owning processes consuming those processors.

The Performance tab shows the overall processor usage or processor usage of each logical processor. A logical processor could be a socket, a core, or a simultaneous multithreading (SMT) processor such as Hyper-Threading (HT) or Clustered MultiThreading (CMT) processor. This means that a two-socket system each with four cores and SMT enabled might have 16 logical processors shown in Task Manager.

One of the features that I like about Task Manager is how it can show kernel time (also known as privileged time) because it helps with directing my troubleshooting efforts. High kernel mode usage might indicate a busy or faulty driver, while high user mode might indicate busy or poorly written application code. On Windows 7 and Windows Server 2008 R2 and earlier, select the Performance tab, and then click

View, Show kernel times. This will add a red line to the processor usage that shows how much time is being spent in kernel mode. On Windows 8 and Windows Server 2012 and later, select the Performance tab, select CPU, right-click on the CPU chart, and then select **Show kernel times**. The difference between the overall usage and the kernel line (a red line or different shading depending on the operating system) represents the amount of user mode time that is related to application code. The analyses of high kernel mode processor usage and high user mode processor usage are both covered in more detail later in this chapter.

Next, click on the Details tab (Processes tab on Windows 7 and Windows Server 2012 and earlier) to see statistical data on each of the running processes. Sort by CPU by clicking the CPU column until it is in descending order (highest to lowest) to determine which process is using the most processor time. If the process name is not recognized, then try to identify it by right-clicking the process name and selecting **Open file location** on Windows 8 or Windows Server 2012 or later. On earlier versions of Windows and Windows Server, the executable file of the process can be identified using a file system search or by searching for it online by searching on the process name. Once the process's executable file is located in the file system, right-click and go to Properties of it to learn more. In addition, consider using the Sysinternals tool, Sigcheck, to verify the digital signature of the executable.

If the process has the name, svchost.exe, then it is hosting one or more Windows services. This can make it difficult to identify which service is consuming processor time. The services running within the process can be identified by right-clicking the svchost.exe and then selecting **Go to Service(s)**. This will automatically show the Services tab, and all of the services that are hosted by the svchost.exe will be highlighted.

Unfortunately, other tools are needed for further troubleshooting. With that said, Task Manager can be used to change the base thread priority of a process and/or change the processor affinity of a process. These techniques can help subdue a high CPU process.

SEARCHING THE FILE SYSTEM FOR A PROCESS'S EXECUTABLE FILE

Arguably the easiest way to identify the executable file of a process is to run the following Powershell command: `get-process | select Name, ID, Path | ft -Autosize`. This returns the process name (Name), process id (ID), and the path to the executable (Path). To search the file system for a process's executable file, open Task Manager, go to the Details tab, right-click on the target process, and select Open file location. Once found, navigate to the file using Windows Explorer, and then go to Properties of the file. This should show more information about the executable.

TIP

As a best practice, consider verifying the digital signature of the executable by using the Sysinternals tool Sigcheck.exe. This will check if the manufacturer specified on the executable file is valid. A "not verified" digital signature means that the executable cannot be verified and could indicate malware or the manufacturer failed to obtain a digital signature.

If the properties of the executable file don't provide enough information about it, then consider searching the Internet using a search engine such as Bing (http://www.bing.com). Try to use keywords from the executable's properties in the search. Also, consider using Sysinternals tool, Strings.exe, to show any words that can be used to identify it. According to Mark Russinovich, malware might contain a suspicious URL that can provide a clue to its origin.

In addition, the Sysinternals tool, Process Explorer, can be used to check the signature of running processes against VirusTotal.com, which might help with identifying it.

IDENTIFYING HIGH PROCESSOR USAGE USING PERFORMANCE MONITOR

The processor-related performance counters are helpful when monitoring processor usage on one or more systems, but not so good at identifying the processes and threads involved. This is because Performance Monitor (Perfmon) does not dynamically add counter instances as it goes. For example, if I add the counter instances of **\Process(*)\% Processor Time**, induce a high processor condition by starting up CpuStres.exe, then CpuStres will not show up on the chart. I would have to re-add the counter instances of **\Process(*)\% Processor Time** in order to see it. There are better tools such as Task Manager, Resource Monitor, and Sysinternals Process Explorer that are much better at showing the current/live processes consuming the most processor time. With that said, if a binary (*.blg) or SQL counter log is recorded (TSV and CSV log file formats do not record counter instances that come and go), then we can see all of the process instances.

Be aware that the instances of **\Process(*)\% Processor Time** show all of the processor usage across all of the threads of the process. This means that any single process can consume up to 100% times the number of processors so long as it has enough threads to keep more than one processor busy. For example, an IIS worker process (w3wp.exe) is multithreaded and can consume up to 800% processor time on a system with eight logical processors. Alternatively, a single-threaded process can only consume up to 100% of a single logical processor. The single thread might run on a single processor or it might be evenly distributed across processors depending on the operating system.

Overall processor usage can be measured using **\Processor(*)\\% Processor Time**. This counter measures the percentage of time that the processor was executing a thread or in a running state (an important distinction when working with virtual processors on a virtual machine, VM). Next, add the **\Processor(*)\\% Privileged Time** counter instances to see how much time is being spent in kernel mode in relation to overall processor usage. If the majority of the time is being spent in kernel mode, then a lot of time is being spent in drivers or other kernel-related activities. If a processor is spending more than 10% of its time in **\Processor(*)\\% DPC Time** or **\Processor(*)\\% Interrupt Time**, then there might be a high amount of usage or a problem with a driver or piece of hardware. Go to section "Capturing and analyzing processor interrupts and DPC events using the Windows Performance Toolkit" later in this chapter for more steps on this condition. If the majority of time is being spent in user mode time (\Processor(*)\\% User Time), then it is application code. Go to section "Capturing and analyzing user mode processor events using the Windows Performance Toolkit" later in this chapter for this condition.

Next, the threads of the process can be tracked using Performance Monitor, but you must be careful. First, just like the Process instances, the instances are not dynamically added when viewing them live. They would need to be re-added again and again, which is inconvenient and tedious. Therefore, it is best to record them in a binary (*.blg) or SQL counter log. Unfortunately, a system can easily support thousands of threads and this would bloat the counter log considerably. Therefore, only record the Thread counter object for short periods of time. The benefit to recording threads is we can view the processor usage and get the thread ID (TID) using **\Thread(*)\\ID Thread**. The TID can be very helpful when the counter log's recording corresponds to a debug dump of the process. In the debug dump, we can go to the TID and get the call stack to see what it was doing at that time. A call stack is the modules and function calls that a thread is executing and can be very valuable to the developer of the code.

IDENTIFYING HIGH PROCESSOR USAGE USING RESOURCE MONITOR

Resource Monitor is a tool built into Windows and Windows Server that provides more detail about processor usage than Task Manager. It was first introduced in Windows Vista and Windows Server 2008 and then updated with more detail in Windows 7 and Windows Server 2008 R2.

Open Resource Monitor by clicking the Open Resource Monitor link or button at the bottom of the Performance tab in Task Manager or by clicking or pressing the Start button and typing in "Resource Monitor" or "Resmon."

In Resource Monitor, navigate to the CPU tab. This tab provides details about processor usage such as Name, PID, Description, Status, Threads, CPU, and Average CPU. The rows of data can be sorted in ascending or descending order.

In Figure 10.1, the process, powershell.exe, is consuming the most CPU and the most Average CPU. Average CPU is the average over 60 s, while CPU is the current usage updated every second. In addition, Resource Monitor can provide more details about the process by selecting it using the check box next to it.

TIP

Resource Monitor shows file names and version information of files loaded in a process. This is helpful in determining if a process is running the expected versions of DLLs and EXEs such as a hotfix update or service pack.

Resource Monitor also provides the amount of power usage of the processors relative to the maximum clock speed. A processor consuming 70% utilization at 30% of its maximum clock speed is actually a much lower load level than running at 40% utilization at 105%. Yes, the clock speed can exceed 100% when in an over-clocked state. There is a small amount of time needed to bring a processor from a low-power state to a high-power state, so some processors temporarily over-clock in order to make up for the power transition delay.

TIP

The current clock speed of the processor relative to its maximum clock speed can be measured using the performance counter \Processor Information(*)\% Maximum Frequency.

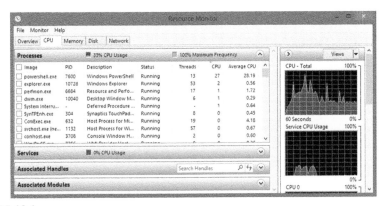

FIGURE 10.1

Resource Monitor showing processor usage.

IDENTIFYING HIGH PROCESSOR USAGE USING PROCESS EXPLORER

Process Explorer is a Microsoft Windows Sysinternals tool available for download at http://live.sysinternals.com/procexp.exe. It provides more detail about a process than Task Manager and Resource Monitor especially if the Microsoft Debugging Tools for Windows are on the system. The debugging tools with the proper symbols (See Appendix C "Debug Symbols" for more information) allow Process Explorer (Procexp) to show the current modules and function calls of the threads—a very helpful feature when identifying the cause of high processor usage. It is arguably the best tool for monitoring and managing live processes on a system.

In Figure 10.2, it shows VirtMemTest64.exe consuming high processor usage (CPU). When I go to the properties of VirtMemTest64.exe and then go to the Threads tab, it shows currently executing modules and functions of the threads. In this case, the threads are executing the function "_threadstartex" (without the double quotes). Keep in mind that only the currently running function is being shown for each thread (Figure 10.3).

To see the stack (instruction set) that leads up to "_threadstartex" being called, we need to look at the full call stack. Think of the current function as the minion doing the work and we want to see which "boss" ordered the work. Select one of the threads consuming CPU, and then click the Stack button (Figure 10.4).

In this case, the stack shows the function "_threadstartex" called "_callthreadstartex" and it is called "CpuHogThread." Therefore, the function "CpuHogThread" would be the one to investigate for optimization.

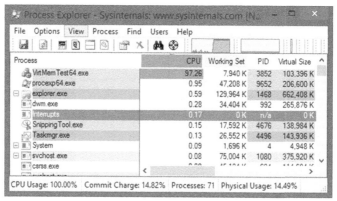

FIGURE 10.2

Process Explorer showing CPU usage of VirtMemTest64.exe.

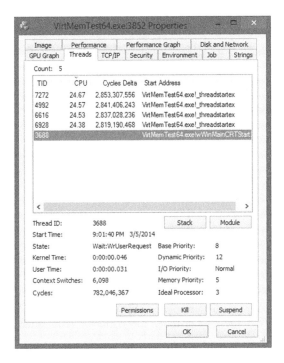

FIGURE 10.3

Threads of VirtMemTest64.exe in Process Explorer.

FIGURE 10.4

The call stack of a thread in Process Explorer.

TIP

The numbers to the right of the functions such as "+0×c5" indicates the offset within the function. This isn't a line number due to compilation optimizations, but it can give you an idea of how far the instruction is in the function.

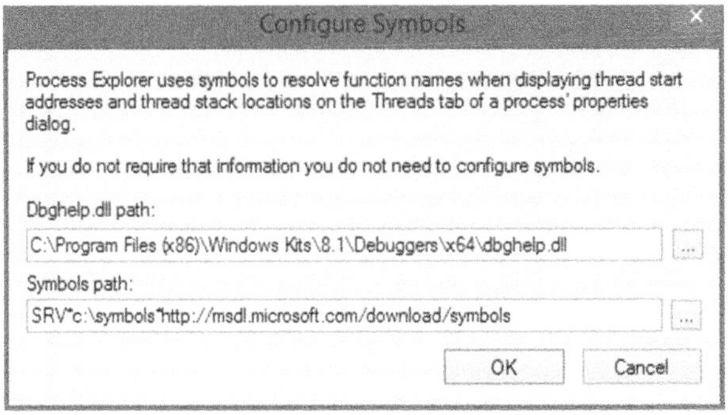

FIGURE 10.5

Configuring symbols for Process Explorer.

The Threads tab of Process Explorer requires configuring its symbol path and pointing it to the dbghelp.dll file from the Microsoft Debugging Tools for Windows. Figure 10.5 shows the location of the 64-bit (x64) version of dbghelp.dll on my laptop. In this case, it was installed to "C:\Program Files (x86)\Windows Kits\8.1 \Debuggers\x64" folder when I installed the Windows Assessment and Deployment Kit (ADK).

For production systems where product installation is limited, the debugging tools can be installed on a non-production system of the same operating system version and architecture, and then the installation directory of the debugging tools can be copied to the production system. Obtaining and installing the Microsoft Debugging Tools for Windows is explained in Appendix A "Tools."

The symbol path is pointing to the HTTP address of the Microsoft public symbol server at http://msdl.microsoft.com/download/symbols and then caching the downloaded symbols to c:\symbols. This symbol path can be used generically on any system. Debug symbols are discussed in more detail in Appendix C.

Process Explorer has far more features than discussed in this chapter. The "Windows Sysinternals Administrator's Reference" book by Mark Russinovich and Aaron Margosis has more information on Process Explorer.

INTRODUCING THE MICROSOFT WINDOWS PERFORMANCE ANALYZER

The Microsoft Windows Performance Analyzer (WPA) tool is an Event Trace Log (ETL) analysis tool and is quickly becoming the favored tool by Microsoft Support and just about anyone who is a Windows performance enthusiast. My friends, Yong Rhee and Jeff Stokes, refer to it as "debugging without the debugger" since it allows us to visually immerse ourselves in the data.

WPA doesn't record ETL files. Tools such as the Microsoft Windows Performance Recorder (WPR), Xperf.exe (discussed later in this chapter), and Performance Monitor take the part of recording the activity. Recording too much can make the ETL file unnecessarily large, while recording too little can prevent us from finding the root cause to a problem. The "just right Goldilocks" approach is a balance between recording the appropriate ETW events, buffering, and duration for the given problem you are investigating.

First, ensure that processor data (CPU events) have been captured into an ETL file of when the processor bottleneck was occurring. If you do not have an ETL file to analyze yet, then follow the steps in the "capturing" sections covered later in this chapter.

Next, if WPA is not installed, then download the latest version of the Windows Performance Toolkit (WPT). As of this writing, the WPT ships with Windows ADK from Microsoft.com and the latest version is 8.1 at http://www.microsoft.com/download/details.aspx?id=39982. Only the WPT is needed in the context of this book.

TIP

As of this writing, the WPA tool requires the Microsoft .NET Framework 4.0. Therefore, consider installing WPA on a non-production workstation.

Finally, on a non-production system, open the ETL file in WPA. This can be done by using the File, Open menu in WPA or by double-clicking the ETL file assuming that ETL files are associated to WPA. Files with the ETL extension are associated with WPA after installing the Microsoft Windows Performance Toolkit.

The loading of the ETL file in WPA can be processor, memory, network, and disk intensive and might require an amount of physical memory of more than four times the size of the ETL file. For example, Jeff Stokes (a WPA expert) was unable to open an 8 GB ETL file on his 32 GB of physical memory system. If you are unable to open an ETL file, then try searching the internet for Microsoft Knowledge Base (KB) articles, articles, and blogs on the subject. If you are still unable to solve it, then consider asking Jeff or I for help on Twitter—@WindowsPerf and @ClintH, respectively.

Once the ETL file is loaded, WPA presents several charts on the left and an analysis work area on the right, which is initially empty—an example of this view is shown in Figure 10.6. The charts that show depend on the ETW events found in the ETL trace file. This is why proper data capture is very important. Charts with the same color are displaying the same data but in different views. This means that the charts can be altered to suit your needs. For now, let's walk through a basic data gathering and analysis using Microsoft Xperf and Microsoft WPR in the next few sections.

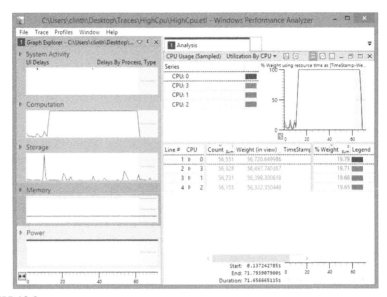

FIGURE 10.6

Microsoft Windows Performance Analyzer (WPA).

INTRODUCING MICROSOFT XPERF.EXE

Microsoft Xperf.exe is a command line tool that collects ETW data in physical memory and then writes it to an ETL file. The advantage of using Xperf.exe is that it requires only two files that can be copied to a system, making this tool convenient for capturing data on a production system. As a matter of fact, I am experimenting with running Xperf continuously in production customer environments for full analysis of problems the first time they occur.

TIP

Xperf.exe and WPR.exe are both command line data capture tools with similar features, but as of this writing, Xperf.exe provides more control over physical memory usage.

Xperf was publicly released for collection and analysis on Windows Vista and Windows Server 2008 and later operating systems. With that said, Xperf.exe can be used to collect data on Windows XP and Windows Server 2003 operating systems so long as the system has hotfix KB938486 (http://support.microsoft.com/kb/938486) installed. As of this writing, this hotfix is several years old (October 2007) and may be rolled up into a service pack (SP) or cumulative update (CU). Otherwise, the hotfix must be installed and requires a reboot.

The amount of physical memory (in the form of Pool NonPaged kernel memory) usage of Xperf will greatly depend on the event subscriptions, frequency of those events, and the duration of the capture. For example, an ETL trace collecting most of the providers will be roughly 50-100 MB per minute on a relatively small system depending on the workload and profiles selected—larger systems will likely collect more data per second. Therefore, Xperf shouldn't be run for long periods of time unless it is in a circular buffer mode. A circular buffer constantly overwrites the oldest data in its buffer to maintain a specified file or buffer size.

TIP

Other than the configurable physical memory overhead, ETW tracing has relatively low processor, network, and disk overhead by design (again depending on the workload and profiles selected) but often produces large trace files when the physical memory buffer is written to disk. These large trace files can be written to removable media such as a USB drive to alleviate the disk IO on the production disk drives.

The following command line is an example often used by Microsoft Support for troubleshooting problems (Figure 10.7 shows a sample screenshot):

```
xperf -on Base+Diag+Latency+FileIO+DPC+DISPATCHER -stackwalk Profile
+CSwitch+ReadyThread+ThreadCreate  -BufferSize  1024  -MinBuffers  256
-MaxBuffers 256 -MaxFile 256 -FileMode Circular
```

The command prompt will immediately return after this command is issued. Therefore, another command must be used to stop the tracing.

In this case, this uses a 256 MB circular physical memory buffer (a relatively small buffer for this amount of data collection—roughly 5 min worth), which can be changed by adjusting the MinBuffers, MaxBuffers, and MaxFile parameters.

It provides deep details of resource usage such as, but not limited to, the following:

- Details of disk IO such as the processes and files involved
- Process memory usage such as Virtual Size (virtual address space usage), Commit, Working Set, and Private Working Set
- Processes, threads, and thread stacks of processor usage

FIGURE 10.7

Example usage of Xperf.exe.

In this case, it does "not" provide call stacks for disk IO, kernel stacks, or memory usage. Those can be added later if needed.

WARNING

The "drivers" ETW provider is very helpful with troubleshooting drivers and other kernel-related activity by providing kernel mode call stacks. With that said, the "drivers" ETW provider has a high risk of crashing (bug check) older operating systems (Windows 7 and Windows 2008 R2 and earlier).

After the problem has been reproduced, wait roughly 10 s, and then use the following command to write the physical memory buffer to disk as an ETL file:

```
xperf -stop -d result.etl
```

The 10 s wait is to provide a reasonable amount of time to collect all of the significant "end" events of when the problem occurred to be included in the ETL trace file.

Another advantage of using Xperf is that it is a command line tool, making it scriptable. This means that it can be scripted to be run by the system Task Scheduler without the need for an administrator to be logged in.

Xperf.exe has many more features that are not covered in this book. For more information on Xperf.exe, consider the following articles:

- Xperf Command-Line Reference http://msdn.microsoft.com/en-us/library/windows/hardware/hh162920.aspx
- Video: Using Xperf to root cause CPU consumption http://blogs.msdn.com/b/ntdebugging/archive/2010/03/22/using-xperf-to-root-cause-cpu-consumption.aspx
- Use Xperf's Wait Analysis for Application-Performance Troubleshooting http://devproconnections.com/development/use-xperfs-wait-analysis-application-performance-troubleshooting
- Xperf Wait Analysis-Finding Idle Time http://www.altdevblogaday.com/2012/05/06/xperf-wait-analysisfinding-idle-time/

CAPTURING AND ANALYZING PROCESSOR INTERRUPTS AND DPC EVENTS USING THE WINDOWS PERFORMANCE TOOLKIT

Interrupts and DPCs (deferred procedure calls) are related to hardware and driver resource usage. If the processors of a system are consistently spending more than 10% of their time servicing interrupts (**\Processor(*)\% Interrupt Time**) or DPCs (**\Processor(*)\% DPC Time**), then it is worth gathering an ETW trace to investigate.

The following command will gather detailed data on interrupts, DPCs, and user mode (application) call stacks:

```
xperf -on PROC_THREAD+LOADER+INTERRUPT+DPC+PROFILE -stackwalk profile
```

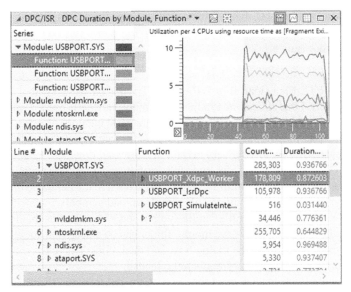

FIGURE 10.8

DPC and interrupt usage in WPA.

After the problem has been reproduced, use the following command to stop tracing where any file name can be used in place of InterruptsAndDpcs.etl:

```
Xperf -d InterruptsAndDpcs.etl
```

Next, open the resulting ETL file in Microsoft WPA (it is recommended to use WPA on a non-production system due to resource usage during analysis), and details of the amount of DPCs and ISRs (interrupt service routines) and the corresponding drivers and function calls will show. Keep in mind that symbols are needed to get function calls. Symbols are covered in more detail in Appendix C "Debug Symbols."

In the case in Figure 10.8, USBPORT.SYS is consuming the most DPC/ISR time, and symbols show us that the functions USBPORT_Xdpc_Worker and USBPORT_IsrDpc are using the most DPC/ISR time.

CAPTURING AND ANALYZING USER MODE PROCESSOR EVENTS USING THE WINDOWS PERFORMANCE TOOLKIT

A user mode processor event is application code that is executing on a processor. The following procedure captures user mode processor usage and can show the processes, threads, and thread stacks (symbols are required for thread stacks) consuming processor time.

The following command captures detailed data of processes, threads, and thread stacks of every process on the system:

```
xperf -on PROC_THREAD+LOADER+PROFILE -stackwalk profile
```

After the problem has been reproduced, wait at least 10 s, and then use the following command to stop tracing where any file name can be used in place of UserModeProcessing.etl:

```
Xperf -d UserModeProcessing.etl
```

Once the ETL file is loaded in WPA, click Trace, Configure Symbol Paths. This opens a dialog box that allows you to adjust the symbol path that is needed when needing non-Microsoft symbols. Symbols are needed to translate memory offsets within DLL, EXE, or SYS files into the closest function. Since a file might contain hundreds or thousands of functions, symbols are very helpful in narrowing down the related code. See Appendix C "Debug Symbols" for more information about resolving symbols.

If you do not have any custom symbols, then leave it to the default symbol path of "srv*C:\Symbols*http://msdl.microsoft.com/download/symbols," which points to the HTTP address of Microsoft's public symbol server and caches the downloaded symbols to C:\symbols. The "C:\symbols" folder can be changed to another folder if needed. Next, click OK on the dialog box, and then, click Trace, Load Symbols. It will take several minutes for symbols to be loaded.

Once symbols are loaded, open the chart on the left labeled "Utilization by Process, Stack" by double-clicking the chart or by dragging it to the Analysis pane on the right. Select a portion of the line chart where there is significant processor usage. This should cause lines in the table to be highlighted. Alternatively, select the process with the highest Count or % Weight. In the example in Figure 10.9, the process with the highest Count and % Weight is VirtMemTest64.exe—a load generation tool written by Aaron Margosis. Expand the Stack field respective to the process you selected. Continue expanding the stack until the Count or % Weight significantly changes such as a difference of more than 50% of the previous entry. The Count indicates the number of times that the function was found on a thread stack, while % Weight is the frequency of the function in relation to other functions. Keep in mind that the stack is showing how often the functions were found on the stack at the time it was sampled and not a direct translation of code coverage. For example, if Function1 called Function2 and the thread was sample while Function2 was executing, then Function1 and Function2 would show up in the stack, but if Function3 was called by Function2 shortly after being sampled, then Function3 might not show up in the sampled stack.

Once the most commonly found functions are discovered, consider sharing this information with the developer of the application associated with the process. This often accelerates the time needed to identify the code responsible for the high processor usage.

CAPTURING PROCESSOR EVENTS USING MICROSOFT WPR

WPR is arguably the most user-friendly tool for collecting ETL traces. Open WPR by pressing or clicking the Start button and typing "Windows Performance Recorder." Alternatively, it can be opened by executing wprui.exe in Windows Explorer. Once running, you should see a list of profiles and scenarios. To collect processor events,

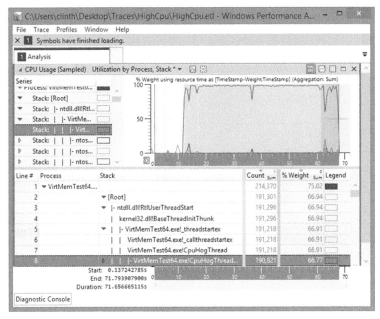

FIGURE 10.9

WPA showing CPU utilization by process and stack.

clear all of the other providers and enable "CPU usage." Keep "First level triage" enabled since this is a general profile. The default settings on the right will make WPR capture in a continuous physical memory buffer until it is stopped and closed. The size of the physical memory buffer within Pool NonPaged memory will depend upon the profiles selected and the amount of physical memory installed (Figure 10.10).

TIP

When starting a WPR capture, you might be prompted to disable the kernel from being paged out by setting the registry key DisablePagingExecutive. If changed, a reboot is required for it to take effect. With that said, this is only required for capturing device IO data, which may or may not be needed depending on what you are analyzing. WPR might require it to be enabled, but Xperf.exe does not require it.

Click the Start button to allow WPR to capture data while the processor problem is occurring. We typically like to have a trace with at least 30 s of data (enough for the data to be relevant), but not more than 20 min (ETL traces can become very large). Once the problem has occurred, wait at least 10 s before stopping the trace. This is because WPA needs respective end events of the problem in order to show them.

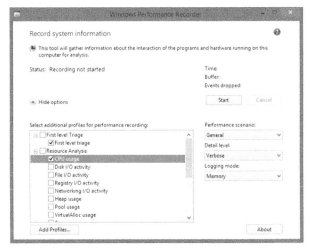

FIGURE 10.10

Windows Performance Recorder (WPR) configured for general and CPU collection.

Click the Save button when finished collecting. Optionally, change the output file name and path using the Browse button, and then click Save. Once saved, click the Open in WPA button to automatically open the trace in WPA. Otherwise, click OK. In this case, I created a file called DARKSTEEL.03-05-2014.23-14-09.etl (Figure 10.11).

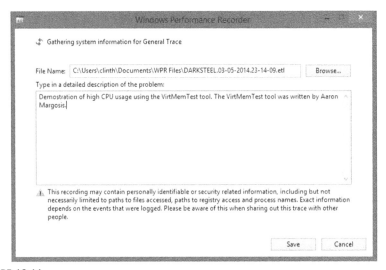

FIGURE 10.11

Saving an ETL file in WPR.

WARNING

ETL files contain a large amount of data and often contain, but not limited to, sensitive data such as the computer name and company where the trace originated. Protect the ETL trace file as appropriate.

VM CONSIDERATIONS

Virtualization of IT is a common practice in the modern world. It allows an administrator to take advantage of underutilized physical hardware by running more than one virtual machine (VM) on it. In general, I treat VMs running on any virtualization platform just like any physical computer, but there are some distinctions you should be aware of when it comes to performance analysis.

Virtual processors (the logical processors assigned to a VM) are effectively thread schedulers. This means that a single virtual processor is only able to schedule a single thread to run at a time, and therefore, it cannot use more than one physical processor on the host hardware. Adding the same number of virtual processors to a VM as the number of physical processors would allow the VM to potentially use all of the processors at the same time. With that said, it is rare for a single computer to use 100% processor usage 100% of the time. Therefore, it is more economical to run multiple VMs with multiple processors. Unfortunately, if there are more virtual processors at 100% than the physical processors can properly execute, then the virtual processors are not getting all of the processing time that they believe they have. All the VM knows is that it scheduled a thread and the thread is in a "running" state. This is why it is important to monitor counters such as **\VM Processor\CPU stolen time**, which according to the description is the time in milliseconds that the VM was runnable, but not scheduled to run.

In Microsoft Hyper-V, once the Hyper-V role is added to a server and rebooted, the host machine becomes a specialized VM called a parent partition. The physical processor usage is only visible by using the **\Hyper-V Hypervisor Logical Processor(*)\% Total Run Time**. All other processor monitoring tools such as Task Manager and the Processor-related counters are only showing the parent partition's own processor time as a VM—not as a physical host. In general, use the Hyper-V-related performance counters first when considering the processor usage of the physical processors. All other resources such as physical memory, disk, and network usage are reliable using the same techniques used throughout this book.

Finally, ignore the **\System\Processor Queue Length** performance counter value on VMs. This counter measures the number of threads that are waiting in a "ready-to-run" state. Unfortunately, this counter is almost always high (greater than 10) even when the virtual processor's usage is low. It has to do with the way in which the threads are scheduled on virtual processors and how the counter data is collected. This is too bad because this counter would normally be helpful in determining if there are enough virtual processors to accommodate all of the ready threads waiting to run state.

CONCLUSION

In this chapter, we introduced processor concepts, how to identify and troubleshoot a high processor usage conditions in both user mode application and kernel mode drivers using various tools. The Microsoft WPT is quickly becoming the favored tool for troubleshooting processor issues.

The following are experts in this field and their contact information:
Jeff Stokes

Twitter @WindowsPerf (https://twitter.com/WindowsPerf)

Yong Rhee

Twitter @YongRheeMSFT (https://twitter.com/YongRheeMSFT)

Boot performance

11

INTRODUCTION

Tired of waiting forever for your laptop to boot up? Have you ever wondered "why" for the sake of humanity is it taking so long to log in? Well, this chapter discusses common causes of boot performance and practical tools to help identify the problem. There are no boot-related performance counters, so boot trace tools are needed.

COMMON CAUSES OF POOR BOOT PERFORMANCE

Services that don't flag when started: If any service does not notify the Service Control Manager (SCM) right away that it started, then the system will wait until a time-out is reached.

Synchronous group policies: Synchronous means to wait, so group policies set to this mode can cause delays. If you are implementing group policies, then consider using asynchronous mode.

Improper BIOS settings: If the BIOS of a laptop or desktop is set to a "quiet" or compatibility mode, then it can dramatically affect the disk performance and hence the boot performance. This can be detected in an ETL boot trace analyzed by Windows Performance Analyzer (WPA) discussed later in this chapter.

Boot scanners: Some antivirus software packages include a boot scanning feature that can dramatically slow down boot performance. These are implemented as disk filter drivers and can be detected in an ETL boot trace with the File IO profile.

Superfetch disabled: Superfetch is a core operating system service on Windows that helps to optimize the interaction of physical memory and disk IO. If the Superfetch service is disabled, then ReadyBoot cannot optimize the boot time IO.

Disk encryption software: Disk encryption software can cause significant delays. Ensure best practices of the software and hardware vendors are followed.

Network delays: Delays can be caused by a network or network adapter not being available. In addition, connections to resources such as home drives, roaming profiles, or Sync mode group policies can induce delays.

Unnecessary log-on scripts: I once came across a log-on script that enumerated all of the files on the hard drive in order to inventory the system. This had the unfortunate effect of making the user wait at least 10 minutes before their log-on finished. Again, this can be detected with an ETL boot trace with the File IO profile that is discussed later in this chapter.

Windows Performance Analysis Field Guide. http://dx.doi.org/10.1016/B978-0-12-416701-8.00011-9

Too many startup items: Use tools such as Autoruns to detect and manage all of the drivers, services, and other applications that start up on the system. This is discussed in more detail later in this chapter.

Go SSD: If all else fails, go with a solid-state drive (SSD). Boot performance is most commonly dependent on disk performance. A SSD is one of the fastest and practical storage devices going from a few hundred IOPS to a few thousand IOPS.

STARTUP IMPACT IN TASK MANAGER

The newly designed Task Manager first introduced in Windows 8 and Windows Server 2012 has a Startup tab that shows items that automatically start and their relative impact on the system (Figure 11.1).

Each item has options:

- *Enable/Disable*: This option allows or prevents the item from automatically starting on the next log-on or reboot. The item remains in the list when enabled or disabled.

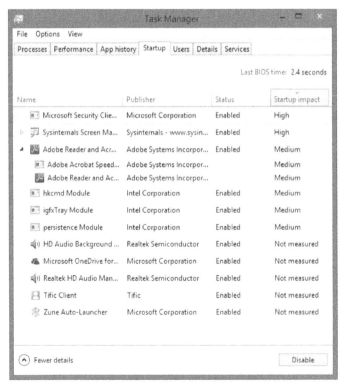

FIGURE 11.1

The Startup tab of Task Manager.

- *Open file location*: This option opens File Explorer to the folder where the executable is located and automatically selects the file. The installation directory of the executable can provide clues as to its origin. Go to properties of the executable to learn more about it such as checking its digital signature and other details.
- *Search online*: This option opens a web browser and automatically searches the Internet using the executable file name and title.
- *Properties*: This option opens the executable's file properties. This is the same as going to the file properties after using the **Open file location** option.

TIP

Validating the digital signatures of executables that automatically start is a very important step in detecting malware.

USING AUTORUNS TO VALIDATE STARTUP DRIVERS, SERVICES, AND APPLICATIONS

Validating startup drivers, services, and applications is something I commonly do with my enterprise customers, friends, and family simply because an overwhelming number of startup items frequently cause delays in startup, normal usage of the system, and shutdown. Autoruns is my tool of choice for discovering all of the nooks and crannies where executables can be started. Disabling or removing items from starting can be very helpful for boot performance, general performance, and malware removal.

NOTE

Autoruns shows more detail of each startup item than Task Manager, but Autoruns does not show impact of the startup items.

DOWNLOAD AND RUNNING AUTORUNS.EXE

Like many of the other Sysinternals tools, Autoruns.exe can be directly downloaded from http://live.sysinternals.com/autoruns.exe. I often use this link in my e-mail replies when helping people. Save it to the Desktop or another location that is easily accessible. Double-click on it to run it.

NOTE

Administrator rights are not required unless you intend to make changes to the system. Also, you might be prompted for administrator credentials or other User Access Control (UAC) prompts depending on your settings.

Autoruns will begin to gather system information. For now, press the ESC key to stop the gathering of data since we will be rescanning the system shortly. Otherwise, wait for the status bar to report, "Ready."

FILTER AUTORUNS

This step will remove common entries that are relatively safe and enable verification of the signatures of the drivers, EXEs, and DLLs of software targeted for startup on the system.

NOTE

Microsoft drivers are certainly not immune to problems, but they are generally written well enough to not be on the list of usual suspects.

In the menu, click Options, Filter Options (Figure 11.2).

Enable/check **Verify code signatures**, **Hide Microsoft entries**, and **Hide Windows entries**. These will have Autoruns verify the code signatures of all of the drivers, executables, and DLLs and hide common Microsoft and Windows startup entries. Click the Rescan button and wait for the hour glasses to go away. This might take a few minutes depending on the resources of the system.

VALIDATE DRIVERS

Let's start with drivers since they are generally the most problematic since they have full rights to the system. This step checks the digital signatures of non-Microsoft and non-Windows drivers.

Click the Drivers tab and look for drivers that are "Not Verified." This will show up in the Publisher field. According to the Windows Sysinternals Administrator's Reference, "Verifying a digital signature associated with that file gives a much higher degree of assurance of the file's authenticity and integrity."

NOTE

When a driver is verified, the Publisher field changes from the company name to the name on the signed certificate.

FIGURE 11.2

Autoruns filter options.

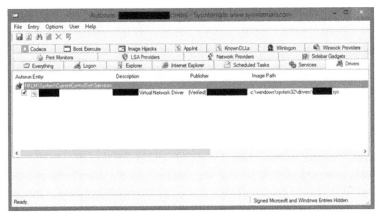

FIGURE 11.3

The Drivers tab of Sysinternals Autoruns.exe.

In my case, I found one driver that is not Microsoft, but it was verified to be a virtual networking vendor. Portions of the screenshot in Figure 11.3 were censored to protect privacy.

If any of the drivers are highlighted and come up as "Not Verified" in the Publisher field, then the driver does not have a valid digital signature or the driver has been modified. It doesn't mean that the driver is malware. It just means that the driver cannot be verified to be from the publisher that it claims to be from. For example, the driver might have been written by a small company that didn't bother to have their driver signed. With that said, malware commonly installs a driver to gain privileged access to the system and it could be exposed through this procedure. My advice is if the system is not functioning properly, then I would uninstall all of the unverified drivers.

When the checkbox next to the driver is unchecked, the driver will not be loaded on the next system start, and a backup of the entry is made by Autoruns. This means that you can close Autoruns, reboot, and then bring up Autoruns again and the entry will still be there. This is very helpful in situations where the entry ends up being needed. Just check/enable the checkbox next to it to re-enable the entry. If the entry is not needed, remove the entry by selecting the entry and pressing the Delete key or Ctrl-D to remove it. A confirmation dialog box will show to verify the deletion.

NOTE

64-bit versions of Windows and Windows Server require all drivers to be signed when loaded, but this setting can be by-passed by an administrator.

VALIDATING EVERYTHING ELSE

Each startup item is categorized on a tab (Figure 11.4).

FIGURE 11.4

Autoruns categories are displayed as tabs.

In general, look for entries that are highlighted in pink. These items cannot be verified and are worthy of more investigation. Entries in yellow indicate that the entry exists, but the resource that it is pointing to is not found.

Disable (uncheck) all items that are unknown to the user (even non-technical users should be able to tell you if they are using certain applications or not) and then reboot the system for the changes to take effect.

The following is a short description of each category according to the Windows® Sysinternals Administrator's book:

- *Log-on*: This tab lists the "standard" autostart entries that are processed when Windows starts up and a user logs on.
- *Explorer*: The Explorer tab lists common autostart entries that hook directly into Windows Explorer and usually run in-process with Explorer.exe.
- *Internet Explorer*: Internet Explorer is designed for extensibility, with interfaces specifically exposed to enable Explorer bars such as the Favorites and History bars, toolbars, and custom menu items and toolbar buttons.
- *Scheduled Tasks*: The Scheduled Tasks tab displays entries that are configured to be launched by the Windows Task Scheduler.
- *Services*: Windows services run in noninteractive, user-mode processes that can be configured to start independently of any user logging on and that are controlled through a standard interface with the SCM.
- *Drivers*: Drivers are also configured in the subkeys of HKLM\System \CurrentControlSet\Services, but they run in kernel mode, thus becoming part of the core of the operating system.
- *Codecs*: The Codecs category lists executable code that can be loaded by media playback applications.
- *Boot Execute*: The Boot Execute tab shows you Windows native-mode executables that are started by the Session Manager (Smss.exe) during system boot.
- *Image Hijacks*: Image Hijacks is the term used to run a different program from the one you specify and expect to be running.
- *AppInit*: DLLs that will be loaded into every process that loads User32.dll.
- *KnownDLLs*: KnownDLLs help improve system performance by ensuring that all Windows processes use the same version of certain DLLs, rather than choosing their own from various file locations.
- *Winlogon*: The Winlogon tab displays entries that hook into Winlogon.exe, which manages the Windows log-on user interface.

- *Winsock Providers*: Windows Sockets (Winsock) is an extensible API on Windows because third parties can add a transport service provider that interfaces Winsock with other protocols or layers on top of existing protocols to provide functionality such as proxying.
- *Print Monitors*: The entries listed on the Print Monitors tab are DLLs that are configured in the subkeys of HKLM\System\CurrentControlSet\Control\Print \Monitors.
- *LSA Providers*: This category of autostarts comprises packages that define or extend user authentication for Windows, via the Local Security Authority (LSA).
- *Network Providers*: The Network Providers tab lists the installed providers handling network communication, which are configured in HKLM\System \CurrentControlSet\Control\NetworkProvider\Order.
- *Sidebar Gadgets*: On Windows Vista and newer, this tab lists the Sidebar Gadgets (now called Desktop Gadgets on Windows 7) that are configured to appear on the user's desktop.

For more information on Autoruns, see Chapter 5 Autoruns in the "Windows® Sysinternals Administrator's Reference" book at http://technet.microsoft.com/sysinternals/hh290819.

RECORDING A BOOT TRACE USING WINDOWS PERFORMANCE RECORDER

This procedure is considerably more complicated than Autoruns but provides the most comprehensive analysis on boot performance. This procedure is intended for users who have a strong understanding of Windows architecture.

Windows Performance Recorder (WPR) is part of the Windows Performance Toolkit. The toolkit is part of the Windows Assessment and Deployment Kit (ADK). Download and start the installation of the latest version of the Windows ADK. As of this writing, the latest version is 8.1 at http://www.microsoft.com/download/details.aspx?id=39982. In the context of this procedure, check the Windows Performance Toolkit, uncheck all other options, and then finish the installation wizard.

Once installed, run WPR by pressing or clicking the Windows Start button and then type "WPR." Press Enter or click the WPR application (Figure 11.5).

Once WPR is running, enable "First level triage," "CPU usage," "Disk I/O activity," "File I/O activity," and "Networking I/O activity." These profiles collect the necessary data to diagnose the most common boot-related conditions. Change the Performance scenario to Boot. The number of iterations is asking the number of times to reboot with a trace. For this case, I set it to 1, so only the next reboot is traced (Figure 11.6).

Once ready, click the Start button. WPR will prompt for a location to write the trace file (*.ETL). Choose a location that you're currently logged in account has

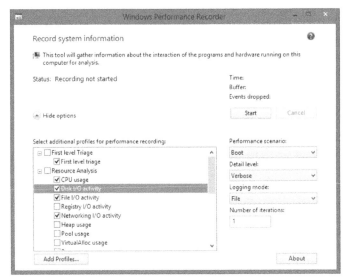

FIGURE 11.5

Windows Performance Recorder (WPR) setup for a boot trace.

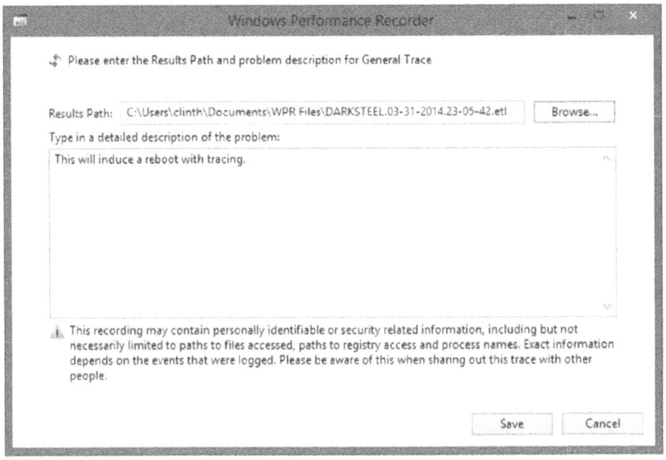

FIGURE 11.6

Where to save the boot trace.

write access. Optionally, provide a description of the problem. Click Save (Figure 11.7).

WPR prompts one last time to confirm the reboot and begin tracing.

Once the system has rebooted and you have logged in again, WPR continues to trace. This is because some systems are not usable right away and may need to be

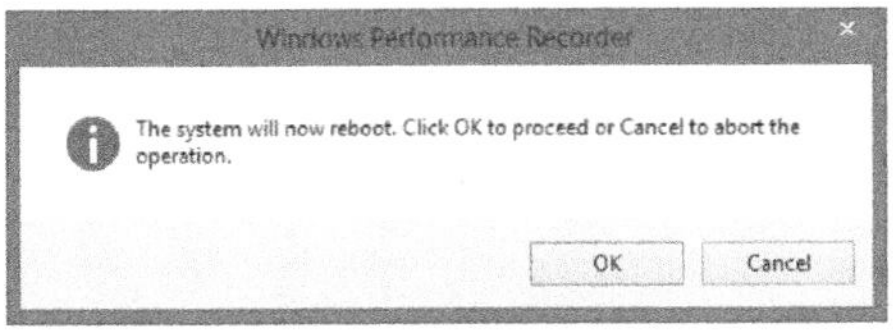

FIGURE 11.7

Confirmation to reboot.

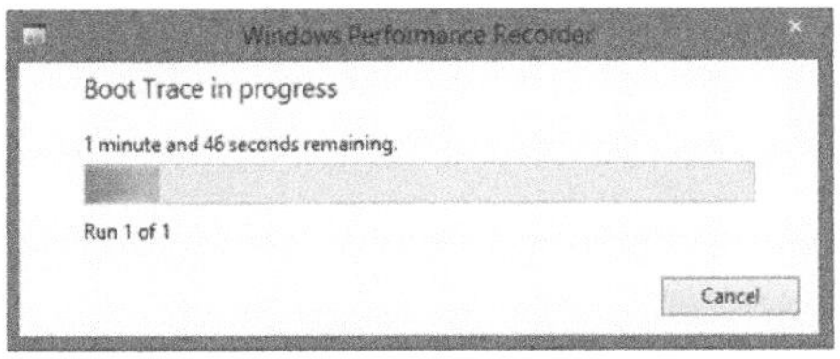

FIGURE 11.8

WPR continuing to trace after a reboot for post-log-on tracing.

analyzed for post-log-on problems. Warning: If the Cancel button is selected, then the entire trace is aborted. Let the trace finish on its own (Figure 11.8).

Once the trace is finished, find the ETL file. It should be in at the Save location specified earlier. The default location is C:\Users\<Account>\Documents\WPR Files.

TIP

ETL files often contain personally identifiable or security related information. Protect the file as appropriate such as only using encrypted file transfer protocols.

TIP

ETL files have a high compression ratio of roughly 80%. Consider compressing the file before sending it out.

ANALYZING A BOOT TRACE USING WPA

This procedure introduces and uses the WPA tool to analyze a boot trace. WPA is one of the most comprehensive tools in the industry for boot trace analysis and is intended for users who have a strong understanding of Windows architecture.

After using WPR to record a boot trace, open the trace (*.ETL) in WPA. Opening the file can take a significant amount of resources, so it is recommended to do the analysis on a non-production system such as a workstation (Figure 11.9).

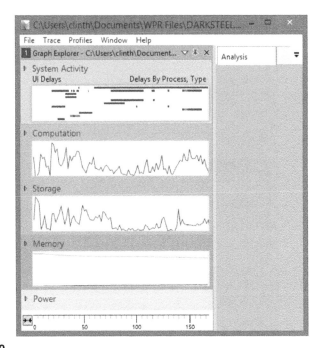

FIGURE 11.9

The initial view of boot trace in WPA.

The initial view of the trace shows several categories of resource usage "rolled up." Each category expands into other charts showing the data in a different view.

The "boot phases" chart is the first chart to look at in a boot trace. It tells us how much time was spent in each phase of boot. Expand System Activity and double-click on the "boot phases" chart. This will show more detail about the boot phases on the right pane (Figure 11.10).

BOOT PHASES IN WPA

- *Pre Session Init*: The BIOS firmware does a power-on self-test and executes preboot instructions. The system is looking for bootable media during this time. An excessive amount checking for bootable media can cause unnecessary delays in this phase.
- *Session Init*: Loading the kernel and preboot-related services. Long delays can be video BIOS or driver related—a BIOS update might be needed.
- *Winlogon Init*: Starting more services, authenticating the machine account, logging on the user.
- *Explorer Init*: The user has been authenticated, but the user's desktop is being created. At the end of this phase, the desktop appears.

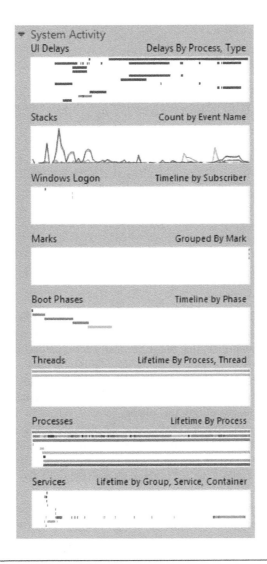

FIGURE 11.10

System Activity-related charts in WPA.

- *Post Boot*: The desktop has appeared, but the system might not be in a usable state yet due to things such as an overwhelmed disk from applications and services starting up.

A healthy or performant boot is considered less than 60 seconds. Figure 11.11 is an example of a healthy boot. In this trace, my desktop was visible at 43 seconds according to the End Time of the Explorer Init phase. My system is a Microsoft corporate laptop joined to the Microsoft network. If any of the phases are taking longer

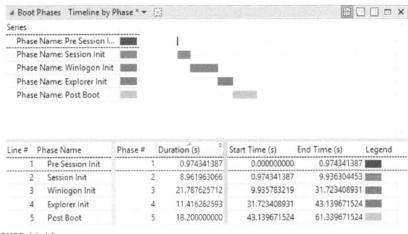

FIGURE 11.11

Timeline by boot phase in WPA.

than expected, then select the boot phase in the Timeline by Phase chart, right-click on the boot phase, and click Filter to Selection. This will change the focus of the chart to only that phase and select that phase vertically across all of the charts on the left pane of WPA. In my trace, the Winlogon Init phase took the longest at 21 seconds. With the phase selected, look through the other charts to see if there is heavy usage of resources during that time frame. A commonly used resource is disk, so let's take a look at disk performance during this phase.

Expand Storage and expand Disk Usage. Double-click or drag to the right pane the chart with the name Service Time by Process, Path Name, Stack. If this chart does not show, then use another chart with significant resource usage.

In my case, the svchost.exe (1244) process used the most disk activity during this time and the file path most often accessed is related to the Windows Management Interface service with a reference to C:\Windows\system32\wbem directory. Optionally, add (if not already on the table) and expand Stack to see which modules were involved with the disk IO (Figure 11.12).

TIP

The function calls can be exposed by selecting Trace, Load Symbols on the main WPA menu. Go to Appendix C Debug Symbols in this book for more information about resolving symbols.

Processor usage is also a commonly used resource during boot, so with the Winlogon Init boot phase still selected, close the "Service Time by Process, Path Name, Stack" chart, expand Computation on the left pane, expand CPU Usage (Sampled), and double-click or drag to the right pane the Utilization by Process, Stack. In the "Utilization by Process, Stack" chart, use the mouse pointer to hover over the lines consuming the most CPU. Select one of them and it will automatically be

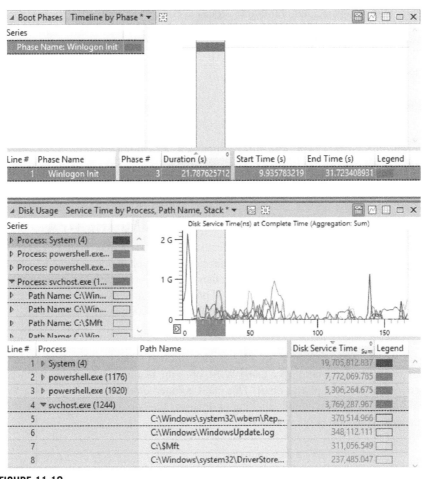

FIGURE 11.12

Disk usage details of the Winlogon Init boot phase.

highlighted in the table below. Expand the highest entry in the Stack column until there is a significant change in % Weight. This stack is considered the most frequently used.

THE FOLLOWING ARE PUBLIC RESOURCES FOR LEARNING MORE ABOUT BOOT PERFORMANCE ANALYSIS USING EVENT TRACING FOR WINDOWS

How Many Coffees Can You Drink While Windows 7 Boots?

http://channel9.msdn.com/Events/TechEd/NorthAmerica/2012/WCL305

The blog of Jeff Stokes

http://blogs.technet.com/b/jeff_stokes

Why do I have long boot times? Pt 1

http://blogs.technet.com/b/jeff_stokes/archive/2009/12/18/why-do-i-have-long-boot-times.aspx

The blog of Yong Rhee

http://blogs.technet.com/b/yongrhee

RunAs Radio Podcast: Jeff Stokes Improves Our Boot Times!

http://www.runasradio.com/default.aspx?showNum=264

AN EXAMPLE OF A BAD BOOT TRACE USING THE WPA

Matthew Reynolds is a colleague on my team in Microsoft Premier Field Engineering. He recreated this trace to demonstrate a real customer problem that he solved. In a tech savvy enterprise, a customer realized that they had a major boot performance problem and they were losing millions of minutes of productivity time by waiting what seemed forever for their systems to boot. These were Windows 7 computers and they were very surprised by what was found.

This example was created using WPR. See "Recording a boot trace using Windows Performance Recorder" of a basic walk through of recording a boot trace.

After capturing a boot trace using WPR, open the resulting ETL file in WPA and then look at the boot phases chart. This chart is found on the left by expanding System Activity and then double-clicking or dragging the boot phases chart to the right pane (Analysis tab) (Figure 11.13).

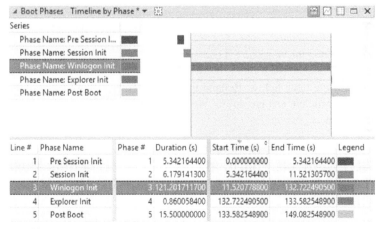

FIGURE 11.13

WPA showing the boot phases by duration in seconds.

In this example, the Winlogon Init phase is much longer than what we expect—it should have been less than 30 seconds, but in this case, it is 121 seconds. Based on the Duration (s) column, we can calculate that the desktop was visible at around 133 seconds just after the Explorer Init phase. This means that resources went to idle shortly after the desktop appeared at roughly over 2 minutes of waiting. Two minutes doesn't sound like much until you find yourself waiting for your system to boot up. Now multiply it times all of the people in the company.

I selected the WinLogon Init phase in the table below the chart and it highlights the phase in blue in the chart showing when that boot phase was active. Next, I right-clicked on the Winlogon Init entry in the table and selected "Filter to Selection." This selects this boot phase on all of the other charts and removes all other entries in this chart.

We can see on the left side of WPA that the Winlogon Init boot phase is highlighted in blue on the other charts (Figure 11.14).

Services that don't flag the SCM are a common cause of slow boot performance, but in this case, there were no services that correlated to the boot delay.

Disk usage is also very common during boot up and we see a lot of disk activity during this phase of the boot (Figure 11.15).

In the Utilization by Process, Path Name, Stack chart, we can see that the System process is the most active process using disk resources and there are a lot of activities related to corporation video bin files (Figure 11.16).

Next, I dragged the Path Name column to the left of the Process column, so that the chart is grouped by the Path Name first and then the Process name.

This showed a pattern of Robocopy.exe with a process ID of 2424 involved with these files.

Next, I simply looked at other charts that show a relatively high amount of resource usage that correlates with the Winlogon Init boot phase. One of them is the "DPC (Deferred Procedure Call) and ISR (Interrupt Service Request) Usage by Module, Stack" chart (Figure 11.17).

This chart shows a relatively high number of DPC usage and the stack shows a lot of network-related activity. At this point, we know there are a lot of disk usage and network usage during the Winlogon Init boot phase (Figure 11.18).

Getting back to the Robocopy.exe process, I opened the chart Lifetime By Process, Image chart under System Activity, and Images to find out more about this instance of Robocopy. Robocopy is a command-line tool built into Windows 7 and WPA is able to provide the command line that initiated Robocopy and the parent process that started it. These fields are not shown by default, so I had to right-click on one of the column headers and select the Process Command Line field, the parent process ID, and unselect all other fields except for the Process field as shown in Figure 11.19.

The parent process (PID 2124) is a cmd.exe (command-line process) and we can see that it is calling the CMD file "\\contoso\netlogon\download-executive-video-messages.cmd."

Come to find out these are corporate videos for all of the employees to watch. Instead of having them downloaded on demand, they had set up the videos to be

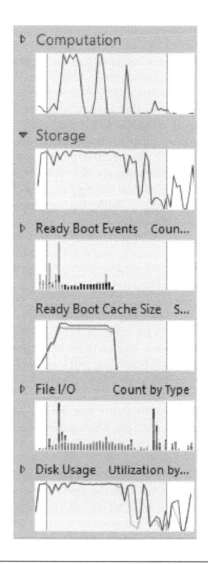

FIGURE 11.14

The Winlogon Init phase is selected in all of the charts for reference.

downloaded during "every" log-on. This ultimately slowed down everyone's log-on sequence. This specific ETL was a reproduction of the problem. In the real case, the customer had purchased an agent software to do the downloads during log-on (Figure 11.20).

Once the video download configuration was moved to an on-demand solution, the boot performance went to less than one minute and the problem was solved.

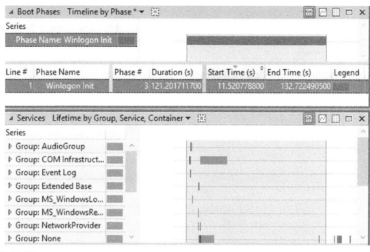

FIGURE 11.15

The services starting up during the Winlogon Init boot phase.

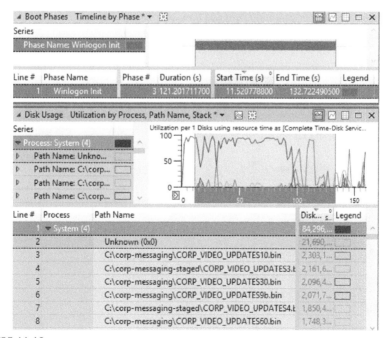

FIGURE 11.16

WPA showing a lot of system process activity with video bin files.

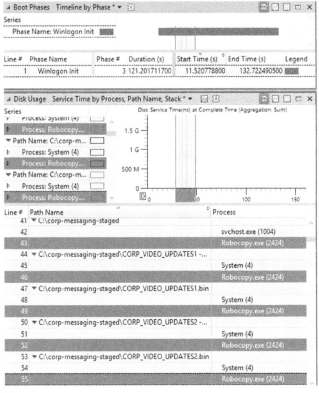

FIGURE 11.17

WPR showing an instance of Robocopy.exe involved the bin files.

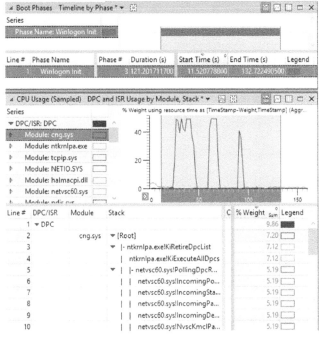

FIGURE 11.18

The DPC and ISR Usage by Module, Stack chart in WPA.

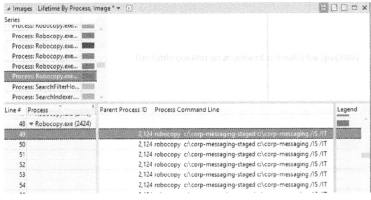

FIGURE 11.19

The "Lifetime By Process, Image" chart showing the parent process ID and command line of Robocopy.exe.

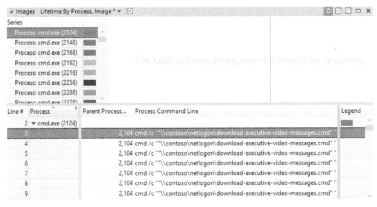

FIGURE 11.20

PID 2124 is a cmd.exe with an interesting command.

Matthew Reynolds, Vadim Arakelov, and Stephen Rose have a very entertaining video of this analysis of the boot trace called "TechEd 2012: How Many Coffees Can You Drink While Windows 7 Boots?" at http://channel9. msdn.com/Events/TechEd/NorthAmerica/2012/WCL305, but this was several years ago and they are using an older version of the WPA tool. They also cover several other boot tracing scenarios. They have an updated version of their session at http://channel9.msdn.com/Events/TechEd/NorthAmerica/2013/WCA-B317.

CONCLUSION

This chapter discussed common causes of boot performance and introduced tools of varying complexity to help with identifying the causes of slow boot performance.

The following are experts in this field and their contact information:

Matthew Reynolds

Twitter @MatthewMWR (https://twitter.com/MatthewMWR)

Jeff Stokes

Twitter @WindowsPerf (https://twitter.com/WindowsPerf)

Yong Rhee

Twitter @YongRheeMSFT (https://twitter.com/YongRheeMSFT)

Performance Analysis of Logs (PAL) Tool

12

INTRODUCTION

The Performance Analysis of Logs (PAL) tool is an open-source project that I started in 2007. The idea came to me when I was teaching both the Vital Signs workshop (training focused on Performance Monitor log analysis) and VBScripting. There is a lot to keep in mind when analyzing performance counters, and VBScript was there to automate things, so it just made sense to write a tool that would automatically analyze counter logs.

I originally wrote the tool for myself, but my friends and colleagues wanted to use it as well. I don't know everything about Windows performance analysis for all products, so I decided to make it an open-source project on Microsoft's open-source website, Codeplex.com, to allow other subject matter experts to contribute to the tool. It paid off well because today, the tool has many subject matter experts who have created threshold files for their respective areas. In addition, fans of the tool are helping with bug fixes and features. All of the work that has gone into the tool has been voluntary.

The tool has been mentioned in books, podcasts, TechEd sessions, SQL PASS, and magazines and is regularly used by Microsoft Support professionals.

The PAL tool uses all of the performance counter thresholds mentioned in this book, analyzes a counter log, and produces an HTML report showing warning and critical alerts. Think of it as the "easy" button to performance analysis. With that said, the tool is designed to be a time-saving tool, not a replacement of performance analysis.

INSTALLATION AND PREREQUISITES

The PAL tool was designed to be free and easy to install. It is very resource-intensive and designed to be used on a non-production system where it is okay to use system resources. To download the tool, go to http://pal.codeplex.com and browse to the Downloads page. From there, download the latest 32-bit version (the file with x86 in the name) or the latest 64-bit version (the file with x64 in the name) depending on the architecture of the operating system. The 64-bit version is preferred since the PAL tool often needs to address more than 2 GB of virtual address space. If you are unsure of the architecture of your system, then run the following command:

Wmic PATH Win32_OperatingSystem GET OSArchitecture

This command should work on Windows XP, Windows Server 2003, or later systems.

As of this writing, PAL 2.x is the latest major version. It requires Microsoft Powershell 2.0 or later and the Microsoft Chart Controls for the .NET Framework 3.5 Service Pack 2. Windows 7 and later ship with Powershell 2.0, so on most systems, only the chart controls are needed. Systems with the .NET Framework 4.0 may already have the chart controls installed.

If the prerequisites are not installed, then the PAL tool installer will mention the missing prerequisite and it will automatically bring up a web browser to the download location for the component. Install the component, and then repeat the PAL tool installation until it finishes the installation.

Once installed, the PAL Wizard (user interface) can be run by clicking or pressing the Windows Start button, and search for the application named "PAL."

NOTE

The PAL Wizard is simply a glorified batch file creator and is not required. The analysis engine is PAL.ps1 and it can be run directly from a Powershell session. With that said, PAL.ps1 requires many parameters that the PAL Wizard automatically provides.

CREATING A COUNTER LOG USING A PAL TEMPLATE

Not sure of which counters to collect? Let the PAL tool help.

The first step in using the PAL tool's full potential is to export a PAL threshold file to a counter log data collector template. The template (depending on how it was exported) can be used on any Windows or Windows Server system to collect counter data into a counter log that can later be analyzed by the PAL tool.

When a PAL template is exported, it recursively combines all of the threshold files that it inherits from with the currently selected threshold file. This means that if a threshold file such as SQL Server 2012 is selected, then it will combine it with System Overview and Quick System Overview. This model allows a single change to a threshold file, and that change is automatically included in all of the other threshold files that inherit from it.

Use the following procedure to create a performance counter log using a template from the PAL tool:

1. Open the PAL Wizard (PALWizard.exe):

    Click or press the Windows Start button and search for the application called "PAL." Execute it by clicking on it. The PAL Wizard user interface should show.

2. Select a threshold file:

    Navigate to the Threshold File tab and select the drop-down list of threshold files. Most of the major Microsoft server products are there with some third-party products such as VMware, Citrix XenApp, and Philips. If a combination of more than one threshold file is desired such as SQL Server and Exchange Server, then select one of the threshold files and then click the Add button. Navigate to the PAL installation directory and choose the other threshold file (*.xml). It should show up in the inherited box as well as all of the threshold files that it recursively inherits from.

WARNING

Changes to the inheritance of a PAL threshold file are permanently written to the respective file.

---

3. Export to a data collector template:

Once the combination of threshold files is selected, click Export to Perfmon template file button. A save dialog box will show. Navigate to a writable location such as your Desktop folder and save the file.

NOTE

If SQL Server performance counters are found during export, then you will be prompted with the option to name any SQL Server named instances. Named instances of SQL Server have performance counters that are unique to named instance such as \MSSQL$MyNamedInstance:Buffer Manager(*)\Page life expectancy.

Choose the XML file extension for target systems running Windows Vista, Windows Server 2008, or later. Choose the HTM file extension for target systems running Windows XP, Windows Server 2003, or earlier. For more information, on performance counter data collector templates, go to Chapter 2 "Performance Monitor".

4. Create and start a data collector from the template on a target production system:

Once the data collector template is created, move the template file to a target production system or use the Logman.exe command line to create a data collector remotely (Example: logman import <Name> -xml <PathToTemplateFile> -s <TargetServer>). For more information, go to section "Creating and starting a data collector set using a template" in Chapter 2.

NOTE

I generally recommend creating a circular data collector log file as discussed in section "Creating a circular data collector" in Chapter 2.

Also, consider making the data collector automatically start after a reboot by following the steps in section "Automatically starting a data collector set after a reboot" in Chapter 2.

5. Once a performance problem occurs, stop the data collector:

If a counter log file is copied or moved while it is still being written to, then it will corrupt the file. Therefore, stop the data collector first, and then move or copy the log file to a non-production system with the PAL tool installed. A non-production system is recommended due to the high resource usage during analysis.

6. Optionally restart the data collector:

If using a circular data collector as discussed in section "Creating a 'black box' data collector" in Chapter 2, then restart the data collector to continue monitoring the system.

7. Analyze the counter log file using the PAL tool:

On a non-production system with the PAL tool installed, use the PAL Wizard to analyze the counter log. Keep in mind that the analysis is very processor and memory intensive.

USING THE PAL WIZARD

Once you have one or more counter logs (whether it was created with a PAL template or not), it can be analyzed by the PAL tool. This is the primary purpose of the tool—to make counter log analysis as easy as possible without the need to know or understand the counters or their thresholds. With that said, the intention of the PAL tool is to be a time-saving tool—not a replacement of normal performance analysis techniques.

START THE PAL WIZARD

Click or press the Windows Start button and search for the application called "PAL." Execute it by clicking on it. The PAL Wizard user interface should show.

WELCOME

This is the start page of the PAL Wizard showing general information about the tool and the author. After I had visited a few customers who were fans of the tool, they ultimately didn't know who wrote it. This inspired me to put my information at the front of the tool similar to an "About the Author" section at the beginning of a book. Yes, that is a picture of my Xbox Live Avatar (Figure 12.1).

COUNTER LOG

On the Counter Log page, specify the absolute path to one or more counter log files in CSV or BLG format such as "C:\Users\clinth\Desktop\SQLDIAG\SQLDIAG.BLG." If you wish to merge two or more counter logs, then specify the full path to all of the counter logs on the same line separated by semicolons (;) such as "C:\Perflogs\Admin \VitalSigns_000001.blg;C:\Perflogs\Admin\VitalSigns_000002.blg."

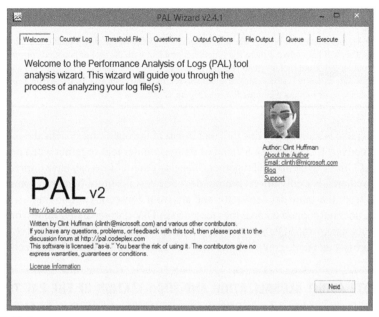

FIGURE 12.1

The Welcome page of the PAL Wizard.

FIGURE 12.2

The Counter Log page of the PAL Wizard.

NOTE

If the PAL tool is unable to process one of your counter logs, then try using the built-in sample counter log. This will help prove if there is a functional problem with the tool or potential corruption in your counter log. Counter logs often become corrupted if they are copied or moved from a system while the data collector is still writing to it. For this reason, always stop the respective data collector before copying or moving a counter log file (Figure 12.2).

Relog.exe is a command line tool that is part of the operating system and is used by PAL to convert BLG files to CSV and/or merge counter logs together when needed—only BLG files can be merged together. Merging counter logs can have unpredictable results and are generally not recommended. For best result, only merge counter logs that are from the same data collector and are from consecutive time frames.

PAL does not support counter logs recorded in TSV (tab-separated values) or SQL (a data source name to an SQL Server table) formats. With that said, the PAL tool is an open-source project and code contributions with this functionality would be appreciated.

A NOTE ABOUT GLOBALIZATION AND LOCALIZATION OF THE PAL TOOL

In order for the PAL tool to match the counter paths in a counter log, the counter log data collector must record using an English (US) locale. This is because the counter path matching is done using English. Non-English locales are certainly possible, but the counter paths would require translation to English or at least be matched to the respective English equivalents. Many efforts have gone toward translation, but it is very difficult to get all of the language translations for a single counter, let alone thousands of counters. I've considered adding a collection tool into the PAL tool for those users who are willing to add their localized counter paths to the project.

Even if we got all of the operating system counters, there are always the product specific counters to deal with as well. Currently, the PAL tool is an open-source project personally owned and developed by me and I don't have the resources to add localization as a feature at this time. Again, I accept code contributions toward this effort. Keep in mind that this is considered "globalization" where the PAL tool will work with non-English counter logs but still show an English report.

Full localization of the PAL tool would require reports in the native language of the operating system. At one time, I added a feature (never published) to the tool that would do a machine translation of the PAL reports into the language of choice of the user. The reaction from my international friends was surprising. Antonio Neves mentioned how "horrible" the Portuguese translation was and how he preferred the original English version. The overwhelming feedback was the same, so I gave up on localizing the PAL reports. I might try to take it on again sometime. Post your feedback to http://pal.codeplex.com.

Optionally, a data time range within the counter log(s) can be specified. This will use the "begin" (-b) and "end" (-e) parameters of Relog.exe to create a new log from the existing log(s) filtered on the time range specified. When the Restrict to a Data Time Range is selected, PAL will use Relog.exe to examine the counter log(s) and populate the Begin Time and End Time with the start and end times of when the counter log was collected.

THRESHOLD FILE

On the Threshold File page, choose a threshold file that best matches the products or roles of the counters captured in the counter log. I am considering an "autodetect" feature in the future. Many of the threshold files inherit from other threshold files.

The Microsoft Internet Information Services 5.x/6.x/7.x threshold file inherits from the ASP.NET and System Overview threshold files. System Overview inherits from Quick System Overview and so on. Therefore, when you select one threshold file, it might inherit from many others to produce a comprehensive analysis and report.

The PAL tool compares the counters in the combined threshold files to the counters in the counter log. Counters that do not match on either side are ignored and not included in the report.

If you find that the PAL analysis takes too long, then consider using a threshold file combination that has less counters in it such as the Quick System Overview threshold file. Many of the other threshold files inherit from the System Overview threshold file that analyzes all of the Process counter object instances with multiple analyses. Analyzing these instances can be very resource-intensive and time-consuming. The Quick System Overview threshold file only analyzes the _Total instance of the Process object making it much faster and less resource-intensive. This allows an overall operating system analysis, but it will not report on individual processes. Try to find a balance between detail, resources, and time.

NOTE

If you want to ensure that all counters in a counter log make it into the report, then consider using the AllCounterStats feature discussed on the Output Options tab.

The PAL threshold files are the most valuable resources of the entire project. Subject matter experts of nearly every discipline of Microsoft server products and a few third-party products have established counter thresholds and prescriptive guidance with their names and reputations on the line. The **Content owner(s)** field shows the name and contact information of the subject matter expert who created and maintains the threshold file. Keep in mind that the content owner of a threshold file only owns the counters in the threshold file chosen. The content owner does not necessarily own the inherited threshold file(s). In the example in Figure 12.3, I am the content owner of the System Overview threshold file and the Quick System Overview threshold file, but Jeff Stokes is the content owner of the VMware threshold file.

TIP

Mix and match threshold files as needed. If the counter log has counters from Microsoft Exchange Server and Microsoft SQL Server, then add the needed threshold files using the Add button. This is a permanent change to the threshold file.

QUESTIONS

The Questions page of the PAL Wizard has changed over the years to reflect the growing complexity of performance analysis. Currently in 2.4.1, the operating system, amount of physical memory, and the UserVa setting (if used) must be specified. If these values are unknown, then use the defaults. In some cases, a Powershell command is provided in the Question field that will return the value that this question is asking.

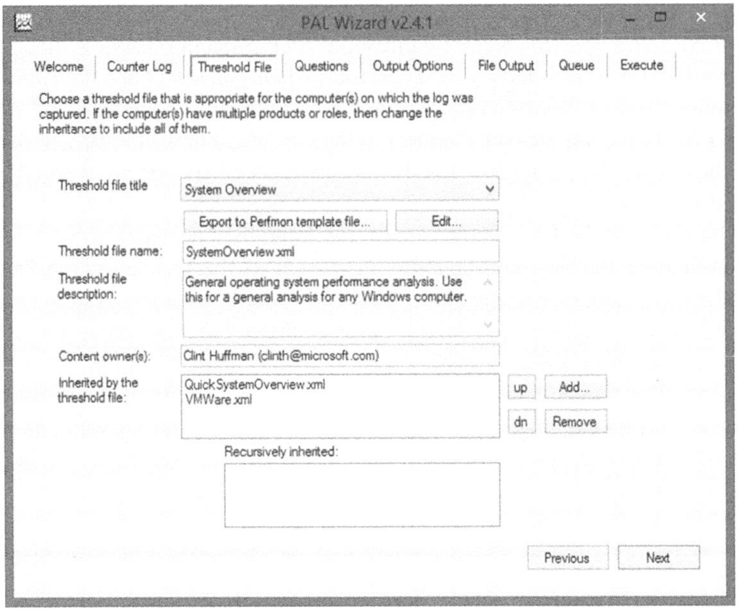

FIGURE 12.3

The Threshold File page of the PAL Wizard.

Why doesn't the PAL tool just collect this data? Well, the PAL tool is designed to be an analysis tool—not a collection tool. This might change in future versions of the tool. I am already experimenting with a PAL Collector tool. Watch the forums at http://pal.codeplex.com for updates on this.

In addition, there are no counters that specify the version or architecture of the operating system in which it was captured, the same with the amount of physical memory accessible to a system and the UserVa setting. These values are critically needed for a proper analysis of a counter log because they can dramatically change the respective counter thresholds.

OUTPUT OPTIONS

The analysis interval is "not" the interval in which the counter log was captured. That is called the sample interval. The analysis interval is how you want the tool to slice up the counter log in regard to a time range. When AUTO is used, I divide the counter log up into 30 time slices. A 30 h counter log would have 1 hour time slices. A 30 minute counter log would have 1 minute time slices. Each time slice has a calculated minimum, average, maximum, and trend values. These statistics are used against the respective thresholds. This allows the tool to reduce the analysis to 30 statistical data points versus every data point. Now, one might suggest that I will miss spikes—not true. Keep in mind that maximum and minimum values are nearly always included in ever threshold analysis, so spikes and valleys will not be missed. This also means that if there is only one data point per time slice, then that one data point becomes the minimum, average, and maximum values, which is not statistically significant. Therefore, when choosing an analysis interval, pick an interval that includes at least three data points in each time slice.

If an analysis interval is selected that is less than the sample interval in which the counter log was collected, then the tool will revert the analysis interval to the same as the sample interval. This isn't ideal, but will still work (Figure 12.4).

If there are counters in the counter log that are unknown to the select threshold files, then they are ignored. If you want to ensure that all of the counters in a counter log make it into the report, then create a threshold file that has the counters and include that threshold file in the analysis. In the meantime, the AllCounterStats feature can be used. This feature ensures that all counters in the counter log make it into the report as statistical data—charts and statistics of the counter instances, but no thresholds, alerts, or gradients in the chart. It is more resource-intensive to have all of the unknown counters in the report, and this is why this feature is not enabled by default.

FILE OUTPUT

The output directory is the file system location where the resulting HTML report will be written and the respective resource directory contains all of the chart images in PNG format. This location must be a location in which you have write access such

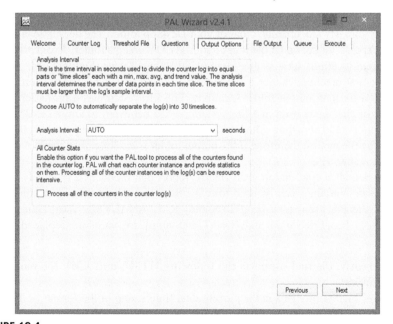

FIGURE 12.4

The Output Options page of the PAL Wizard.

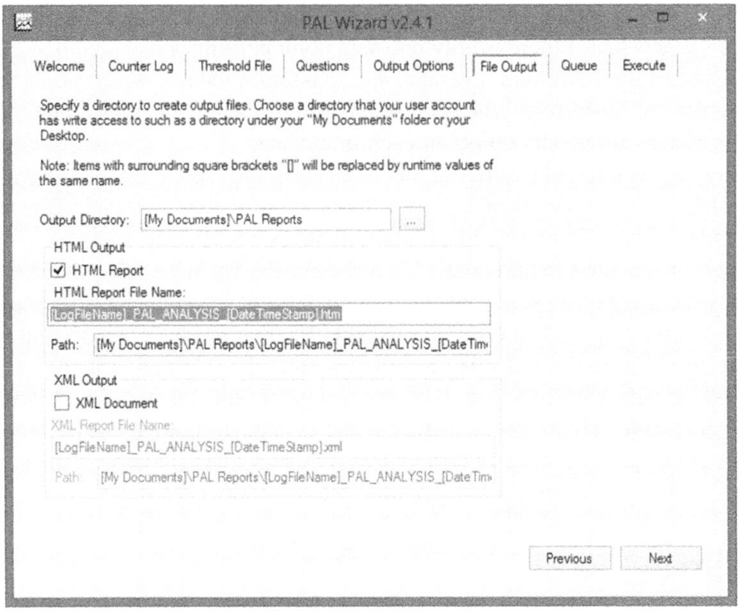

FIGURE 12.5

The File Output page of the PAL Wizard.

as under your My Documents folder or your Desktop folder. The default location is a "PAL Reports" folder under the root of your My Documents folder. Avoid privileged file system locations such as the %windir%\Perflogs folder (Figure 12.5).

As a best practice, choose a file system location that is relatively short. Avoid unnecessarily long output folder locations. The file system has a limitation on the number of characters used in a file system path. I believe it is limited to 256 characters, but I could be wrong. The PAL tool creates a lot of uniquely named chart files with large file names; therefore, if the output folder is too long, then the tool will fail to write a chart file.

The default output option is an HTML report that produces a relatively easy to read report. Variables can be used to make the file name of the report unique. By default, the PAL tool uses [LogFileName]_PAL_ANALYSIS_[DateTimeStamp]. htm where [LogFileName] and [DateTimeStamp] are variables replaced during run time.

Currently, the tool supports the following HTML and XML file name variables:

[DateTimeStamp] This is the current data time stamp in the format of YYYY-MM-DD_hh-mm-ss.

[LogFileName] This is the file name of the counter log specified.

[GUID] This is a randomly generated but guaranteed to be unique number.

Currently, the tool supports the following output directory variables:

[DateTimeStamp] This is the current data time stamp in format of YYYY-MM-DD_hh-mm-ss.

[LogFileName] This is the file name of the counter log specified.

[GUID] This is a randomly generated but guaranteed to be unique number.

[My Documents] This is the folder path of the currently logged in user's My Documents folder.

If you are using a separate tool to parse the PAL output, then consider using the XML output. The XML file is a file version of the primary data structure (an XML document) used during analysis.

At least one kind of output (HTML, XML, or both) must be selected.

QUEUE

The PAL Wizard is actually just a glorified batch file creator. This page represents what is being written to a batch file (*.bat) that will eventually call the PAL.ps1 Powershell script. Each paragraph is reformatted into an executable line. More "lines" can be added to the batch file by selecting the **Add to Queue** option on the Execute page.

The last item (line in the batch file) can be removed by clicking the **Remove Item From Queue** button (Figure 12.6).

FIGURE 12.6

The Queue page of the PAL Wizard.

The PAL Wizard creates a batch file with all of the items (groupings of counter logs and parameters) at %temp%\{GUID}_RunPAL.bat file where {GUID} is a uniquely generated number created at the time the PAL Wizard is finished.

TIP

If the PAL analysis fails, the most recently created %temp%\{GUID}_RunPAL.bat batch file can be modified and restarted instead of running through the PAL Wizard again.

EXECUTE

If the Execute option is selected when the Finish button is clicked, then the tool will write the current Queue data to a batch file in the %temp% directory and then close the PAL Wizard (Figure 12.8).

NOTE

More than one PAL instance can be running at the same time without affecting each other (Figure 12.7).

If the Add to Queue option is selected when the Finish button is clicked, then the PAL Wizard will append another line of execution to the resulting batch file. Use this option if you intend for the PAL tool to analyze several counter logs in succession without stopping.

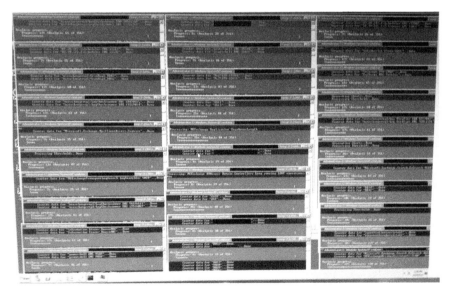

FIGURE 12.7

30 instances of the PAL tool running at the same time.

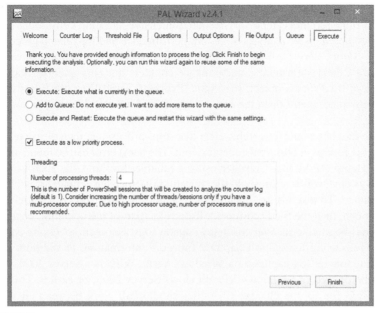

FIGURE 12.8

The Execute page of the PAL Wizard.

If the "Execute and Restart" option is selected when the Finish button is clicked, then the PAL Wizard will save the queue data to a batch file in the %temp% directory and will restart the PAL Wizard effectively creating another batch file while the other is executing (Figure 12.8).

If "Execute as a low priority process" is enabled (this is the default for PAL 2.4.1 and later), then all of the threads of the Powershell-associated sessions will run at priority Low. Most threads such as your user interface run at Normal priority, so this means that the PAL analysis threads will not slow down any other applications or system services unless they are running at Low priority as well.

The Number of processing threads is the number of Powershell sessions to create toward processing. Powershell sessions are single-threaded, so a separate Powershell session has to be created for each processing thread. The analysis is very processor-intensive; therefore, the optimal setting is to set it equal to the number of logical processors on the system. In PAL 2.4.1 and later, the PAL Wizard detects the number of logical processors on the system and uses it as the default value.

FINISH

Click the Finish button when ready to begin processing. Processing can take anywhere from a few minutes to a few days. The amount of time greatly depends on the number of counter instances that matched to the combined PAL threshold files selected.

The System Overview threshold file analyzes every Process counter instance multiple times, so this can be very resource-intensive and time-consuming but provides a comprehensive analysis of system performance and the related processes. If Quick System Overview is used by itself, then it is significantly faster since it analyzes all of the system-related performance counters but only analyzes the _Total instance of the Process object. If it finds **\Process(_Total)\Private Bytes** is on an increasing trend, then I open the counter log in Performance Monitor to investigate further.

If the tool has an unrecoverable error that stops processing, then please report the error to the forums at http://pal.codeplex.com. The latest error can be found in the log file at %temp%\PAL.log. Consider using a reliable threshold file such as just the Quick System Overview threshold file. If it still fails, then the counter log itself might be corrupted. To test this, try opening the counter log in Performance Monitor. If it fails to open, then the file is corrupted. Relog.exe (part of the operating system) can sometimes be used to recover corrupted counter logs. See section "Fixing corrupted counter logs using Relog" in Chapter 2 for more information. In addition, keep in mind that counter log captured on Windows Vista, Windows Server 2008, or later cannot be opened on Windows XP, Windows Server 2003, or earlier. This is due to the BLG file format change. CSV files should still work between all versions of Windows and Windows Server.

INTERPRETING THE REPORT

The primary purpose of the PAL tool is to analyze a counter log and produce a detailed report as easy as possible. The top of the report has the file name of the counter log that was analyzed and the PALv2 logo that has a link to the PAL Web site http://pal.codeplex.com (Figure 12.9).

The report is an HTML file with an HTM extension. The choice of this format was so that the report can be viewed on most consumer operating systems and be viewed over the network using the HTTP protocol. I considered using MHT files (files in which the HTML and resource data are all in a single file), but the internal document links (links that point to other parts of the same document) failed to work in Internet Explorer unless the HTM format was used. For compatibility and internal linking functionality, I am continuing to use the HTM format.

An HTML report (if selected in the output options) will automatically open in the default web browser of the system. The output is only tested using Microsoft Internet Explorer 8 and 9 but should work on any web browser that uses standard HTML.

FIGURE 12.9

The header of a PAL report.

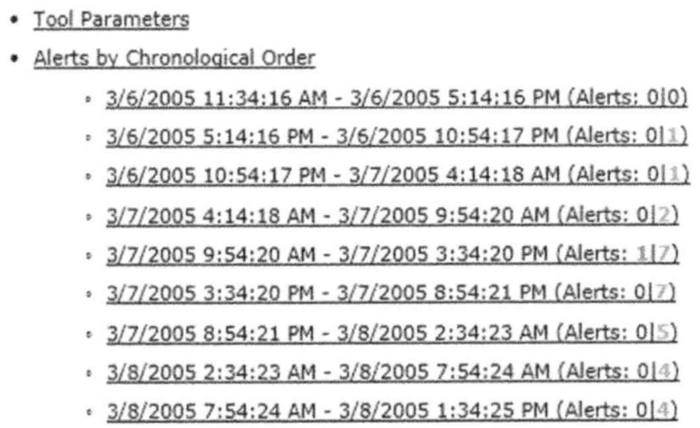

- Tool Parameters
- Alerts by Chronological Order
  - 3/6/2005 11:34:16 AM - 3/6/2005 5:14:16 PM (Alerts: 0|0)
  - 3/6/2005 5:14:16 PM - 3/6/2005 10:54:17 PM (Alerts: 0|1)
  - 3/6/2005 10:54:17 PM - 3/7/2005 4:14:18 AM (Alerts: 0|1)
  - 3/7/2005 4:14:18 AM - 3/7/2005 9:54:20 AM (Alerts: 0|2)
  - 3/7/2005 9:54:20 AM - 3/7/2005 3:34:20 PM (Alerts: 1|7)
  - 3/7/2005 3:34:20 PM - 3/7/2005 8:54:21 PM (Alerts: 0|7)
  - 3/7/2005 8:54:21 PM - 3/8/2005 2:34:23 AM (Alerts: 0|5)
  - 3/8/2005 2:34:23 AM - 3/8/2005 7:54:24 AM (Alerts: 0|4)
  - 3/8/2005 7:54:24 AM - 3/8/2005 1:34:25 PM (Alerts: 0|4)

FIGURE 12.10

Table of contents showing alerts by chronological order.

Microsoft Internet Explorer is installed by default on Windows 7 and Windows Server 2008 R2.

TIP

Add the parameter "-DisplayReport $False" to the end of a PAL.ps1 command line to prevent the HTML report from automatically opening. As of this writing, this parameter is not yet exposed in the PAL Wizard.

The HTML report begins with a table of contents (Figure 12.10) with links within the document. The first part of the report shows the parameters passed into the PAL. ps1 script followed by all of the alerts from each of the time slices in chronological order. This view is helpful when correlating many critical (red) and warning (orange) alerts that occurred within the same time slice but from different analyses. For example, if the report shows a critically low available memory alert, a high pages/sec warning alert, and a critical alert that the logical disk hosting the page file is overwhelmed, then the alerts can be correlated to indicate a low memory condition that is causing system-wide delays.

After the "Alerts by Chronological Order" section, the table of contents shows each of the analyses and the number of critical (red) and warning (orange) alerts in each. Generally, analyses with a high number of critical alerts are important to look at. Analyses with no alerts indicate that one or more counters were analyzed and did not break any thresholds. Analyses with the phrase "Stats Only" indicate that the analysis has no thresholds and is providing statistical data only. In the case of Figure 12.11, Memory Pool Paged Bytes has a one critical and one warning alert. All other analyses show no alerts.

Clicking on an analysis in the table of contents takes you to the details of the analysis. The description of the analysis often provides the reason why the analysis exists and what it is checking for followed by references to other documents on the Internet such as Microsoft TechNet articles, Microsoft Developer Network (MSDN) articles,

- Memory
  - Memory Available MBytes (Alerts: 0|0)
  - Memory Free System Page Table Entries (Alerts: 0|0)
  - Memory Pool Non-Paged Bytes (Alerts: 0|0)
  - Memory Pool Paged Bytes (Alerts: 1|1)
  - Memory Pages/sec (Alerts: 0|0)
  - Memory System Cache Resident Bytes (Alerts: 0|0)
  - Memory Cache Bytes (Alerts: 0|0)
  - Memory % Committed Bytes In Use (Alerts: 0|0)
  - Memory Pages Output/sec (Stats only)
  - Memory Committed Bytes (Stats only)
  - Memory Commit Limit (Stats only)
  - Memory Pages Input/sec (Alerts: 0|0)

FIGURE 12.11

Table of contents showing memory analyses.

Microsoft Knowledge Base (KB) articles, or reputable blog articles. Eventually, I will try to write Microsoft TechNet Wiki articles for each analysis providing prescriptive guidance on how to solve the detected problem.

Some charts have a warning (gold) and/or critical (red) gradient indicating if/ when a counter exceeds a threshold. These gradients are optional for content owners to add to their analyses and not all have them. In the case of Figure 12.12, it shows

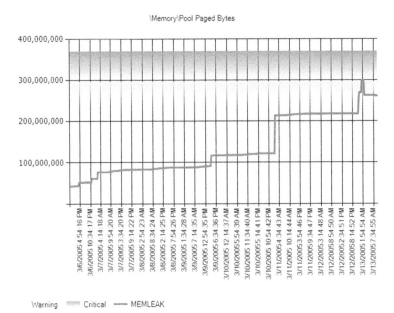

FIGURE 12.12

Chart showing Pool Paged Bytes leaking over time.

the **Memory\Pool Paged Bytes** is on an increasing trend toward the critical zone. The corresponding alerts indicate that this condition is important and should be investigated further using the guidance in the analysis description.

Below the chart is a set of overall counter instance statistics showing the condition, counter instance name, and statistics of each counter instance that spans the entire counter log (Figure 12.13).

Explanation of values of overall counter instance statistics:

- *Min*: This is the minimum (lowest) value of the counter instance observed throughout the counter log.
- *Avg*: This is the average of all of the values of the counter instance observed throughout the counter log.
- *Max*: This is the maximum (highest) value of the counter instance observed throughout the counter log.

Overall Counter Instance Statistics

Condition	\LogicalDisk (*)\Avg. Disk sec/Read	Min	Avg	Max	Hourly Trend	Std Deviation	10% of Outliers Removed	20% of Outliers Removed	30% of Outliers Removed
Greater than 25 ms logical disk READ response times	SQL01/C:	0	0	.063	0	.001	0	0	0
OK	SQL01/G:	0	0	0	0	0	0	0	0
Greater than 25 ms logical disk READ response times	SQL01/H:	0	.001	.466	0	.016	0	0	0
Greater than 15 ms logical disk READ response times	SQL01/I:	0	.007	.025	0	.003	.006	.006	.006
Greater than 600 ms - Slower than a 3.5 inch floppy drive	SQL01/U:	0	.011	5.198	0	.163	0	0	0
Greater than 25 ms logical disk READ response times	SQL01/W:	0	0	.064	0	.001	0	0	0
Greater than 25 ms logical disk READ response times	SQL01/X:	0	0	.028	0	.001	0	0	0

FIGURE 12.13

Overall counter instance statistics.

- *Hourly Trend*: This is the hourly increase of the counter instance observed from the beginning to the end of the counter log. Specifically, each of the average values of each time slice (based on the analysis interval) is compared, and the difference is the adjusted for an hourly time. A value of 10 would indicate an average increase of 10 every hour likewise a value of −10 would indicate an hourly decrease of 10.
- *Std Deviation*: This is the standard deviation of all of the values of the counter instance throughout the counter log. My interpretation of standard deviation is the average distance of the data points to the average value. If you have the values of 5,5,5,5,5,5,5,5,5,5, then the average is 5 and the standard deviation is 0. If you have the values of 0,10,0,10,0,10,0,10,0,10, then the average is still 5, but the standard deviation is 5—meaning each of these values is 5 away from the average of the values. Effectively, the lower that standard deviation, the more reliable the average. The higher the standard deviation, the more unreliable the average.
- *10% of Outliers Removed*: This is an average value calculated with 10% of the data points that are furthest from the average removed. If you have the values of 5,5,5,5,5,5,5,5,5,999999, then the average is 100004, which doesn't represent most of the values. When 10% of the outliers are removed—meaning the 999999 value is removed from the array of numbers—and a new average is calculated, then the new average is 5. The point of this value is to remove 10% of the "noise" values that occasionally happen in performance counters due to dramatic spikes in a counter instance.
- *20% of Outliers Removed*: This is the same as 10% of Outliers Removed except 20% of the data points furthest from the average are removed and a new average is calculated.
- *30% of Outliers Removed*: This is the same as 10% of Outliers Removed except 30% of the data points furthest from the average are removed and a new average is calculated.

Finally, each alert that occurs in the analysis is listed under Alerts. The alert shows the Time Range (the time slice) that the alert occurred and is "clickable" to go to that time slice for all of the alerts that occurred in the same time range, the Condition (red for critical or yellow for warning), the counter instance, and statistics (Min, Avg, Max, and Hourly Trend) similar to the overall counter instance statistics. In the case of alerts though, the statistics are in the context of the time slice only. The Hourly Trend is increasing or decreasing hourly trend of the average values of all of the time slices from the current time slice to the beginning of the counter log. To see specifically how this value is calculated, look at the function CalculateTrend in PAL.ps1. The point of the Hourly Trend is to detect resource leaks such as process private committed memory or handle leaks.

In the example in Figure 12.14, the alerts show an overall (_Total) increase of 116 MB of which the processes sxxxxxxxmw#10 and sxxxxxxxmw#11 are contributing increases of 15,989,001 bytes and 21,295,631 bytes, respectively.

3/7/2005 9:54:20 AM - 3/7/2005 3:34:20 PM	Condition	Counter	Min	Avg	Max	Hourly Trend
	Possible Memory Leak: More than 500 MB between overall Min and overall Max and an increasing trend of more than 100 MB per hour	\\MEMLEAK\Process (_Total)\Private Bytes	3,302,518,784	3,890,004,450	4,248,690,688	116,944,777
	Possible Memory Leak: More than 250 MB between overall Min and overall Max and an increasing trend of more than 10 MB per hour	\\MEMLEAK\Process (sxxxxxxxmw#10) \Private Bytes	312,483,840	397,022,148	441,339,904	15,989,001
	Possible Memory Leak: More than 250 MB between overall Min and overall Max and an increasing trend of more than 10 MB per hour	\\MEMLEAK\Process (sxxxxxxxmw#11) \Private Bytes	403,726,336	514,481,453	566,173,696	21,295,631

FIGURE 12.14

Time slice-related alerts.

DISCLAIMER

The PAL reports are provided in an "as-is" condition—meaning the project cannot be held responsible for any damages physical or intellectually. This tool is designed to help, but is by no means perfect. Trust, but verify.

RUNNING THE PAL TOOL WITHOUT THE PAL WIZARD

The PAL Wizard is a VB.NET application that is just a glorified batch file creator. The true analysis engine of the tool is the Powershell script, PAL.ps1. Therefore, the Powershell script can be called directly without the need for the PAL Wizard.

The best approach to automating the PAL tool is to first run the PAL Wizard and examine the batch file that it creates. The wizard creates a batch file in the %temp% folder with the naming convention of {GUID}_RunPAL.bat such as {cdb231bb-296b-46b5-845b-b3d986bc3bb6}_RunPAL.bat.

Editing the batch file will show similar output to this:

```
C:
cd "C:\Program Files\PAL\PAL"
start /LOW /WAIT Powershell -NoProfile ".\PAL.ps1" -Log "C:\Program Files\PAL
\PAL\SamplePerfmonLog.blg"   -ThresholdFile   "C:\Program   Files\PAL\PAL
```

\SystemOverview.xml" -Interval 'AUTO' -IsOutputHtml $True -HtmlOutputFileName '[LogFileName]_PAL_ANALYSIS_[DateTimeStamp].htm' -IsOutputXml $False -XmlOutputFileName '[LogFileName]_PAL_ANALYSIS_[DateTimeStamp].xml' -AllCounterStats $False -NumberOfThreads 4 -IsLowPriority $True -OS '64-bit Windows Server 2008 R2' -PhysicalMemory '4' -UserVa '2048'

This example shows nearly all of the syntax that PAL.ps1 supports. To see a full list of all of the parameters that the PAL.ps1 supports, edit PAL.ps1 using a Powershell editor or a text editor and examine the first line of parameters.

From here, it is just a matter of copying and modifying the values in the sample batch file. Some users have gone so far as to have the output placed on Microsoft SharePoint servers since the reports are in HTML.

EXAMINING THE PAL LOG

If the PAL analysis fails, then consider looking at the log produced. For ease of accessibility, the log is located at %temp%\PAL.log and overwrites this file with each new analysis. If PAL.log is in use by another analysis session at the time, then PALx.log will be written to where x is the lowest number available.

The log is generated using the Start-Transcript feature of Powershell. This means that all of the output that shows on the console will be in the log. Unfortunately, the Start-Transcript Powershell feature prevents the script from being debugged. Therefore, if you are trying to debug the PAL.ps1 script on your own, then you must first disable the Start-Transcript function calls. Do this by commenting out the StartDebugLogFile and StopDebugLogFile function calls at the bottom of the script.

If no %temp%\PAL.log file is present or the output is difficult to understand, then contact the forums at http://pal.codeplex.com or Twitter me at @ClintH with the question.

HOW TO CREATE A THRESHOLD FILE FOR THE PAL TOOL

The number of products covered by the PAL tool is limited only by those willing to create a threshold file to define it. If you need a threshold file for a product, then consider making one.

First, open the PAL Wizard as you normally would to analyze a counter log and navigate to the Threshold File tab and click "Edit. . .." It doesn't matter which threshold file is selected at this time. The PAL Editor will show (Figure 12.15).

In the PAL Editor, go to the upper left and click File, New (Figure 12.16).

This clears the editor but hasn't created a new threshold file just yet. We will get to that. For now, let's create a new analysis by clicking the "New" button at the lower left of the editor (Figure 12.17).

This will show the "New Analysis" dialog box. An analysis is the primary container for one or more data source counters that you want to analyze, the thresholds that are applied to the "Counter to Analyze," and the charts generated for the data source counters (Figure 12.18).

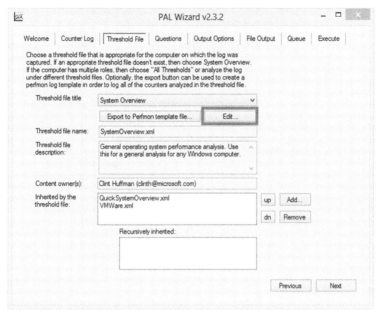

FIGURE 12.15

The Threshold File tab in the PAL Wizard.

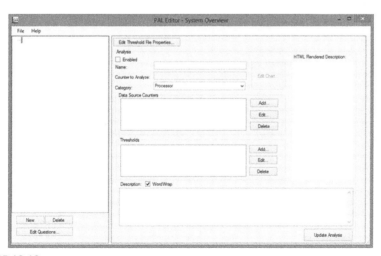

FIGURE 12.16

The PAL editor after clearing it with File, New.

FIGURE 12.17

The New Analysis dialog box.

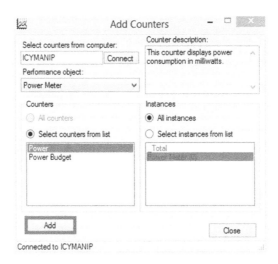

FIGURE 12.18

The Add Counters dialog box showing the buttons to click to add new counters to a new analysis.

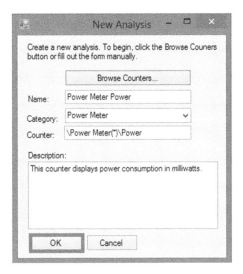

FIGURE 12.19

Click OK on the New Analysis dialog box after selecting a counter path.

Click the Browse Counters button and this will open the Add Counters dialog box. This interface allows you to connect to a computer either locally or remotely that has the performance counter that you want to add. It's important that the PAL tool connects to computer that has the counter to ensure that the counter path is exact (Figure 12.19).

Click Close or OK to all of the open dialog boxes to continue.

Once at the main editor again, notice that many of the fields have been populated with data from the selected counter. This is a good opportunity to update the description of the analysis to tell the end users the purpose of this analysis, what is being checked and why, and what do to if the thresholds are exceeded. The description field supports the use of HTML tags and the rendered HTML can be previewed on the right pane. The text in the description will always show in the PAL report with this analysis. Once finished with editing the description, click the Update Analysis button to set the change and click File, Save to permanently save the changes to the threshold file.

In this case, I am adding all of the instances of the **\Power Meter(*)\Power** performance counter. Once I click OK, you are returned to the main PAL editor and should now see the performance counter that you added on the left pane.

EXCLUDING COUNTER INSTANCES

In some cases, it is necessary to exclude specific instances of a performance counter. For example, the _Total counter instance of the LogicalDisk counter object is commonly excluded because the _Total instance is the sum of all of the logical disk

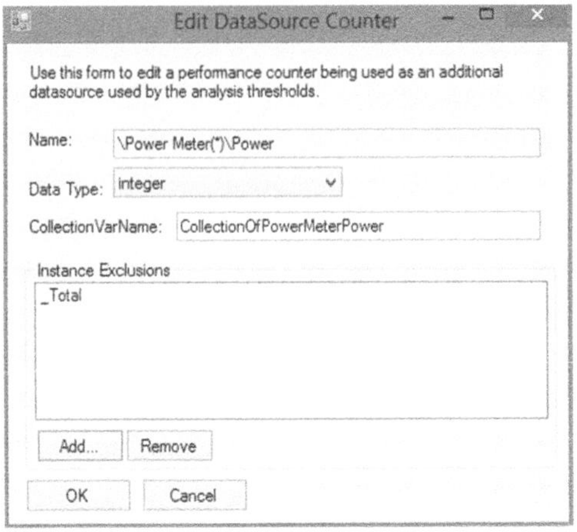

FIGURE 12.20

The Edit DataSource Counter form in the PAL editor.

counter values, which is not helpful when trying to analyze each disk. To exclude a counter instance, select the data source counter to edit, and then click the Edit button.

The Edit DataSource Counter form will show. Click the Add button and specify the counter instance to exclude. Repeat as many times as necessary to define all of the counter instances to exclude. In this case, I excluded the _Total instance. Click OK when finished (Figure 12.20).

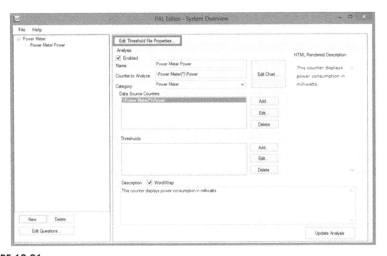

FIGURE 12.21

The PAL editor with a new analysis.

Now is the time to save the work as a new threshold file. At the top left, click File, Save As. This opens the Save As dialog box that will allow you to save the work you've done so far to an XML file that is the new threshold file. Navigate to a folder that you have write permissions to such as your Desktop or a location under your My Document folder. In the File Name field, type in a file name that you want the threshold file to have and click Save. Once saved, move the file to the folder where PAL is installed. This typically requires elevated privileges. The default installation folder for PAL is C:\Program Files\PAL\PAL. Saving files directly to this folder is typically prevented by Windows unless you use elevated privileges. In this case, I saved the threshold file as PowerStates.xml and I copied it to the PAL installation folder (Figure 12.21).

Next, let's give the threshold file a name and other information. Click the Edit Threshold File Properties... button. In the Threshold File Properties dialog, change the Title field to a more presentable name. In this case, I named mine, "Windows power states" (Figure 12.22):

- *Title*: This is the name of your threshold file that will be shown. This must be a unique name relative to the other threshold file names. A title with the name of the manufacturer, product, and product version that the threshold file focuses on such as Microsoft IIS 8 is recommended.
- *Version*: This starts off as 1.0. Increment the major and/or minor version numbers when significant changes are made to your threshold file.

FIGURE 12.22

The Threshold File Properties dialog box.

- *Content owner(s)*: You are the content owner—the one whose reputation is behind this threshold file. Put your name and the names of other contributors in this field.
- *Feedback email addresses*: Put your email address or addresses separated by semicolons (;) that you would like users to contact you for support or questions. Twitter handles and/or URLs are fine as well. Whichever you feel is appropriate.
- *Threshold file description*: This is a sentence or two describing the purpose of the threshold file.
- *Threshold file inheritance order*: There is no need to recreate all of the thresholds of the other threshold files. Simply inherit them from all of the threshold files that you want. I generally recommend inheriting from at least the Quick System Overview threshold file because it contains all of the threshold for the core operating system. For example, Microsoft BizTalk Server depends on SQL Server and IIS, so it inherits from the SQL Server and IIS threshold files. When a change is made to any of the inherited threshold files, your threshold file automatically gets those changes allowing your threshold file to evolve with the other threshold files.

The order that the threshold files are listed is used to resolve conflicts where the two or more threshold files have an analysis with the same name or same identifier (in the XML only—not exposed by the editor). Your threshold file is always applied last, meaning it will always win conflicts unless another threshold file is inheriting this one. This means that if you don't agree with the logical disk latency thresholds defined in the Quick System Overview, then all you have to do is define an analysis with the same name and create your own thresholds that will override the inheritance. This is what the Microsoft Exchange Server threshold files do because they have more restrictive threshold for disk latency than what the Quick System Overview threshold has defined. With that said, the Exchange Server threshold file still gets all of the other thresholds defined in the Quick System Overview threshold file.

To add a threshold file to inherit from, click the Add button, browse to the PAL installation folder, select one of the threshold files listed there, and then click Open. You should see the threshold file name listed in the inheritance order. If necessary, use the Move up and Move down buttons to change the order in which the threshold files are applied. Remember, your threshold file will be applied last allowing it to win any conflicts in analysis names.

In my case, I added the QuickSystemOverview.xml file. Click OK when finished. For good measure, save your work so far by clicking File, Save in the main PAL editor.

At this point, the threshold file is usable and you should find it in the drop-down menu on the PAL Wizard, but when no thresholds are defined, the counter will only show a chart and statistics only.

Next, let's add question variables to the threshold files.

QUESTION VARIABLES (OPTIONAL)

Question variables allow you to ask the end user more information about the computer system(s) where the counter log was captured that cannot be retrieved by any other means. The answer provided by the user can be used by thresholds in your threshold file for a more thorough analysis. For example, you could ask the user what phase of the moon it was when the counter log was captured.

To add a question variable, click the Edit Questions button on the main PAL editor. Edit Questions will show. Click Add and "-Needs Updated-" will show. Click "-Needs Updated-" and replace the default data on the right as appropriate (Figure 12.23).

- *Question Variable Name*: This is the variable name that will be used in the threshold code. Ensure that the name meets the variable naming requirements of Powershell such as no spaces in the name.
- *Question*: This is the question that is presented to the end user.
- *DataType*: Choose Boolean or String. Boolean provides a true or false value type for the variable. String provides a text value type for the variable.
- *Default Answer*: If no answer is provided by the end user, then this is the default response to the question.

Click Update, then OK when finished and do another File, Save for good measure.

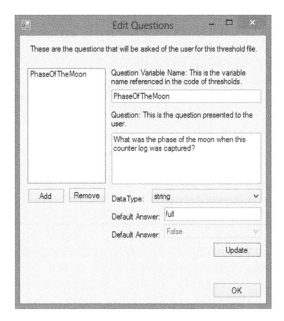

FIGURE 12.23

The Edit Questions form.

ADDING A THRESHOLD (OPTIONAL)

To add a new threshold to an analysis, click the Add button in the Thresholds group. This will open the Add Threshold Properties.

- *Name*: This is the name of the threshold and is the text that shows with all alerts generated by this threshold. Make this a concise description.
- *Condition*: Choose Warning or Critical. Use Warning to alert the user that a critical threshold is near, there might be an ambiguous condition that could lead to a larger problem, or when the threshold is experimental. Use Critical when it is clear that there is a problem or a condition that the user must be made aware of. Notice that when the condition is changed, the priority changes. This is because Critical conditions are more important than Warning conditions.
- *Color*: This will always be yellow for Warning or red for Critical conditions.
- *Priority*: You can add as many thresholds as you want to an analysis, but if more than one threshold is broken, then only one threshold will win to produce an alert. When multiple thresholds in an analysis are broken, the threshold with the highest priority will win—meaning the name, condition, and color of the "winning" threshold will be used in the alert generated from the broken threshold(s).
- *Variables*: This is a list of variables and descriptions of those variables that can be used in the Powershell Threshold Code. These could be question variables such as the $PhaseOfTheMoon variable that I created earlier.
- *Powershell Threshold Code*: This is where nearly any Powershell code can be added toward analyzing the "counter to analyze" data source counter. It can be as simple or as advanced as you prefer. By default, PAL provides a "ready-to-use" threshold by automatically adding the appropriate arguments to the StaticThreshold function. It defaults with a threshold of greater than 10. All of the lines that precede with "#//" are comments and can be removed. They are there only to provide as help.

NOTE

Please keep in mind that the threshold code can be much more advanced than the standard StaticThreshold. For an example of advanced threshold code, explore the Process Private Bytes analysis of the System Overview threshold file.

- *StaticThreshold*: This is a function inside of PAL.ps1 that will automatically compare the operator and threshold arguments to all of the statistic values of the "counter to analyze" (Min, Avg, and Max, and respective overall statistics with the same name) counter and will generate an alert each time the threshold is exceeded.
- *CollectionOfCounterInstances*: This value must be the variable that contains all of the instances of the "counter to analyze" counter that is automatically named and provided.

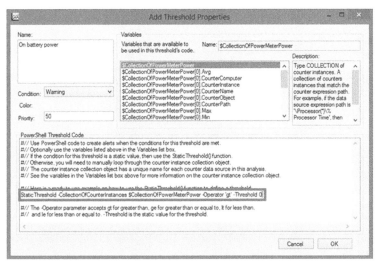

FIGURE 12.24

The Add Threshold Properties form.

- *Operator*: This is a string type that accepts less than "lt," less than or equal to "le," greater than "gt," or greater than or equal to "ge."
- *Threshold*: This must be an integer or double type that will be compared against the values of the "counter to analyze" counter (Figure 12.24).

Click OK when finished and the threshold should appear in the Thresholds section of the main PAL editor. Click the Update Analysis button on the lower right of the PAL editor, and then click File, Save to save your changes.

At this point, the threshold file can be used, and if any of the thresholds are exceeded, then they will throw an alert with the corresponding conditions of the threshold.

ADDING VISUAL THRESHOLDS TO THE CHART (OPTIONAL)

If you are adding thresholds to an analysis, then it is recommended to add corresponding visual thresholds into the chart or charts generated for the analysis. On the main PAL editor form, click the Edit Chart... button on the upper right (Figure 12.25).

This will show a new form that allows you to create a Warning threshold and/or a Critical threshold into the chart or charts generated for this analysis. These thresholds will show as yellow and red gradients with the ranges specified in this form. Like the counter thresholds, by default, the visual chart thresholds of Warning and Critical are automatically generated and usable. You can enable one or both of them by clicking the Enabled combo box next to the respective threshold (Figure 12.26).

FIGURE 12.25

The main PAL editor form highlighting the Edit Chart... button.

FIGURE 12.26

The Edit Chart form in the PAL editor.

- *StaticChartThreshold*: This is a function in PAL.ps1 that can be called to create the visual thresholds seen as gradients on the analysis charts.
- *CollectionOfCounterInstances*: This argument requires the variable that contains all of the counter instances of the "counter to analyze." It is recommended to only use the variable already provided.
- *MinThreshold*: This is the lowest value of the respective Warning and/or Critical chart threshold.
- *MaxThreshold*: This is the highest value of the respective Warning and/or Critical chart threshold. If the maximum value of Critical or Warning (if Warning is the only threshold) is 30 and if none of the counter values reach 30, then the chart will automatically expand to 35, which makes the placement of the gradient seem off. Therefore, consider using a value ending in .999 such as 29.999 to represent 30.
- *IsOperatorGreaterThan*: This is a Boolean (true|false) argument. If true, then it is assumed that the greater the counter value, the worse the condition leading from yellow [Warning] to red [Critical] as the value increases. If false, then the effect is inverted—meaning lower values are considered a worse condition leading from yellow to red in a downward view.
- *UseMaxValue*: This is a Boolean (true|false) argument. If true, then if this chart threshold is exceeded by the counter value, then this chart threshold is increased automatically to match the counter value. If false, then the chart threshold values will not change on the chart. When using both Warning and Critical chart thresholds, it is recommended to set the Warning chart threshold to false and set the Critical chart threshold to true allowing the Warning threshold to stay in place and the Critical threshold to continue to increase matching the counter value if it had exceeded the MaxThreshold value for Critical.

Once finished, click OK to return to the main PAL editor and click Update Analysis on the lower right and then File, Save to permanently save your changes to the threshold file.

At this point, the analysis should be relatively complete and should be tested. When working with many analyses within a threshold file, consider using the Enabled combo box near the top of the analysis to enable or disable the analysis. This is helpful when needing to test some, but not all of the analyses in your threshold file.

GENERATED COUNTERS (OPTIONAL)

The PAL tool has the unique ability to create "fake" counters that don't normally exist in a performance counter log but can be analyzed, charted, and processed with thresholds exactly like normal performance counters. Unfortunately, the PAL editor does not provide a way to create a generated performance counter. It must be created by manually editing the XML code of the threshold file using a text or XML editor.

The "Network Interface % Network Utilization" analysis is an example of a generated counter. In this analysis, the values of the counters **\Network Interface(*) \Bytes Total/sec** and **\Network Interface(*)\Current Bandwidth** are put through a formula that produces a percentage value of the amount of network bandwidth used based on the amount of data passing through compared to the current bandwidth of the network interface. In the PAL report, the % Network Utilization performance counter appears as if it was a real performance counter.

The technique of creating generated counters based on other counters was used a lot in the SQL Server threshold file to compare full scans/sec to batch requests/sec in a ratio. Once the generated ratio counter was created, it is easy to add thresholds and chart thresholds for it.

Examine the XML code of the analysis mentioned above as an example of creating your own generated performance counter.

PAL VERSION IS INCOMPATIBLE

If you receive the following error, "CheckPalXmlThresholdFileVersion: The threshold file specified is not compatible with PAL v2.0," then the threshold file is missing the PALVERSION attribute. This is a bug with the editor. Open the threshold file in an XML or text editor and add the XML attribute PALVERSION to the PAL XML node with a value of "2.0." It should look similar to this:

```
<?xml version="1.0"?>
<PAL PALVERSION="2.0" NAME="Quick System Overview" ...
```

Save the threshold file and try again. This was discussed on the PAL forum at: https://pal.codeplex.com/discussions/468305

For the latest version of this procedure, go to my blog article at http://blogs.technet.com/b/clinth/archive/2013/01/08/how-to-create-a-threshold-file-for-the-pal-tool.aspx

CONVERTING A PERFMON TEMPLATE TO A PAL THRESHOLD FILE

If you want to have all of the counters in a counter log be represented in a PAL report, then use the AllCounterStats feature in the PAL Wizard. This will use all of the thresholds in the PAL threshold files and ensure that all of the counters are in the report at Stats Only.

With that said, if you deal with many unique counters and don't want to create your own threshold file yet, then consider using the script discussed in this blog entry as a starting point. http://blogs.technet.com/b/clinth/archive/2013/01/08/pal-collector-script-palcollector-ps1.aspx.

Due to popular demand, I created a Powershell script that will convert a performance counter data collector template into a PAL threshold file. The script is called a non-imaginative PerfmonTemplateToPalThresholdFile.ps1. Be forewarned that the threshold file produced from this will not have any thresholds in it—it will only be statistics only but can serve as a base to start from.

For now, I consider it to be beta. It can be downloaded from http://aka.ms/clinth, and then go to PAL/BetaTesting

HOW TO USE THE SCRIPT

1. Ensure Powershell is set to unrestricted. Warning: this can be a potential security risk:
   a. At an administrator Powershell session run: Set-ExecutionPolicy unrestricted
2. Place a performance counter data collector template file (it must be in XML format) in the same directory as the script.
3. Unblock the script file. Files downloaded from the internet are considered high risk, so go to the properties of the script file and click the Unblock button. Otherwise, the script will not be permitted to run.
4. Run the script:
   a. Start a Powershell session and change directory to the script location.
   b. .\PerfmonTemplateToPalThresholdFile -PerfMonTemplate .\SysTemplate. xml.
   c. A PAL threshold file will be created in the same directory. It will use the DataCollector Name attribute in the template file as the file name.
5. Copy the PAL threshold file to the PAL installation directory:
   a. Once the PAL threshold file is created, copy it to the PAL installation directory.
   b. Run the PAL Wizard and you should see the file in the list of threshold files.

CONSIDERATIONS

- This script is designed for PAL v2.0 and later.
- The PAL threshold file produced will only create statistics only—no thresholds.
- If your goal is to have all of the counters in a counter log to be represented in the PAL report, then use the AllCounterStats feature.

  For the latest version of using this script, go to my blog http://blogs.technet.com/clinth.

CONCLUSION

In this chapter, I introduced the PAL tool and how to use it to its full potential. If you have questions on the tool, then please post the questions to http://pal.codeplex.com or contact me on Twitter @ClintH (https://twitter.com/clinth).

Tools

This book refers to a large number of tools. This appendix is intended to help guide you to the tools that are best for a given resource and/or technical level. This is not a comprehensive list of all performance-related tools. All of the tools mentioned are owned by Microsoft Corporation and are free to use. These tools are the same ones that Microsoft support professionals might ask for you to run.

The chart in Table A.1 ranks each tool based on the details it can provide for the given resource.

- **Blank [ ]:** If a field is blank, then it means that the tool provides no benefit to the resource.
- **1:** The tool provides an overview of the resource, but provides no further details.
- **2:** The tool provides a moderate level of detail of the resource.
- **3:** The tool provides a high level of detail of the resource, but does not show call stacks of threads related to the resource.
- **4:** The tool provides the highest level of detail of the resource and includes call stacks.

DEBUG DIAGNOSTIC TOOL (DEBUGDIAG) V2.0

http://www.microsoft.com/download/details.aspx?id=40336

The Debug Diagnostic Tool (DebugDiag) is designed to assist in troubleshooting issues such as hangs, slow performance, memory leaks or fragmentation, and crashes in any user-mode process. The tool includes built-in analysis rules focused on Internet Information Services (IIS) applications, web data access components, COM+, SharePoint, and related Microsoft technologies (Figure A.1).

In my opinion, it is best when needing detailed information about why a process is consuming system committed memory.

MICROSOFT NETWORK MONITOR 3.4 (NETMON)

http://www.microsoft.com/download/details.aspx?id=4865

Microsoft Network Monitor 3.4 is a tool that allows capturing and protocol analysis of network traffic. It allows you to capture network traffic and view and analyze it.

Table A.1 A Chart of the Level of Detail Provided by Each Tool

Name	User Technical Level	Processor	Memory Leak	Physical Memory	Disk	Network Capacity	Network IO	Native to OS	Installation Required	.NET Framework Stacks
DebugDiag	4	3	4	4				N	Y	Native and 2.0+
Network Monitor	4					4	4	N	Y	
PathPing	2						2	Y	N	
Performance Monitor	2	1	1	1	1	1		Y	N	
Poolmon	3		4	3				N	N	
Process Explorer	2	4	2		2	1	3	N	N	Unmanaged, 4.0+
Process Monitor	2				4		4	N	N	Unmanaged, 4.0+
RAMMap	3			4	3			N	N	
Resource Monitor	2	2	1	2	3	2	2	Y	N	
Server Performance Advisor (SPA)	2	2		1	3	1	3	WS2008+	WS2003+	2.0
Task Manager	1	Y				1	1	Y	N	
TCPView	2						3	N	N	
VMMap	3		4	3				N	N	
Windows Debugger	4	4	4	4				N	Y	All with sos.dll or psscor.dll
Windows Performance Analyzer (WPA)	3	4	4	4	4	4	4	N	Y	Unmanaged, 4.0+

FIGURE A.1

DebugDiag opening screen.

Microsoft is working on its successor, Microsoft Message Analyzer, and is available from http://www.microsoft.com/download/details.aspx?id=40308.

Network Monitor is best for recording and detailed examination of network packets (Figure A.2).

PATHPING

The PathPing tool is a route tracing tool that combines features of Ping and Tracert with additional information that neither of those tools provides. It was first introduced as part of the operating system on Windows 2000 and Windows Server 2000. PathPing sends packets to each router on the way to a final destination over a period of time and then computes results based on the packets returned from each hop. Since PathPing shows the degree of packet loss at any given router or link, you can pinpoint which routers or links might be causing network problems. For more information on PathPing, go to http://technet.microsoft.com/library/cc958876.aspx.

PathPing is best for identifying packet loss and latency of network nodes using TCP/IP ping requests (Figure A.3).

PERFORMANCE MONITOR (PERFMON)

http://technet.microsoft.com/library/cc749154.aspx

Microsoft Performance Monitor is part of the operating system and applies to many aspects of collecting performance data in Windows and Windows Servers such as live

FIGURE A.2

Network Monitor 3.4.

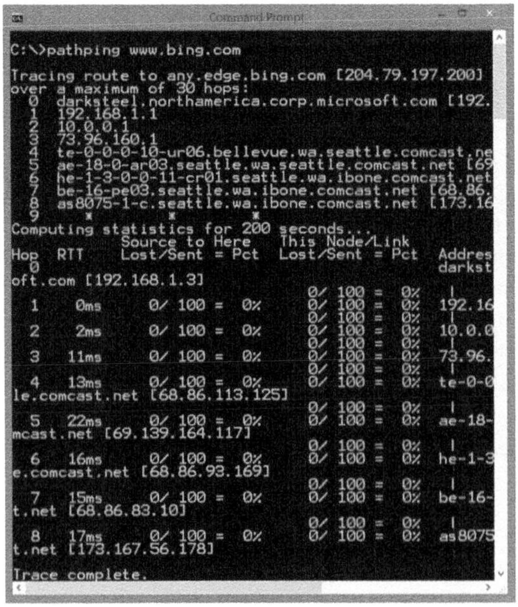

FIGURE A.3

PathPing tracing against www.bing.com.

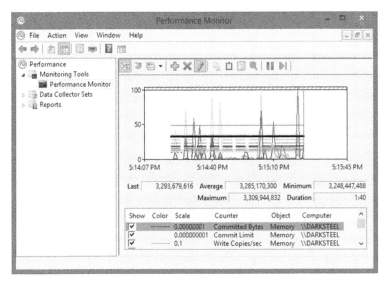

FIGURE A.4

Microsoft Performance Monitor.

monitoring, data collection, data management, and reporting of performance counter data, event tracing for Windows (ETW) data, and system information data. Perfmon and performance counters are discussed throughout this book as appropriate (Figure A.4).

POOLMON

http://www.microsoft.com/download/details.aspx?id=7911

This command-line tool displays data that the operating system collects about memory allocations from the system paged and nonpaged kernel pools and the memory pools used for Terminal Services sessions. The data are grouped by pool allocation tag. Poolmon is most often used to detect memory leaks.

Poolmon is best for identifying the driver tags consuming the most kernel memory (pool paged and pool nonpaged) (Figure A.5).

Poolmon is part of the Windows Server 2003 Support Tools that was last published in 2005. The installer still works on x64 Windows 8.1. If the download link fails, then go to my personal OneDrive at http://aka.ms/clinth and then go to the Tools folder.

PROCESS EXPLORER

http://technet.microsoft.com/sysinternals/bb896653

Process Explorer is a Windows Sysinternals tool that shows you detailed information about the processes actively running on a system including which handles and DLL processes have opened or loaded (Figure A.6).

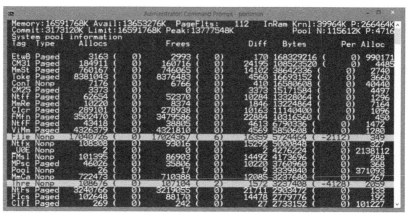

FIGURE A.5

Poolmon.exe showing driver tags and usage sorted by Bytes.

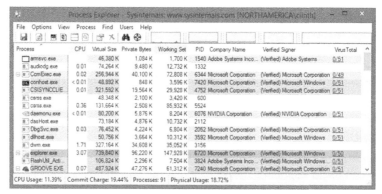

FIGURE A.6

Process Explorer showing memory, CPU, and digital signature information.

Process Explorer combines many of the Windows Sysinternals tools together for a powerhouse of detail on running processes, system memory, IO, thread stacks, handles, DLLs, and processor usage. Version 16 includes a helpful feature that sends the hashes of images (DLLs and EXEs) and files shown in the process and DLL views to VirusTotal and if they have been previously scanned. It reports how many antivirus engines identified them as possibly malicious.

PROCESS MONITOR

http://technet.microsoft.com/sysinternals/bb896645

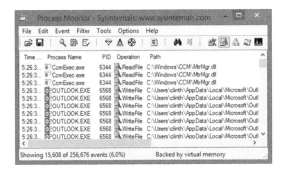

FIGURE A.7

Process Monitor showing file activity.

Process Monitor is an advanced Windows Sysinternals monitoring tool for Windows that shows real-time file system, Registry, and process/thread activity. It is part of the Windows Sysinternals suite of tools.

Process Monitor is best for pinpointing problems with registry key IO, file IO, and network IO. It is probably the tool that solves the most function problems such as installation failures but is also very good for identifying poorly performing disk filter drivers (Figure A.7).

RAMMap

http://technet.microsoft.com/sysinternals/ff700229

RAMMap is a Windows Sysinternals tool. Use RAMMap to gain understanding of the way Windows manages memory, to analyze application memory usage, or to answer specific questions about how RAM is being allocated.

RAMMap is best for identifying where all of the physical memory usage has gone such as Driver Locked, AWE, and working set usage (Figure A.8).

RESOURCE MONITOR (RESMON)

Resource Monitor is a tool that you can use to monitor the usage of CPU, hard disk, network, and memory in real time. It is part of the operating system and can be opened by clicking the Start button. In the search box, type Resource Monitor, and then, in the list of results, click Resource Monitor. Administrator permission required. If you're prompted for an administrator password or confirmation, type the password or provide confirmation (Figure A.9).

Resource Monitor is best for getting a general overview of system resources while still getting deep enough to identify many problems by showing active network connections and active file IO.

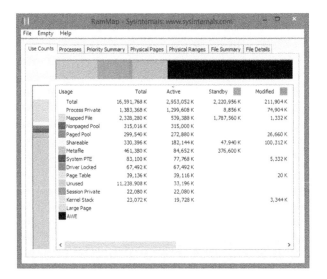

FIGURE A.8

RAMMap showing physical memory usage.

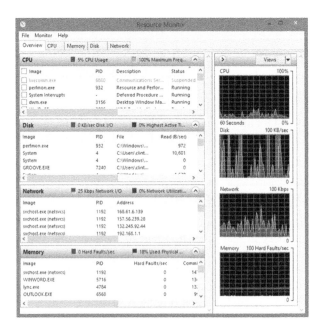

FIGURE A.9

Resource Monitor showing CPU, disk, network, and memory usage.

MICROSOFT SERVER PERFORMANCE ADVISOR

http://msdn.microsoft.com/windows/hardware/dn481522#BKMK_DownloadSPA

Microsoft Server Performance Advisor (SPA) helps IT administrators collect metrics to identify, compare, and diagnose potential performance issues in a Windows Server 2012 R2, Windows Server 2012, Windows Server 2008 R2, or Windows Server 2008 deployment. SPA generates comprehensive diagnostic reports and charts and provides recommendations to help you quickly analyze issues and develop corrective actions. As of Windows Vista, Windows Server 2008, and later, the SPA tool is part of the operating system and can be accessed through Performance Monitor. It is best if there is a performance problem actively occurring and if you have console access to the system in which to start data collection (Figure A.10).

The first version of Microsoft SPA tool was originally created as a free download for Windows Server 2003. It records and provides performance counter and ETW data in its report. For example, it can show the web pages running on IIS that are consuming the most processor time.

Download for Windows Server 2003: http://www.microsoft.com/download/details.aspx?id=15506

TASK MANAGER

Task Manager is part of the operating system and provides a general overview of system resources and processes with tabs that provide more detail of each system resource. It can be started by right-clicking the task bar and then clicking Start Task Manager or by pressing Ctrl+Shift+Esc. The user interface of Task Manager changed significantly between Windows 7 (Windows Server 2008 R2) and Windows 8 (Windows Server 2012) (Figure A.11).

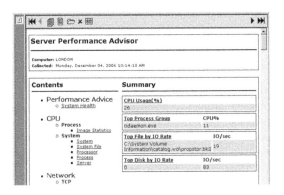

FIGURE A.10

A Server Performance Advisor (SPA) report.

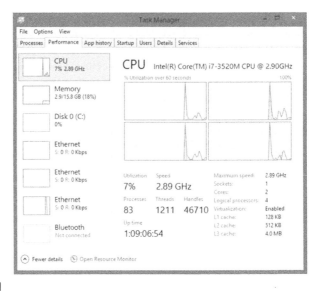

FIGURE A.11

The Performance tab of Task Manager on Windows 8.1.

TCPVIEW

http://technet.microsoft.com/sysinternals/bb897437.aspx

TCPView is a Windows Sysinternals tool that will show you a list of all TCP and UDP sessions on your system, including the local and remote addresses and state of the TCP connections. On Windows Server 2008, Vista, and XP, TCPView also reports the name of the process that owns the session. TCPView provides a more informative and conveniently presented subset of the Netstat program that ships with Windows (Figure A.12).

VMMap

http://technet.microsoft.com/sysinternals/dd535533.aspx

VMMap is a process virtual and physical memory analysis utility that is part of the Windows Sysinternals suite of tools. It shows a breakdown of a process's committed virtual memory types and the amount of physical memory (working set) assigned by the operating system to those types. Besides graphic representations of memory usage, VMMap also shows summary information and a detailed process memory map. Powerful filtering and refresh capabilities allow you to identify the sources of process memory usage and the memory cost of application features (Figure A.13).

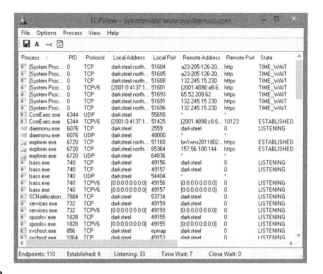

FIGURE A.12

Sample output from TCPView.

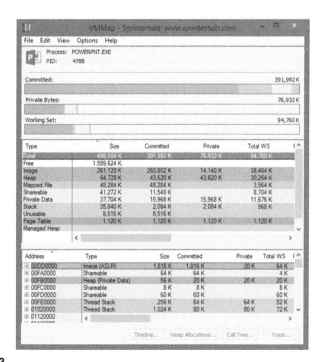

FIGURE A.13

VMMap attached to a 32-bit version of Microsoft PowerPoint 2013.

This tool is great for identifying the amount of contiguous free virtual address space within an active process. This is important because it helps determine if an application will be running out of virtual address space and if the address space is highly fragmented.

WINDOWS DEBUGGER (WinDBG)

http://msdn.microsoft.com/windows/desktop/bg162891

This tool is the tool that can often get or show data that no other tool can. With that said, it is also the most technical tool that can be used. It is most frequently used by senior support professionals and senior developers. Don't be afraid to use it, but know that there is a high learning curve to use this tool effectively (Figure A.14).

WinDBG is part of the Debugging Tools for Windows. The Debugging Tools for Windows is part of the Windows Software Development Kit (SDK). If you want to download only Debugging Tools for Windows, install the Windows SDK, and, during the installation, select the Debugging Tools for Windows box and clear all the other boxes.

The Windows Debugger and many other related tools have the ability to create a user-mode dump—meaning to dump the memory usage of a process to a file called a dump file with the extension of DMP. This dump file is a snapshot in time of everything the process was doing at the time of the dump. In addition, it can attach to the kernel invasively or noninvasively in order to query it for things like virtual memory structures.

This tool is best used to go deep into a process such as looking at thread stacks, memory usage, and processor usage.

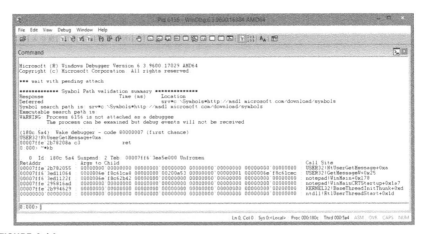

FIGURE A.14

WinDBG attached to Notepad.exe.

For more information on Windows debugging, consider the book "Advanced Windows Debugging" by Mario Hewardt and Daniel Pravat at http://www.advancedwindowsdebugging.com.

WINDOWS PERFORMANCE ANALYZER

http://www.microsoft.com/download/details.aspx?id=39982

The Window Performance Analyzer tool is arguably the best tool for identifying the root cause of performance problems in nearly all areas of performance (disk, processor, memory, startup, and shutdown). It is discussed throughout this book when appropriate.

WPA is part of the Windows Performance Toolkit that includes tools such as Windows Performance Recorder (user interface recorder) and xperf.exe (command-line recorder). The Windows Performance Toolkit is part of the Windows Assessment and Deployment Kit (ADK), which is a collection of tools that you can use to customize, assess, and deploy Windows operating systems to new computers (Figure A.15).

To install WPA, install the Windows ADK, and during setup, select the Windows Performance Toolkit, and clear all other boxes.

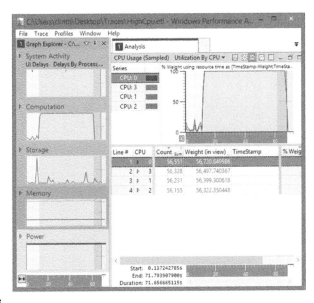

FIGURE A.15

Windows Performance Analyzer (WPA) showing a high CPU trace.

Collecting Process Memory Dumps

B

Dump files are often needed by Microsoft support professionals to assist customers with process hangs and crashes, so it's important to know how to properly gather a process memory dump.

This appendix briefly discusses process memory dumps and introduces many tools that can be used to collect process memory dumps. This appendix does not cover kernel memory dumps also known as bug checks or blue screens of death.

One of the most reliable ways of gathering data on a process is to take a memory dump of it. A memory dump suspends all of the threads of the target process and writes all of the memory usage of it to a dump (*.dmp) file on disk. The dump file can then be analyzed to see what was going on with the process at the time the dump was taken. This procedure is very helpful when an application hangs or crashes because the thread stacks can often provide clues as to the reason why the process hung or crashed.

Dump files are highly compressible, so it is encouraged to compress them before transferring them. Windows and Windows Server natively support compression by right-clicking on selected files and folders and selecting Send to Compressed (zipped) folder in File Explorer.

For more detailed information about user-mode debugging, I recommend "Advanced Windows Debugging" and "Advanced .NET Debugging" by Mario Hewardt (Twitter @MarioHewardt) and Daniel Pravat.

There are many tools that can create a dump file from an actively running process. I will briefly describe each tool, how to use it to collect a process memory dump, and any other important facts about it.

USING TASK MANAGER

Task Manager (part of the operating system) has the feature of creating a process memory dump of most processes. This is arguably the easiest way to get a process dump since Task Manager is part of the operating system and readily available. With that said, dump files created by Task Manager on x64 versions of Windows and Windows Server will be 64-bit dump files even if the process is 32-bit running in a wow64 host. This can make 32-bit process dumps difficult to read. Therefore, on 64-bit versions of Windows and Windows Server, avoid using Task Manager to create dump files of 32-bit processes. Also, some processes such as System and System Idle Process are excluded from creating a dump file.

In Windows Vista, Windows Server 2008, Windows 7, and Windows Server 2008 R2, open Task Manager by right-clicking the task bar and selecting Task Manager or press Ctrl+Shift+Esc.

Click the Processes tab, right-click one of the processes you wish to target, and select Create Dump File. If you are prompted for an administrator password or confirmation, then type your password or click Continue. A dump file for the process is created in the user temporary folder specified by the %temp% environment variable. When you receive a message that states that the dump file was successfully created, click OK. These instructions came from the Microsoft Knowledge Base (KB) article 931673 at http://support.microsoft.com/kb/931673.

In Windows 8, Windows Server 2012, Windows 8.1, and Windows Server 2012 R2, open Task Manager by right-clicking the task bar and selecting Task Manager or press Ctrl+Shift+Esc. Click the Details tab, right-click one of the processes you wish to target, and select Create Dump File. If you are prompted for an administrator password or confirmation, then type your password or click Continue. A dump file for the process is created in the user temporary folder specified by the %temp% environment variable. When you receive a message that states that the dump file was successfully created, click OK.

USING DEBUGDIAG

The Debug Diagnostics tool is a free tool from Microsoft. It must be installed and is not part of the operating system. It provides a user interface "wizard" to make creating process dumps easier. DebugDiag 2.0 can be downloaded from http://www.microsoft.com/download/details.aspx?id=40336.

Once installed, run DebugDiag 2.0 Collection, and a Select Rule Type wizard will show. To create a hang dump (an instantaneous process dump), click Cancel on the Select Rule Type dialog box and navigate to the Processes tab. Right-click on a process and select either Create Full Userdump or Create Mini Userdump. The type of dump to create should be discussed with the person who will be analyzing the dump file. If unsure of which to use, then create a full userdump or both.

In addition, rules can be created in DebugDiag to create attach to a process and capture a crash dump if the process crashes.

USING ADPLUS

ADPlus is a tool that is included in the Debugging Tools for Windows suite of tools. This tool was one of the first tools of its kind to make the gathering of process dumps easier.

The Debugging Tools for Windows is bundled with the Windows Software Development Kit (SDK). To install a standalone version of the debugging tools, install the Windows SDK, and during installation, select Debugging Tools for Windows, clear all other check boxes, and finish the installation wizard.

ADPlus can be used to create many different kinds of process dumps. See the KB article 286350 for details on how to use it at http://support.microsoft.com/kb/286350.

USING PROCDUMP

ProcDump is a Windows Sysinternals command-line utility whose primary purpose is monitoring an application for CPU spikes and generating crash dumps during a spike that an administrator or developer can use to determine the cause of the spike.

For more information on how to use this tool to collect process dumps, go to http://technet.microsoft.com/sysinternals/dd996900.aspx.

Also, it can be directly downloaded from http://live.sysinternals.com/procdump.exe. No installation is required.

USING WINDOWS ERROR REPORTING

Starting with Windows Server 2008 and Windows Vista with Service Pack 1 (SP1), Windows Error Reporting (WER) can be configured so that full user-mode dumps are collected and stored locally after a user-mode application crashes. Applications that do their own custom crash reporting, including .NET applications, are not supported by this feature.

For more information on how to use this operating system feature, go to http://msdn.microsoft.com/library/windows/desktop/bb787181(v=vs.85).aspx.

USING PROCESS EXPLORER

Process Explorer is part of the Windows Sysinternals tools and can be used to create a process memory dump. It can be downloaded directly from http://live.sysinternals.com/procexp.exe and no installation is required. Execute Procexp.exe to run the tool. Once running, it displays a list of the active processes running on the system. To create a process memory dump, right-click on a process, select Create Dump, and then select Create Minidump or Create Full Dump depending on what the person who will be analyzing the dump prefers. If unsure of what to gather, then gather either a full dump or both. For more information about Process Explorer, go to http://technet.microsoft.com/sysinternals/bb896653.aspx.

USING WINDBG

WinDBG is a Windows Debugger tool that is part of the Debugging Tools for Windows, which is a suite of debugging support tools. The Debugging Tools for Windows is bundled with the Windows SDK. To install a standalone version of the debugging tools, install the Windows SDK, and during installation, select

Debugging Tools for Windows, clear all other check boxes, and finish the installation wizard.

Once WinDBG is running, use the .dump command to create a process memory dump. For more information on the .dump command, go to http://msdn. microsoft.com/library/windows/hardware/ff562428(v=vs.85).aspx.

VERIFYING THE PROCESS MEMORY DUMP FILE

Before sending a process memory dump file to someone to be analyzed, it's important to check the dump file to ensure it is valid and not corrupted.

Dumpchk.exe is a command-line tool that is part of the Debugging Tools for Windows, which is a suite of debugging support tools. Use this tool to ensure that a process memory dump file (*.dmp) is not corrupted and is valid. At a command prompt, run dumpchk.exe followed by the path to the DMP file. If the dump file is valid, then it will show a lot of output. Otherwise, if there is an error, then the file is likely corrupted.

The Debugging Tools for Windows is bundled with the Windows SDK. To install a standalone version of the debugging tools, install the Windows SDK, and during installation, select Debugging Tools for Windows, clear all other check boxes, and finish the installation wizard.

For more information about Dumpchk.exe, go to http://technet.microsoft.com/library/ee424340(v=ws.10).aspx.

Debug symbols

INTRODUCTION

To say that the problem is with foo.dll certainly helps, but DLLs and EXEs can have thousands of function calls in them. This would be similar to saying that the person you are looking for is somewhere in a city—it doesn't help much. Symbols are files associated with a specific build of DLL or EXE that translate memory offsets to function calls such as VirtMemTest64.exe+0x232a7c to VirtMemTest64.exe! CpuHogThread where the bang (!) separates the module from the function call. This gives the developer of the application a much more specific location to look at in their code similar to providing a street name to search. It still doesn't get it down to a line number (similar to an address on a street), but it is as close as we can get when it comes to post-production debugging. Now, one might say just look at the memory offset and that tells you how far down in the file to look. Well, code is often optimized during compilation that effectively scrambles the offsets. This means that memory offsets alone can be misleading (Figure C.1).

Once symbols are loaded, we can see that it resolves to VirtMemTest64.exe! CpuHogThread.

Now, the developer can review the code in that function call and try to identify how the high CPU usage is occurring. This means that having symbols makes your and the developer's life much easier at resolving performance problems.

For more detailed information about user-mode debugging, I recommend "Advanced Windows Debugging" and "Advanced .NET Debugging" by Mario Hewardt (Twitter @MarioHewardt) and Daniel Pravat.

USING SYMBOL PATHS

A symbol path is a string that points the tool to file system locations where it can try to match DLLs and EXEs to their respective symbol file.

In the example in Figure C.2, I used the following symbol path:

```
srv*c:\Symbols*http://msdl.microsoft.com/download/symbols;C:\Users
\clinth\Desktop\Desktop\Tools\VirtMemTest\x64;
```

The syntax is as such:

Srv*<SymbolCache>*<SymbolServer>

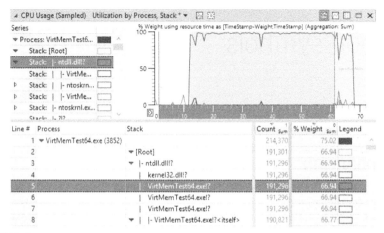

FIGURE C.1

Windows Performance Analyzer showing VirtMemTest64.exe without symbols.

or

<DirectPathToSymbols>

Each entry is separated by a semicolon (;).

<SymbolServer> is a specialized folder structure (not a process or service) that can be a local file system path, file share, or an HTTP address. In this case, http://msdl.microsoft.com/download/symbols is Microsoft's public symbol server. It likely contains terabytes of symbol files because nearly every build of each file that Microsoft ships has a symbol file at this location. Therefore, when a symbol file is not

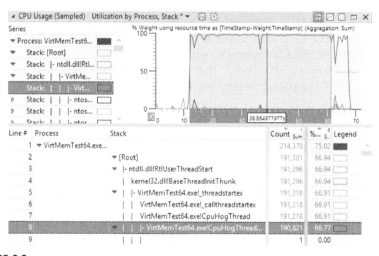

FIGURE C.2

Windows Performance Analyzer showing VirtMemTest64.exe with symbols.

located in the <SymbolCache>, which should be faster to access than the <SymbolServer>, it downloads the symbol file from the <SymbolServer> location and stores it at the <SymbolCache> location as a symbol server (a specialized folder structure). Therefore, if/when a debugging tool needs the symbol file again, it can quickly load it from the <SymbolCache> location.

My <SymbolCache> folder is a symbol server folder, which in this case is C:\Symbols. Figure C.3 shows how the folder structure looks like.

Each folder is for a DLL or EXE with a subfolder of unique GUIDs to indicate each build with symbols are within each folder.

A sample symbol path is as follows:

```
C:\Symbols\1394OHCI.pdb\39D04E6E457F4C9E8001D7FAF62CDBE51\1394OHCI.
pdb
```

The second path, <DirectPathToSymbols>, is a direct file system path to one or more symbol files without a specialized folder structure. In my case, I have the following files at "C:\Users\clinth\Desktop\Desktop\Tools\VirtMemTest\x64":

VirtMemTest.pdb
VirtMemTest.sln
VirtMemTest.exe

Name	Date modified	Type
1394OHCI.pdb	3/10/2014 10:00 PM	File folder
AcGenral.pdb	3/10/2014 11:07 PM	File folder
AcLayers.pdb	4/7/2014 10:54 AM	File folder
aclui.pdb	3/11/2014 3:35 PM	File folder
acpi.pdb	3/10/2014 9:56 PM	File folder
acpiex.pdb	3/10/2014 11:05 PM	File folder
acpipmi.pdb	4/7/2014 10:52 AM	File folder
acppage.pdb	4/7/2014 10:53 AM	File folder
ActionCenter.pdb	3/10/2014 10:02 PM	File folder
ActivationVDev.pdb	3/11/2014 3:25 PM	File folder
activeds.pdb	3/10/2014 10:00 PM	File folder
ActXPrxy.pdb	3/10/2014 11:10 PM	File folder
AdhApi.pdb	3/10/2014 11:05 PM	File folder
AdhSvc.pdb	3/10/2014 11:05 PM	File folder

FIGURE C.3

A sample of a specialized folder structure known as a symbol server.

In this case, only the VirtMemTest.pdb file is the symbol file that was created when VirtMemTest.exe was compiled.

Each tool that uses a symbol path often has a unique dialog box to set the path. A system environment variable can be set that debugging tools will automatically use as the symbol path. It is "_NT_SYMBOL_PATH." The most common value for this variable is "SRV*C:\Symbols*http://msdl.microsoft.com/download/symbols," which downloads public symbols from Microsoft's public symbol server to the local cache of C:\Symbols when the symbol file doesn't exist in the local cache. For more information about creating this environment variable, go to "Use the Microsoft Symbol Server to obtain debug symbol files" at http://support.microsoft.com/kb/311503.

> **NOTE**
>
> Some tools such as Windows Sysinternals Process Explorer require the dbghelp.dll from the Debugging Tools for Windows in order to resolve symbols of actively running processes. On production systems, consider installing the Debugging Tools for Windows on a non-production system and then copying the installed files to the production system.

CREATING SYMBOLS

Symbols are relatively easy to create and use, but requires a lot of planning and cooperation. Symbols can only be created when the executable (EXE) or module (DLL) is compiled and they are unique to the build. This means that once a file is compiled, the developer cannot create symbols for it later. The symbol file must be created at the time of compilation. For this reason, it is a best practice for developers to create symbols with every build.

> **TIP**
>
> Creating symbols does "not" cause any performance degradation in the functionality of the DLL or EXE.

SYMBOLS AND SECURITY CONCERNS

According to "Public Symbols and Private Symbols" at http://msdn.microsoft.com/library/windows/hardware/ff550665(v=vs.85).aspx, symbol files can include any or all of the following data:

- The names and addresses of all functions
- All data type, structure, and class definitions
- The names, data types, and addresses of global variables
- The names, data types, addresses, and scopes of local variables
- The line numbers in the source code that correspond to each binary instruction

Some developers might be uncomfortable with sharing all of this information with others.

Therefore, public symbols can be created to help troubleshoot problems without exposing too much of the source code or how the application was developed. See the article "Public Symbols and Private Symbols" at http://msdn.microsoft.com/library/windows/hardware/ff550665(v=vs.85).aspx for more information on creating public symbols.

MANAGING SYMBOL FILES USING SYMBOL SERVERS

When developers are regularly creating symbols, managing the symbol files can be difficult. For this reason, a specialized folder structure called a symbol server can be used to organize the files and allow tools to quickly find the appropriate symbol files. A relatively easy way of doing this is by using a command-line tool called Symstore. exe, which is part of the Debugging Tools for Windows. Symstore.exe is a command-line tool that will copy a symbol file and place it into the appropriate location on a symbol server, making management of symbols much easier.

For more information on how to use Symstore.exe, go to "Using SymStore" at http://msdn.microsoft.com/library/windows/desktop/ms681417(v=vs.85).aspx.

Index

Note: Page numbers followed by *f* indicate figures and *t* indicate tables.

Printed and bound by CPI Group (UK) Ltd, Croydon, CR0 4YY

03/10/2024

01040322-0002